D1005899

INDUSTRY OF ANONYMITY

INDUSTRY OF ANONYMITY

Inside the Business of Cybercrime

JONATHAN LUSTHAUS

HARVARD UNIVERSITY PRESS

CAMBRIDGE, MASSACHUSETTS

LONDON, ENGLAND

2018

LIBRARY OF CONGRESS CATALOGING-IN-PUBLICATION DATA
Names: Lusthaus, Jonathan, 1984– author.
Title: Industry of anonymity: inside the business of cybercrime / Jonathan Lusthaus.
Description: Cambridge, Massachusetts: Harvard University Press, 2018. | Includes bibliographical references and index.
Identifiers: LCCN 2018009362 | ISBN 9780674979413 (alk. paper)
Subjects: LCSH: Computer crimes. | Hackers. | Online identities. | Organized crime.
Classification: LCC HV6773 .L87 2018 | DDC 364.16/8—dc23
LC record available at https://lccn.loc.gov/2018009362

To my parents

Contents

INDUSTRY OF ANONYMITY

1

Introduction

ON JULY 5, 2014, a thirty-year-old Russian national from Vladivostok named Roman Seleznev was reaching the end of his holiday. He had been in the Maldives with his girlfriend and daughter. At the conclusion of the trip, they boarded a seaplane to travel from their five-star resort to Malé's international airport. As a bus ferried them from the seaplane to the terminal, Seleznev may not have noticed, but he was being watched closely from the rows behind him. When he arrived at the airport, his passport was checked and he began a long journey. But the destination was not the one he had planned. He was on his way to the US territory of Guam, and he began that trip in handcuffs.[1]

Seleznev and his family, in many of their published photos, appear perfectly normal. He cuts a casual and jovial figure who could easily pass for a family-minded IT professional or technology entrepreneur. In a sense, this is an accurate descriptor. But some of the photos hint at something more. One shows Seleznev next to a bright yellow Dodge muscle car parked in Moscow's Red Square; others show him partying with friends; and in another, bundles of cash are clearly visible in the back seat of a vehicle. These pictures are more suggestive of someone with a taste for the high life and whose earnings may be less than legitimate. Taken together, these divergent images create an intriguing illustration of what it means to be one of the leading cybercriminals of recent years, as Seleznev is considered to be.[2]

According to a US indictment, Seleznev was engaged in credit card fraud on a massive scale. His tactic was to gain access to the point-of-sale systems of restaurants and other retail businesses, and infect them with malware. Seleznev and his associates could then obtain the credit card details of myriad customers. Without suggesting it was his only period of activity, the indictment specifies that between November 15, 2010, and February 22,

2011, Seleznev and his associates stole over 200,000 credit card numbers. Through his own websites, he sold around 140,000 card numbers to other cybercriminals, generating at least $2,000,000 in profits.[3] In total, prosecutors estimated Seleznev and company had gained around $18,000,000 from their activities.[4] A later indictment in 2012 listed him as a member of the "Carder.su organization." This forum provided a thriving online marketplace where credit card data, along with other illicit goods and services, could be traded among cybercriminals from around the world. On it, Seleznev would have advertised his wares like any good merchant. The forum as a whole was claimed to be responsible for more than $50,000,000 in victim losses.[5]

Given this background, it is perhaps not surprising that Seleznev chose the Maldives for his vacation. The picturesque island nation might have its appeal for a family man, but for a cybercriminal it had the added charm of having no extradition treaty with the United States. Nevertheless, American Secret Service agents managed to negotiate an ad hoc arrangement with the local authorities. After he was handed over to the Secret Service, Seleznev was flown to Guam where he was charged under US law. Later, he was transferred to Seattle to face trial.[6] In April 2017, he was sentenced to twenty-seven years in prison.[7]

Industry of Anonymity

Roman Seleznev's story makes for an appropriate opening to a book on the sociology of profit-driven cybercrime for a number of reasons, but chief among them is that it puts a human face on the subject. There can be a temptation to think about cybercrime in the abstract, as an almost invisible phenomenon. Attacks occur through cyberspace and are orchestrated by unseen and unknown actors. The only people we tend to picture are the victims. This leads to a mystification of cybercrime and a focus on the technical components rather than the offenders, which makes the phenomenon even more foreign to the average person. The reality, of course, is that every attack has one or more humans behind it. Somewhere in the world, there is a person sitting at a keyboard. As the example of Seleznev shows, that person has a life and exists in a specific social setting. Producing a better understanding of the people behind cybercrime and the contexts in which they operate is an important task for scholars. Part of this book's purpose is to help lift the veil of anonymity that has hidden cybercrime offenders and their activities from view.

Seleznev's story also provides a good starting point for another important reason: it is reflective of shifts that are taking place more broadly in the world of cybercrime. The picture painted above is of a multimillionaire criminal tech entrepreneur who, with his associates, is capable of compromising a large number of businesses and siphoning off hundreds of thousands of card details. The criminal not only exploits these cards himself, but also makes them available to others. He advertises them on a platform with thousands of members and sells them through automated, online shop fronts, netting millions of dollars in the process. This is a far cry from the days when cybercrime was associated with a mental image of a teenager in his mother's basement—a residual memory that still occupies a place in the public imagination. A long evolution has taken place from the earliest days of computer hacking in the late 1950s, when computer scientists with access to university mainframes indulged in harmless side projects largely driven by intellectual curiosity.

The central theme of this book is that cybercrime has matured into a large, profit-driven industry. Hobby hackers still exist and hacktivists have attracted some attention in recent years, but a very significant component is now financially motivated. Contemporary cybercriminals engage in, among other activities, blackmail, extortion, intellectual property violations, phishing, fraud, identity theft, spam, and renting out resources and services (such as hacking services). These enterprises are sophisticated and organized. Although there are significant methodological and data challenges involved in estimating the total cost of global cybercrime, government and private sector studies regularly put it in the neighborhood of hundreds of billions of dollars a year.[8] A study by the United Nations claims that the victimization levels of conventional crime have even fallen behind those of cybercrime.[9]

Applying the term "industry" to cybercrime, however, is more a characterization of how it functions than of how much money it generates for its practitioners and costs its victims. While it is easy to get bogged down in a definitional quagmire, in simple terms, an industry is a set of businesses all operating in similar ways and producing the same types of goods and services.[10] The term need not be restricted to only large, multinational corporations operating within established systems of regulation. While its goods and services are usually illicit, the cybercrime industry operates according to the same foundational principles of industrial organization observed across numerous other contexts.[11] First, there is a clear division of labor by which different activities, from hacking, to coding, to vending, to *cashing out* (which involves turning virtual gains into monetary ones), are handled by different specialists. In fact, there are numerous subspecialties within these specialties. This division of labor has allowed a wide range of people to become involved in cybercrime, with offenders of many ages, demographic groups, skill sets, and backgrounds finding niches in which they can be productive. Second, along with this specialization has come greater professionalization. The old hacker code of intellectual discovery and information sharing has in large part been superseded by professional criminals devising processes to maximize financial gain.

Third, the increasing specialization and professionalization of cybercriminals is mirrored by the growth of virtual marketplaces. Trading platforms that are essentially criminal eBays have become particularly important. In the most popular of these forums, thousands of cybercriminals convene online to buy and sell illicit goods and services. Commonly traded offerings include products such as compromised credit and debit card data, online banking logins, and malware, as well as services such as cashing-out solutions. Finally, cybercriminals increasingly organize themselves into groups which begin to resemble legitimate businesses or, in economics language, *firms.* Many of these are small crews whose members perform particular roles in a joint endeavor, such as producing malware or carrying out elaborate confidence scams online. As we shall see, some of these illicit teams have reached a point of sophistication that makes them almost indistinguishable from licit firms, complete with physical office space and formal organizational hierarchies. Among these are companies that specialize in coordinating spam advertising campaigns or that serve as bulletproof hosts, which are essentially Internet service providers that refuse to take down illegal content.

From the perspective of operational efficiency, the industrialization of profit-driven cybercrime makes perfect sense. But this phenomenon remains puzzling in another way: an industry requires a strong basis of trust among its actors to grow, whereas faceless criminal partners should encourage distrust. Cooperation among conventional criminals has always presented significant obstacles, given that the parties concerned operate outside the law and there is no possible recourse to enforcement by the state should deals go awry. Paolo Campana and Federico Varese summarize these challenges:

> In the underworld, actors face more natural obstacles to be overcome. By definition, one cannot turn to the state to protect stolen or illegal assets. Information about the quality of goods and services is hard to come by as there are no reputable and easily accessible

sources of unbiased information. One cannot even be sure that the person offering a deal is not an undercover agent or a police informant. Regardless of personal inclination to cheat, actors in the underworld are difficult to locate, as they move around frequently. Entrepreneurs in these markets cannot freely advertise their good reputation, creditors disappear, informants consort with the police, and undercover agents try to pass themselves off as *bona fide* fellow criminals.[12]

To explain how cooperation can be sustained in spite of these substantial challenges, a significant body of literature has emerged. It reveals various ways in which cooperation has emerged in seemingly unlikely extra-legal contexts.[13]

Cybercrime, however, takes these complications further by introducing the element of greater anonymity. In offline criminal dealings, actors may try to disguise their true identities, but few, if any, can achieve the depth of anonymity that prevails online in cybercrime. In these settings, cyber-criminals are often dealing with partners whose true identities are unknown to them. In an environment that lacks physical interactions, trustworthiness can be difficult to assess and agreements hard to enforce. Beyond this, if one were able to unmask a collaborator's true identity, that person might be on the other side of the world, offering little hope for threatening the physical violence that has been a favored tool for dissuading traditional criminals from reneging on their commitments.

In light of these major obstacles, it might seem logical that cybercriminals would work primarily on their own. But, in recent years, they have been very successful in building partnerships. Today's cybercrime industry exhibits significant levels of structure and governance, alongside more small-time collaboration.[14]

This book will focus on both these aspects of cybercrime—first, outlining the evolution and nature of this industry, and second, addressing the puzzle of how this industry was able to develop in spite of the challenges of anonymity. To make sense of cybercrime, we must engage with this problem of anonymity on multiple levels. If we want to go beyond viewing cybercrime as a mystical and invisible phenomenon, we must peel back some of the layers of anonymity to see its day-to-day workings. Then we must understand how cybercriminals overcome the challenges of dealing with anonymous partners; this is what has allowed them to build a functioning industry. Finally, we need to examine those situations in which cybercriminals choose not to insist on anonymity and may even prefer to operate with physically known associates. These offline interactions also may be integral to the successful functioning of the broader cybercrime industry.

Before exploring the industrialization of cybercrime in the coming chapters, the remainder of this introduction addresses some contextual concerns that should be of interest to readers. The first section outlines the debates around the very definition of cybercrime, and settles on an appropriate understanding for this book's purposes. The section after will review what is known about cybercriminals in terms of their backgrounds and life circumstances. A following section will survey the relevant literature on the topic of profit-driven cybercrime, along with broader theory supporting this study. The final section of this introduction outlines the approach and structure of the book as a whole. Those with a particular interest in the academic foundations of the study should also engage with Appendix 2, which provides details on data and methods. Readers with less interest in definitions, background on cybercriminal offenders, literature reviews, and theory are invited to skip forward to the last section of this chapter.

Defining Cybercrime

Many early investigations of cybercrime struggled with the realities of limited data availability in conjunction with a subject matter that was rapidly evolving as new technologies emerged. This literature was not necessarily pitched at a theoretical level, but focused on what this new phenomenon of cybercrime meant in relation to traditional approaches to the study of crime. It outlined key aspects of what it was, the technologies being used, and the new threats posed as the Internet came into existence and more and more aspects of human life, such as credit card use and banking, started to go online.[15] The focus of such works was often on cybercrime in general rather than on a specific subgenus like profit-driven cybercrime. Given how far the Internet and associated technologies have now come, it is interesting to look back on this literature as capturing some of the spirit of the time. It was certainly prescient in a number of ways, but it is also true that new technologies evolved in ways authors could not have predicted, and set cybercrime on another course.

One of the enduring contributions of this conceptual literature has been the attempt to define the term *cybercrime* itself. At the intersection of new technologies and crime, there have been a number of competing terms looking at similar, but perhaps distinct, phenomena. These have included:

cybercrime, virtual crime, net-crime, high-tech crime, and computer crime. But, as David Wall notes, whatever "its merits and demerits, the term 'cyber-crime' has entered the public parlance and we are more or less stuck with it."[16] In recent years, cybercrime appears to have become the dominant term used by social scientists working in this area.

The main conceptual question regarding how to demarcate what is (and is not) cybercrime has been whether it constitutes a new type of crime, or is instead a form of existing criminality adapted to a digital environment. Some have argued for the former position. For instance, Wall nods in this direction by arguing that "the Internet, and particularly the cyberspace it creates, is not just a case of 'old wine in new bottles,' or for that matter 'new wine in new bottles,' rather many of its characteristics are so novel that the expression 'new wine, but no bottles!' becomes a more fitting description."[17] Others, however, take the opposite (though still wine-related) view captured in Peter Grabosky's article: "Virtual Criminality: Old Wine in New Bottles?" According to Grabosky:

> "virtual criminality" is basically the same as the terrestrial crime with which we are familiar. To be sure, some of the manifestations are new. But a great deal of crime committed with or against computers differs only in terms of the medium. While the technology of implementation, and particularly its efficiency, may be without precedent, the crime is fundamentally familiar. It is less a question of something completely different than a recognizable crime committed in a completely different way.[18]

In line with this approach, a consensus has formed around defining cyber-crime not as a particular subset of crimes, but rather as a range of illegal activities taking place within the realm of cyberspace. As Thomas Holt and Adam Bossler note in their review of the field, while there is "no single, agreed-on definition of cybercrime, many scholars argue that it involves the use of cyberspace or computer technology to facilitate acts of crime and deviance."[19]

There is one further element linked to this debate, however, that some-what muddies the definitional waters. This is the distinction some scholars and practitioners draw between those cybercrimes that are "traditional" crimes, such as fraud or theft, now facilitated and enhanced by new technologies, and those cybercrimes that could not exist at all without these new technologies—such as computer or network intrusions, distributed denial of service (DDoS) attacks, and the spread of malware—because computers or networks are themselves the targets of such crimes.[20] Based on my interactions with law enforcement agencies and policymakers, it would seem that this categorization has been fairly widely adopted.

While this distinction between *cyber-enabled* and *cyber-dependent* crimes is logical, for application in the social sciences it does not appear particularly helpful. All crimes are simply behaviors that have been criminalized by legal systems; the concept of what is criminal does not necessarily have a theoretical underpinning independent from the law of the land. Legislators might declare specific acts against computers and networks to be criminal, but often what is being newly criminalized is the use of novel tools or methods rather than the behaviors behind them. The older motivations remain. For instance, computer intrusions and the spread of malware can facilitate theft or vandalism, and DDoS attacks can serve the goals of an extortion ring or a group pushing a political agenda. It would be unusual for one of these technical crimes not to be linked to some broader motivation and a more traditional crime type, be it theft, fraud, extortion, harassment, vandalism, or espionage. Legal scholars might find this debate relevant, but for social science–based approaches, this may be a distinction without a difference. As social scientists work to understand the human actors behind such crimes, motivations should probably matter more than legal technicalities.

If there is indeed a true sociological distinction between cyber-enabled and cyber-dependent crimes, this study nonetheless includes both types under the single banner of cybercrime. In this book, I apply a broad functional definition: cybercrime is the "use of computers or other electronic devices via information systems such as organizational networks or the Internet to facilitate illegal behaviors."[21] It is also sensible to specify that, for a crime to be referred to as cybercrime, the use of such technology cannot be only tangential or peripheral to it. Texting one's accomplice, for example, or communicating using any of the electronic means which have become commonplace in contemporary life, does not a cybercrime make—if it did, the term might incorporate virtually all crime. This is largely a return to the approach of Grabosky, who appears in the first instance to have understood matters well.[22]

Cybercriminal behaviors and activities go well beyond hacking, and vary widely. They can include online pedophilia, vandalism, harassment, espionage, fraud, activism, hobby hacking, and cyberterrorism. Wall's typology, which has been widely applied by scholars, separates cybercriminal acts into four broad types based on established legal categories:

1. Cyber-*trespass*, which involves crossing online boundaries into the computers or systems of others, possibly causing damage (for example, by hacking or unleashing a virus).
2. Cyber-*deceptions* and *thefts*, involving fraud or theft of money / property, such as credit card fraud or intellectual property violations.
3. Cyber-*pornography*, consisting of online activities that run counter to obscenity laws.
4. Cyber-*violence*, causing psychological harm to others, such as by stalking, or inciting physical violence against them, perhaps with hate speech.[23]

This book focuses on cybercrime that involves an element of profit, as opposed to cyber-activities with motivations that are more malicious, personal, or political. Profit-driven cybercrime would most closely approximate the second category of Wall's typology. But any given instance might straddle more than one category. For instance, hacking credit card data for profit might also fall under category 1, and launching DDoS attacks (perhaps the closest cyber equivalent to violence) as part of an extortion campaign could meet the requirements for categories 1 and 4 (although in terms of cyber-violence, the psychological harm caused by DDoS attacks may be limited, as many attacks are directed against organizations rather than individuals). Furthermore, there would appear to be profit-driven cybercrimes that do not fit into category 2 at all. One such example would be *market crimes*. These involve the illegal trade in financial data and malware, along with traditional illicit products like drugs, counterfeit products, and weapons that fall on the blurred edges of cybercrime (and are not a focus of this book).[24] Another example would be the provision of a bulletproof hosting service, which involves taking payment from cybercriminal enterprises (such as phishing or illicit pornography websites) to host their illegal content online and refuse to take it down even when directed to by various authorities. In such cases, there is a clear element of profit, but the hosting service is not itself committing the central theft or fraud. In fact, even though many aspects of pornography are legal in a number of jurisdictions, illicit pornography has been traded online through such protected sites (category 3). Based on these various complications, profit-driven cybercrime as a whole might encompass every point in this typology.

Wall's typology is a valuable starting point, but in practice it might be useful to categorize cybercriminal activity by the motivations of its perpetrators.

This may yield, among the broad range of cybercriminals, five common "types": 1) those who are *motivated by personal reasons,* such as a desire for revenge against an old employer, a predilection for child sexual abuse material, or an obsession with an indifferent love interest; 2) recreational hobby hackers *motivated by fun or intellectual challenge,* who intrude into networks or undertake other projects that contravene the law; 3) non-state actors *motivated by political ideology,* such as cyberterrorists or hacktivists; 4) cybercriminals *motivated by financial profit;* and 5) nation-state actors and their affiliates *motivated by military or civilian orders based on geopolitical considerations,* who engage in cyber-espionage against corporate, political, and military targets.[25] For the purposes of this book, the main focus is on the fourth category of profit-driven cybercrime. While there is some crossover, this category should be viewed as quite distinct from other forms of cyber-crime that persist, including hobby hacking, hacktivism, or cyber-espionage. These often (though not always) involve different actors and organizational structures, and as a result are not discussed in much detail in this book.[26]

Who Are Cybercriminals?

Also important as contextual background to the chapters that follow is a grounding in what is known about cybercriminal profiles. This section addresses those involved in cybercrime in a serious way, rather than those who may happen to contravene particular laws in a given jurisdiction accidentally, incidentally, or in a minor way. In the context of profit-driven cybercrime, the focus is on professional and semi-professional cybercriminals attempting to make significant sums of money. Unfortunately, due largely to difficulties of access, the existing literature has not focused on this subject and only provides a sketch.[27] Still, several points can be made.

First, while it is practical to refer to "cybercriminals" in a discussion of cybercrime, it would be wrong to assume that these individuals constitute a homogeneous group. In some sense, profiling the typical cybercriminal is a lost cause. Just as cybercrime as a phenomenon is diverse, so too are the offenders who carry it out. This is a reflection of the strong degree of specialization that has developed in the industry, a topic of Chapter 3. Some offenders are hackers with strong technical skills, while others are organizers who approximate technology entrepreneurs (albeit criminal ones), and still others have little technical ability at all and might simply, for example, make ATM withdrawals with counterfeit cards that have been provided to them. These are just a few roles among many, yet they demonstrate the basic point: given such diverse skill sets, it would be naive to expect participants to conform to one profile. A career fraudster, for instance, is likely to have a very different background from an elite hacker. Rather than attempting to profile cybercriminals, therefore, a stronger approach is to break the industry down into its clearly defined roles, and then assess whether common profiles might emerge among those who carry out specific tasks.

This first point links closely to a second observation: not all cybercriminals are hackers, and vice versa. "Hacking" is obviously an important term within the zeitgeist, but it did not originally have the negative connotations that it does today. As will be discussed in Chapter 2, the original hackers were computer scientists at MIT in the 1950s and 1960s, and in those early days, the term hacker was understood quite differently. It was "someone who does some sort of interesting and creative work at a high intensity level. This applies to anything from writing computer programs to pulling a clever prank that amuses and delights everyone on campus."[28] Since then, the meaning of hacker has shifted to the point that it has become a contested term, often used in the media today to imply criminality rather than a certain skill set or personality. In truth, hackers have a range of motivations, from white hat (good) to black hat (bad) and grey hat (somewhere in between). One Western European hacker I met as part of this study still viewed the term in a neutral way, despite also being a former cybercriminal who made considerable money from his activities:

> Hacking isn't about technology, it isn't about computers. It's about having a hacker's mindset. A mindset to understand things in a different way than other people. It doesn't necessarily mean that you all understand what you are saying. It just means that you are able to understand it differently, to stand out from the crowd. You are able to solve problems in a unique way. You are able to think differently. And usually when you've got that mindset you want to learn. Because without learning you don't know how to do these things (WE-(F)CC-1).

While cybercrime can involve hacking, the two descriptors remain distinct. Some cybercriminals are also hackers, but others are not. Conversely, a great many hackers are not cybercriminals.

A third point to be made with regard to profiling cybercriminals addresses an ongoing debate about whether they, or more specifically the black-hat hackers among them, tend to share common traits in terms of their psychology. Other forms of economic crime have also attracted discussions as to whether offenders have a typical psychological profile that would distinguish them from the broader population.[29] In the case of the criminal hacking population, some suspect there may be a relatively high incidence of autism spectrum disorders, and more particularly of Asperger's syndrome (AS). The argument for a link between AS and cybercrime has gained some traction in recent years, but the evidence is not clear. In a number of high-profile cases, cybercriminals have been diagnosed with AS or related disorders, and some have claimed such psychological factors in their defense. Perhaps the most famous of these is Scottish hacker Gary McKinnon, whose hacking into US military systems led to a protracted, though ultimately unsuccessful, campaign to have him extradited.[30] More recently, a claim of undiagnosed AS came up in Adam Mudd's "Titanium Stresser" case. Mudd, who was a teenager at the time of his offense, was convicted of creating and selling access to a "booter" service that allowed a large number of users to launch DDoS attacks at targets of their choosing.[31] In my informal discussions with a number of prosecutors and law enforcement agents, the notion that AS might be unusually prevalent among cybercriminals resonated strongly with some (although it is also possible that offenders with AS are more likely to come to their attention in the first place). Rebecca Ledingham and Richard Mills confirm that this belief is widespread among law enforcement, but conclude the evidence is not currently sufficient to strongly support the link itself.[32]

Two separate points would need to be established to demonstrate a connection between autism, or AS specifically, and black-hat hacking. One would be to show that this disorder is associated with technical ability or a hacking mentality. The other would be to show that the disorder is even more strongly associated with the criminal application of those skills. Short of establishing the latter, it might only be true that AS is present among cybercriminals to essentially the same degree it is among technical professionals. Speaking from the perspective of the fieldwork undertaken for this study, I cannot claim to have found evidence of pronounced AS incidence. I am by no means a trained expert on the subject, nor is autism the focus of the present research, but most of the cybercriminals I met with did not behave in ways consistent with AS. There were a couple of exceptions, but in most cases my participants were personable and sometimes even charismatic. Of course, my sample may be biased by self-selection in this regard, since those interested in participating might represent a subset that is more socially adept than those who refused my requests. In interviews conducted remotely, it also may be difficult to read the signs of AS. But equally, there may be something about the nature of profit-driven cybercrime, as opposed to other hacking activities, that is less attractive to those who are "on the spectrum." Many of the hackers and former cybercriminals I interviewed believed that strong social skills are important to the business and said they would be surprised to learn that many individuals were involved who lacked such skills (SEA(E)-(F)CC-1; UK-CSP-1). Given the complexity (and medical nature) of the subject, specialist empirical work is required to better understand the link, if any, between AS and cybercrime.[33] It is also important that this work be carried out in different countries and regions, as the findings might vary across societies and economies.

A fourth point to be made about cybercriminals concerns their gender. This appears to be one of the few factors that is consistent among cybercrime offenders. One US law enforcement agent with undercover experience put it this way: "About the only profile that I can probably say is that they're male" (US-LE-2). This appears to hold true across a number of subdisciplines of offending. For instance, while there are some cases of female hackers (US-(F)LE-8), the great majority of those arrested are male. Due to this, I use male pronouns in general discussions throughout this book. Interestingly, there are at least some aspects of cybercrime where women appear to play key roles. Cashing out is one such area (US-LE-2). While some groups are largely male, others make extensive use of women. For example, Chris Aragon, who was the offline partner of elite black-hat hacker Max Butler, employed a number of young women to buy expensive merchandise with counterfeit credit cards.[34] In a slightly different capacity, one cybercriminal I interviewed, Sean, used "drop girls" to provide addresses and receive the delivery of products that had been purchased with stolen funds (WE-(F)CC-1). In the United States, street gangs on the west coast have also been known to make use of women who might otherwise be engaged in prostitution as part of their cashing-out operations. This will be explained in more detail in Chapter 7.

There is little statistical data available on this topic. But below is a tabulation of data from the Cambridge Computer Crime Database, which collates information from the cases of known offenders in the UK.[35] At least in this one jurisdiction, the general claim appears to be supported.

Across all crime types in the database, the gender breakdown is strongly male. In the more technical forms of cybercrime, such as malware and DDoS, the proportion of males is particularly high. (This mirrors broader statistics on female representation in the cybersecurity industry and science, technology, engineering, and mathematics—or STEM—fields of work.) The slightly higher representation of women in the less technical areas also fits with the discussion above. The women involved in cashing out likely fall within the

Table 1

CYBERCRIMINAL GENDER BREAKDOWN

Type of Crime	Total Number (N)	Males		Females	
		N	%	N	%
Malware	100	93	93.0%	7	7.0%
Data or System Breach	127	102	80.3%	25	19.7%
DDoS	44	44	100.0%	0	0.0%
Fraud / Phishing / Social Engineering	132	111	84.1%	21	15.9%
Money Laundering	62	46	74.2%	16	25.8%
Total	465	396	85.2%	69	14.8%

Source: Cambridge Computer Crime Database

category of money laundering. It is also not surprising that the cases of misconduct in public office and breaching data protection laws, which are also included in the database, tend to have a more equal gender distribution.[36]

A fifth point that can be made about cybercriminals concerns their age. The traditional stereotype is of a very young offender, but this appears outdated and unrepresentative. Cybercrime is known to include offenders in their thirties, forties, fifties, and even sixties. BOA, who was a leader of the influential CarderPlanet network (to be discussed in Chapter 2), was in his mid-thirties at the turn of the millennium, despite many of his confreres being in their early twenties or teens. By some accounts he acted as a mentor figure to the group. At the further extreme, in 2016, sixty-two-year-old Charles Eccleston pleaded guilty to attempting to infect US government systems with malware so that he could extract and then sell data to foreign states.[37] There are other cases of people in the same age bracket engaging in cybercrime, including John McHugh (aka Devilman) who was a member of the DarkMarket forum and was arrested for operating a "mini card factory" making use of compromised credit card data.[38]

The fact that offenders vary in age does not mean, however, that they are evenly spread across age ranges. Outside the realm of cybercrime, demographic studies of traditional forms of crime show that offenses are disproportionately committed by people in their teens and twenties.[39] It would not be surprising if cybercriminals fit a similar age distribution. But the more skilled offenders may be at the higher end of that range, given the technical proficiency required and the time it takes to hone one's craft and gain experience in the business. The range may also extend further. If there existed a comprehensive global database of all known cybercrime offenders, it would help answer these questions. There is, however, no such resource and it would be an immense undertaking to create one—which would in any case still fail to capture the ages of those many cybercriminals who never had a brush with the law. That said, accounts based on partial databases from some jurisdictions suggest an average age of around twenty-five or thirty.[40] The former offenders interviewed for this study were often in their twenties when they were at the height of their illicit activities, although a number had a history of (fringe) involvement in cybercrime from their teenage years.

A sixth point concerns the class or social background of offenders—also part of the traditional stereotype of cybercriminals. The common perception is that the middle class accounts for a higher proportion of offenders than it does in other crime types. This belief is rooted in the (formerly) high cost of computers, which meant that the people most likely to commit cybercrime were simply those who had access to the necessary tools. But the world of the 1980s is not the world of today. Computer ownership is much wider, and even those who cannot afford their own devices often have ready access to them through friends, schools, libraries, Internet cafes, and beyond. Mobile technology has also made Internet access more affordable and widespread across the globe. In line with other points made in this section, there appears to be no one-size-fits-all profile with regard to cybercriminal social class. One need only look at the Ghostmarket case to see the range. In that case, Nicholas Webber, the privately educated son of a former Guernsey politician, collaborated with Gary Kelly, who was described as living in "squalid" conditions in council housing.[41] In my own study, I also found a wide variation in the backgrounds of former cybercriminals who participated. Some, like Webber, came from middle-class and more comfortable circumstances, while others described economic struggles and the challenging environments in which they had lived. Of course, many fell somewhere between.

It is very difficult to make accurate claims about the economic circumstances of offenders because, for the most part, the datasets that would allow statistical analysis do not yet exist. This also prevents other important questions from being answered. For instance, my interviews with former cybercriminals point to a possible link between drug use and cybercrime. But this is only suggestive. The presence of drug users may be no higher than among broader criminal populations, or the broader population. Reliable statistics would be required to address this question. Some positive developments are occurring in this regard, including the creation of the Cambridge database mentioned above. But the dearth of data will remain a key difficulty in researching cybercrime, largely because, with a hidden population that has been quite small, surveys are quite difficult to carry out. In this study, it was challenging to access and then interview even a small sample of former cybercriminals, but this approach allowed for a qualitative assessment of whether subjects were genuine cybercriminals or pretenders. To conduct a survey would call for a much larger sample, which would heighten the challenges of access and reliability (as to whether the participants are bona fide cybercriminals). Over time, as the number of cybercrime offenders continues to increase, along with those who are convicted, such surveys may bear fruit. Continued attempts to build usable data sets are also a very valuable endeavor for the academy. But until that is done, many questions relating to the nature of cybercriminals around the world remain unanswered.

A final point to be noted about cybercriminal offenders concerns their motivations. In advocating for routine activity theory, Lawrence Cohen and Marcus Felson famously suggest that "motivated offenders" are one key element of crime, alongside "suitable targets" and the "absence of capable guardians against a violation."[42] This book focuses mainly on financial motivations for cybercriminal activities, which appear strongly tied to aspiration and, for many participants in a variety of places, a lack of suitable employment options. Given later discussions, I will not labor this point here. What is important to note is that rational and economic motivations need not exclude other reasons for involvement in crime. Jack Katz, for example, looking at conventional forms of crime, emphasizes the "seductive qualities" of committing particular offenses.[43] Humans are complex beings, and other more emotional elements likely also play a role in cybercriminals' behaviors.

Throughout this book, there are moments when it is obvious that cybercriminals derive enjoyment or respond to other emotions when committing their crimes. For instance, Chapter 3 features the voices of criminal hackers who clearly prize the intellectual challenge of their work as much as the profits to be gained from it. Succeeding can deliver a kind of rush. A number of former offenders in this study, particularly those with more technical interests, began with curiosity and fun as their primary driver before sliding into crime, whether knowingly or by convincing themselves that their activities fell into a grey area short of illegality (MENA-(F)CC-1, SEA(E)-(F)CC-1, WE-(F)CC-1, WE-(F)CC-3). Many don't regard themselves as "real criminals." In Chapter 6, the case of Andrey, a former cyber-criminal from Eastern Europe, illustrates that the profits made from criminal pursuits are not always spent wisely. He paints a picture of cybercriminals enjoying "good times" with near total freedom: joyriding in expensive cars, drinking, taking drugs, clubbing, and having near-constant sex (EE-(F)CC-2). The former cybercriminal Thiago, a South American, told a similar tale of spending all his gains on travel and female companionship (SA-(F)-CC-1). Even the process of making money can be addictive. Former cybercriminal Tan, a Southeast Asian, explained that "I used to make money a lot every day, it's like a drug you want to have every day" (SEA-(F)CC-2). These and many other complexities in motivation should be noted even though, given the subject matter of this book, much of the focus here will remain on financial gain.

Literature Review and Theoretical Background

This section surveys the relevant literature on cybercrime and provides theoretical background that might be useful to the questions at hand. The review itself is relatively short, given that writings on how cybercriminals have managed to cooperate and industrialize remain somewhat sparse. In fact, the broader social science literature on cybercrime more generally, while growing, is still relatively niche. As the specter of cybercrime has risen over the past decades, scholarly interest in the topic has also developed. But the interest initially was from computer scientists and those from related disciplines: a technical subject area required a technical analysis.[44] Over time, the presence of human actors behind these threats was acknowledged, and more social science–based approaches to the topic slowly emerged. Pioneers in this area have been writing on the topic for decades now, beginning mostly at the turn of the millenium.[45] But recent years have brought a greater flowering of work by criminologists, sociologists, and economists working in this niche discipline of cybercrime.[46]

This growth in the literature results partly from new forms of online data becoming available for analysis, but also mirrors cybercrime's continuing rise as a major public and policy concern. Yet, this budding field still has far to go. Its content is only slowly moving into the academic mainstream and has yet to appear in the pages of many leading social science publications, beyond some respected criminology journals. And while the literature has begun to address some of the novel questions posed by cybercrime, it has only scratched the surface. Numerous topics in the area remain unexplored while the subdiscipline works to determine the best tools to use in each instance. This is certainly the case regarding issues of trust, cooperation, and governance, which are central to understanding the growth of the cybercriminal industry. Therefore, it makes sense to begin with a review of the most pertinent cybercrime literature, before moving to a discussion of relevant theory derived from the broader social sciences that should be more directly helpful in addressing the key concerns of this book.

LITERATURE REVIEW

The most relevant literature for this book is those studies that address the organization of profit-driven cybercriminals. The field is not deep. There are some well-known books on cybercrime.[47] But these offer general overviews of cybercrime rather than specific coverage of financially motivated activities. One of the rare attempts to address this topic directly is Nir Kshetri's *The Global Cybercrime Industry,* which takes an economics-flavored approach.[48] While these works provide interesting conceptual insights, they largely depend on the existing academic literature and open source material, instead of bringing new data to bear on the subject. Given the deficit in general knowledge about cybercrime, such data are essential to a better understanding of the phenomenon. There have also been some good books on profit-driven cybercrime written by journalists, which often rely on a considerable number of interviews and extensive research.[49] While they provide useful sketches in passing, these texts generally focus on the stories of specific cybercriminals, rather than the workings of the industry as a whole.

In scholarly journals, articles on the organization of financially motivated cybercrime have multiplied in recent years. Some of these studies capitalize on the availability of new data, such as from trading forums that are publicly accessible or allow anyone to register for an account.[50] For instance, Thomas Holt and Eric Lampke qualitatively analyze data from discussion threads on six publicly accessible trading forums and describe aspects of these markets including the goods available, the payment systems used, the relationships between users, and the market dynamics.[51] David Décary-Hétu and Benoît Dupont use quantitative methods to study the reputation index of an open-registration, botnet-related forum, and argue that reputation is not randomly distributed, but rather tied to personal characteristics, networking, and behavior.[52]

Such studies shed light on facets of the broader cybercriminal industry, but are often limited to a focus on online forums. As we shall see in chapters to come, there is much more to the organization of cybercrime. And while various studies touch on issues of trust, cooperation, and governance that might help explain how the industry has been able to grow, they rarely deal with these points in detail. Those that do specifically address such concerns appear more interested in levels of trust within certain groupings, rather than in the specific mechanisms used to achieve such levels of trust and subsequent cooperation among cybercriminals. In one study of the social organization of a single hacking group, Dupont examines hacker chat logs provided by Canadian law enforcement.[53] This allowed a rare analysis of private interactions of the group rather than just the communications those hackers were comfortable posting publicly. While the hacking group in question is, by the author's own admission, far from an elite criminal operation, this study is commendable for providing a valuable window into its internal workings. Dupont does consider the role of trust (and distrust) in the group, but his focus is not on the mechanisms that increase trust. Instead, he describes various relationships among members, shifts that took place in them, and why those shifts occurred. In the area of trust and collaboration in cybercrime, the study concludes:

> The social capital that flows through such technology-mediated criminal networks also deserves much closer scrutiny. The scientific literature has, in my view, overestimated the ability and willingness of hackers to collaborate (Taylor 1999: 62; Schell et al., 2002; Holt 2009), assuming that the convergence of the global proliferation of available communication platforms, the semi-anonymity afforded by these technologies, and the jurisdictional boundaries constraining law enforcement agencies have eliminated the barriers that traditionally constrained illicit markets. However, far from creating a frictionless social environment for malicious hackers, these digital tools have a darker side that, under certain conditions, hinders collaboration and fosters distrust.[54]

To date, only a handful of studies have looked at the mechanisms of cybercriminal cooperation in any detail, and this subject has not always been the specific focus of these works.[55] These articles generally examine the key institutions for collective action found in cybercriminal trading forums, such as the power of forum officers to exclude or ban certain members, the provision of escrow services, and the feedback and rating systems that allow users to share information about past dealings. But because these studies analyze data only from forums, they cannot address the subtler interactions and aspects of cooperation that don't take place openly on these sites. These interactions could take place outside forums because users choose to continue communicating via more private means, as discussion becomes more sensitive, or because the cybercriminals in question choose not to join such forums at all. This is not to mention the cooperation that takes place offline, removed from cyberspace itself. Furthermore, to address questions about collaboration, more could be done to connect the cybercrime literature to theories of relevance from the social sciences more broadly, especially those touching on trust, cooperation, or governance that have been successfully applied in other criminal settings.

This book is an extensive investigation of the cybercrime industry and the factors that help explain its growth. It draws on seven years of field research and interviews with 238 participants. It seeks to address some significant gaps in the existing literature, first, by demonstrating the value that fieldwork-driven, qualitative studies can add to cybercrime research, which is often focused on new forms of data rather than on the social science approaches that have traditionally proven effective in studying "hidden populations." Second, in more thematic terms, it aims to increase understanding of profit-driven cybercriminals and their industry at the human level, which remains poorly understood. Third, as a core part of this analysis, it hopes to account for how the growth of the industry could be achieved when cybercriminals face significant challenges to cooperation, most notably when dealing with anonymous criminal partners.

THEORETICAL BACKGROUND

To cooperate with one another and build a functioning industry, cybercriminals must overcome not only the risks of doing business with anonymous fraudsters, thieves, and extortionists, but also the lack of any legal recourse for agreements to be enforced. Leaving aside the literature on cybercrime, broader social science theory might be relevant in helping explain the growth of the industry. Subjects relating to cooperation have been dealt with in some detail across a range of disciplines. But it is common for these approaches to have a rational choice or economics bent. While there is no uniform body of theory that can be drawn on, here I attempt to briefly pull together some of the key concepts that relate to successful collaboration and cooperation that will be relied on throughout this book. These include trust, enforcement, institutions, and governance.

In other criminal settings, trust has been suggested as a possible explanation for co-offending.[56] It is not unreasonable to begin with the same concept in the analysis of cybercriminal cooperation. But first we must define trust. According to Partha Dasgupta, trust consists of "correct expectations about the *actions* of other people that have a bearing on one's own choice of action when that action must be chosen before one can *monitor* the actions of those others."[57] Similarly, James Coleman views it as:

> an incorporation of risk into the decision of whether or not to engage in the action. This incorporation of risk into the decision can be treated under a general heading that can be described by the single word "trust." Situations involving trust constitute a subclass of those involving risk. They are situations in which the risk one takes depends on the performance of another actor.[58]

But it is also vital to differentiate conceptually between trust and trustworthiness. The challenge of trust is that we cannot rely on all others to be trustworthy. To overcome this obstacle, individuals use various mechanisms to assess other people's trustworthiness, which lessens risks within these interactions.[59] In determining trustworthiness, three conventional mechanisms likely apply: appearance, performance, and reputation.[60] The literature on reputation is particularly extensive. In this literature, repeated interactions have regularly emerged as key to how reputations are strengthened and cooperation is enhanced, at least in small-scale interactions among few people.[61] Repeated interactions may be important because they allow for building familiarity, incrementally testing compliance, and sanctioning the other side for defections. Thomas Schelling suggests a slightly different explanation, arguing that the sheer repetition of interaction could in itself perpetuate cooperation:

> Trust is often achieved simply by the continuity of the relation between parties and the recognition by each that what he might gain by cheating in a given instance is outweighed by the value of the tradition of trust that makes possible a long sequence of future agreement. By the same token, "trust" may be achieved for a single discontinuous instance, if it can be divided into a succession of increments.[62]

But trust is not the only way in which cooperation can be achieved. Some forms of cooperation can occur without it, using, for example, the mechanism of enforcement, and related concepts such as monitoring, punishment, and credible commitments. By closely monitoring the actions of a partner, one can ensure that deception does not take place. But such oversight can be very costly in terms of the time and resources required and, in some situations, it might not be possible. Monitoring is more likely to be effective when the burden is shared by a group and information is transferred easily among members.[63] If this fails to encourage compliance, punishment can be applied. Within criminal circles, violence has traditionally been a favored form of punishment, but other means are available. A defector who is sanctioned might come back into compliance, and even if that round of cooperation is already lost, sanctioning might deter future defections by the same male-factor or others who take note of the resulting treatment. Experimental re-search has found empirical support for the *threat* of punishment increasing compliance in later rounds of games.[64] A related means of enforcement is to seek a third party to act as guarantor. This third-party role can be played by the state or its agents, or by various illicit actors with the appropriate skill set.[65]

Cooperation without trust can also be achieved through credible com-mitments, as Karen Cook, Russell Hardin, and Margaret Levi explain: "When there is no ground for trust, we can often establish reliability by dem-onstrating our commitment to take relevant actions. If we, whom you have no reason to trust, wish to convince you that we will be reliable in taking some action that will benefit you, we can try to establish a credible commitment."[66] There are two famous game-theoretic examples of credible commitments to be found in the work of Thomas Schelling: *cutting off options* and *informa-tion hostages*. The idea of cutting off options was originally explored by Schelling in his classic work *The Strategy of Conflict*. He showed that lim-iting one's own options can lead to a strange inversion by which "weakness is often strength, freedom may be freedom to capitulate, and to burn bridges behind one may suffice to undo an opponent."[67] Schelling later settled on an historical example to explain his point using the strategy of the Greek gen-eral Xenophon. When facing the Persians, Xenophon chose to position his army with its back to a ravine. His view was that the enemy could flee in any direction, but by cutting off options, the message to his troops and their opponents was that the Greek army was now bound to fight, and to win. Schelling saw how such commitments could influence others' choices.[68]

Schelling's concept of information hostages is perhaps even more rele-vant to the realm of cybercrime. This idea approximates the historical ex-change of hostages to strengthen relationships and avoid conflict. Instead of swapping people, however, information is exchanged. This enhances co-operation by allowing each party to inform on the other, in case one should defect. Schelling provides a hypothetical illustration:

Both the kidnapper who would like to release his prisoner, and the prisoner, may search desperately for a way to commit the latter against informing on his captor, without finding one. If the victim has committed an act whose disclosure could lead to blackmail, he may confess it; if not, he might commit one in the presence of his captor, to create the bond that will ensure his silence.[69]

Diego Gambetta extended Schelling's idea, suggesting that "deviant" groups could reinforce internal loyalty by having members exchange evidence of their past misdeeds.[70] Campana and Varese examined two traditional organized crime groups, finding that, along with kinship, shared information about violent acts could help enhance trustworthiness and elicit cooperation.[71]

For a suggestion of how the information hostages concept might apply to profit-driven cybercrime, one could consider online pedophile groups. Such groups form largely to share child sexual abuse material online. Gambetta outlines the kinds of tests that must be passed to join these groups, which seek to prove commitment and verify that potential members are not undercover agents.[72] One example is the requirement to supply ten thousand original sexual abuse images. In another, stricter test, members travel to a different country in order to assess potential new recruits in person. Explaining the relevance of this, Gambetta writes that, because "identification is at a premium and must be kept secret, just showing one's face is itself like giving a hostage, namely, the knowledge of one's key sign of identity."[73] In the same way, we might expect some profit-driven cybercriminals, who are very distrustful of others, to vet potential collaborators they have met online by asking to meet face-to-face in a specific location.

So far, the focus has been on trust and enforcement. It is clear how these elements can contribute to cooperation, especially on a small scale. Individuals can assess the trustworthiness of potential partners and act accordingly. They can also seek to enforce matters themselves or rely on trusted figures to provide third-party enforcement. But difficulties emerge if they wish to expand trade by moving beyond the small scale and begin to collaborate with, for instance, strangers about whom they know little and who might disappear before a deal can be completed.[74] In his extensively cited paper "Institutions," Douglass North summarizes the problem in game-theoretic terms:

Wealth-maximizing individuals will usually find it worthwhile to cooperate with other players when the play is repeated, when they

possess complete information about the other player's past performance, and when there are small numbers of players. But turn the
game upside down. Cooperation is difficult to sustain when the
game is not repeated (or there is an endgame), when information
on the other players is lacking, and when there are large numbers
of players.[75]

To understand the development of such a large industry as cybercrime,
something more is required. Cybercriminals come from all over the world
and, online, little is known about them unless they choose to reveal it. There
are many of them, and sometimes an individual wishes to collaborate with
a partner for one deal only. For those challenging examples that Douglass
North examines, the solution can be found in *institutions,* as he defines
them:

> Institutions are the humanly devised constraints that structure po-
> litical, economic and social interaction. They consist of both in-
> formal constraints (sanctions, taboos, customs, traditions, and
> codes of conduct), and formal rules (constitutions, laws, property
> rights). Throughout history, institutions have been devised by
> human beings to create order and reduce uncertainty in exchange.[76]

The key mechanisms relating to trustworthiness and enforcement still drive
cooperation, but effective institutions enhance the operation of these mechanisms and allow them to be scaled up. Institutions lead to an overall ordering of interactions and reduce the costs involved in exchange. Without
them, it would be difficult for actors to move beyond dealing only with
those that are well known to them and with whom agreements can be relatively easily enforced.

From this discussion of institutions we can move to a final point on
governance. These two concepts are closely linked, as those who provide
governance are often responsible for the creation or management of institutions. At a broad theoretical level, there are two ways in which such a
system of governance can emerge. One is in a top-down manner, where order
is imposed by a hegemon, as classically stated by Thomas Hobbes.[77] The
other way is bottom-up, whereby order comes about spontaneously and
without design, and evolves to meet needs among humans but not always
in predictable ways.[78] A related division can be found in discussions of
extra-legal governance, which suggest different possibilities for how economic governance might develop in situations where the state is unable

to protect property rights effectively or enforce contracts. Avinash Dixit argues that in such cases there are two alternative organizational structures that can (at least partially) take the place of the state: private governance and self-governance.[79] Private governance involves paying third-party individuals or groups to enforce contracts and provide protection for property rights, in top-down fashion. Self-governance, by contrast, is akin to a bottom-up approach, and assumes order can emerge and be maintained within a group as long as options for communal punishment exist and information about members cheating each other can be transmitted across the group.

In the literature relating to criminal groups, private governance has generally been assigned a key role. In fact, for a certain school of scholars, the whole concept of organized crime is built around governance. Thomas Schelling's central argument is that organized crime is not simply "crime that is organized."[80] By way of explanation, Schelling offers his now famous distinction between burglars who organize, say, to "work in small gangs," and those involved in true organized crime. Unlike the latter, who seek to monopolize crime, he writes:

> burglars are never reported to be fighting each other in gangs for exclusive control over their hunting grounds. Burglars are busy about their burglary, not staking claims and fighting off other burglars. It is when a gang of burglars begins to police their territory against the invasion of other gangs of burglars, and makes interloping burglars join up and share their loot or get out of town, and collectively negotiates with the police not only for their own security but to enlist the police in the war against rival burglar gangs or nonjoining mavericks, that we should, I believe, begin to identify the burglary gang as *organized crime*.[81]

In Schelling's formulation, genuine organized crime groups attempt to regulate and control some form of illegal industry. This approach is central to the definitions of organized crime and mafias that Varese settles on after surveying the various definitions that have been applied to the subject.[82] For Varese, an *organized crime group* "attempts to regulate and control the production and distribution of a given commodity or service unlawfully." As for the definition of *mafia*, he follows Gambetta.[83] This is a particular type of organized crime group that "attempts to control the supply of *protection*."[84] In effect, a mafia desires to govern all criminal markets.

Empirical evidence supports this governance-centric approach to understanding organized crime. Henry Hill, the mobster who was the inspiration for Martin Scorsese's film *Goodfellas,* provides a street-level definition of the Mafia. In *Wiseguy,* the book from which the film was adapted, Hill explains the function of Paul Vario, the Lucchese crime family *Capo* in his neighborhood:

> The guys who worked for Paulie had to make their own dollar. All they got from Paulie was protection from other guys looking to rip them off. That's what it's all about. That's what the FBI can never understand—that what Paulie and the organization offer is protection for the kinds of guys who can't go to the cops. They're like the police department for wiseguys.[85]

Among the questions this book will explore are whether cybercriminals have achieved a similar level of governance in their dealings and whether this has contributed to the overall success of the industry. Also to be examined is the extent to which traditional organized crime groups like mafias may be involving themselves in cybercrime and providing a degree of governance themselves.

In this section on theoretical underpinnings, I have tried to pull together existing concepts that might help explain how cooperation can be achieved and enhanced on a broad scale. The argument has been that trustworthiness and enforcement play a key role, but that to scale their impact, cybercriminals likely need the help of institutions and a system of governance. The more established and efficient these mechanisms become, the greater levels of cooperation there should be. But it would be naive to expect cooperation to become universal. Even within societies with strong institutions and governance, some defection takes place. In these contexts, laws and formal contracts are employed to reduce the risks and create order. More informal means can also be used, including establishing reputation—by way of, for example, repeated, successful transactions or, in the case of strangers, online reputation systems within e-commerce.[86] Yet even with these measures in place, some risk endures. The court system in a certain jurisdiction might not function efficiently or transparently. A long-standing partner might suddenly decide to make off with your money.

Given the fundamentally distrustful environment of cybercrime, the expectation is that these actors will also face defection, probably to a much higher degree than in transparent and well-functioning societies. After all, they are dealing not only with criminals, but often with anonymous strangers as well. This further weakens trust and any available enforcement options, thereby increasing risks. But to establish the industry that they have managed to build, cybercriminals must have found ways of minimizing these risks. The theoretical concepts described in this subsection offer a strong starting point for investigations into how this success has been achieved, and will be drawn on throughout this study.

Approach and Structure

This book focuses on two key points. First, it argues that cybercrime has evolved into a sophisticated, profit-driven industry. Second, it seeks to understand how this evolution has taken place when anonymity and other challenges would suggest that cybercriminals might be more likely to operate alone or in small groups. The approach undertaken in this book is strongly qualitative, and it is also exploratory. In its attempt to draw a map of the cybercrime industry and how it functions, it enters largely uncharted waters. The preceding section on theory offers some useful guidance to keep us from becoming lost in this expanse. That said, much of this book's contribution is empirical, offering new insights into cybercrime and aiming to provide a detailed overview of the subject based on field research over a seven-year period. Therefore, this study cannot be packaged to fit neatly into popular academic distinctions, such as empirical versus theoretical, deductive versus inductive, or explanatory versus interpretivist. It should rather be seen as a first step in exploring an immense if often hidden world. Perhaps, following this study, it will be easier to read the map and engage in some narrower and more tightly defined investigations that fall within these distinctions. In the meantime, no apologies are made, but further discussion of this point can be found in Appendix 2.

Appendix 2 also includes a more detailed discussion of data and methods. In short, this study of profit-driven cybercrime was an enormous undertaking and is perhaps the most extensive project of its kind to date. Along with legal documents, archived cybercriminal communications, and open-source material, some 238 interviews provide the foundational data. Collecting this information was not an easy feat, but began with a naive student in 2011, who had no knowledge of cybercrime and no contacts at all in the area. To correct this deficiency, over a seven-year period I carried out fieldwork in twenty countries across all the inhabited continents. Through detailed investigations, I tracked down participants and leveraged the further contacts that they and others provided. I built up a network of subjects that gradually edged me from the periphery of the underground economy closer to its heart, constantly driven by tracking down "white whales" and finding others who could verify the information they provided. As part of this effort, I visited suspected cybercrime hotspots in countries including Russia, Ukraine, Romania, China, Nigeria, Brazil, and the United States. In each location, interviews were carried out with law enforcement agents, professionals in the private sector fighting cybercrime, former cyber-criminals, and others with knowledge of the subject. Other interviews were carried out "virtually" through calls, writing, or messaging. This exploration could probably have continued endlessly and gone deeper still; the result is by no means perfect. But it is important now to share the results.

Tables 2 and 3 summarize the distribution of the 238 participants included in this study by geography and profession, respectively. In Table 2, the regional, rather than country, signifiers marked with asterisks refer only to former cybercriminal participants and are used to better protect their identities (discussed further in Appendix 2). In Table 3, the distribution by profession combines both active and former members of each vocation.

To protect the identities of all participants and encourage more open contributions, throughout this text I employ randomly chosen pseudonyms that are not connected to each subject's real name, and also make use of a code to signify each person. The first part of each code lists the country where the participant is based, or region in the case of former cybercriminals. The second part lists that person's profession. In cases where an individual had multiple roles, I have listed the one that is most closely linked to the interview data the subject provided. The final part of each code is the number of that participant type in chronological order. For instance, UK-LE-3 means that the person is based in the UK, is an active law enforcement agent, and is the third of this kind I interviewed. Two complications arise when someone is an expatriate (E) or provides information largely derived from a former profession (F). To illustrate these more complex cases, here is another example: SEA(E)-(F)CC-1. This is the code for someone in Southeast Asia who is an expatriate, a former cybercriminal, and the first of that type I spoke to. The country and regional signifiers should be relatively intuitive but are contained in Table 2, as well as in the headings of Appendix 1, which provides a list of the participants in this study. Table 3 also summarizes the profession signifiers.

Finally, to preview the whole book's structure, the next two chapters address the first concern of the study: how cybercrime has evolved into an industry. Chapter 2 outlines the history of profit-driven cybercrime, and Chapter 3 offers analytical insights that make sense of the topic within the framework of industrial organization. The remaining four body chapters address the second concern: how this industrialization has taken place given the challenges of anonymity. Chapter 4 addresses how cybercriminals

Table 2

DISTRIBUTION OF PARTICIPANTS (GEOGRAPHY)

Code	Meaning	Number of Participants	Code	Meaning	Number of Participants
AUS	Australia	8	NIG	Nigeria	15
BRA	Brazil	9	RDT	Redacted	5
CHN	China	7	ROM	Romania	16
EE*	*Eastern Europe*	5	RUS	Russia	18
GER	Germany	1	SA*	*South America*	1
HK	Hong Kong	7	SEA*	*Southeast Asia*	3
IND	India	3	SGP	Singapore	6
INT	International	6	SWI	Switzerland	2
IRE	Ireland	2	THA	Thailand	4
KOR	South Korea	5	UDL	Undisclosed	2
LAT	Latvia	3	UK	United Kingdom	24
MY	Malaysia	8	UKR	Ukraine	10
MENA*	*Middle East & North Africa*	1	US	United States	41
NA*	*North America*	5	VN	Vietnam	13
NLD	Netherlands	4	WE*	*Western Europe*	4

Table 3

DISTRIBUTION OF PARTICIPANTS (PROFESSION)

Code	Profession	Number of Participants
A	Academic	1
CC	Cybercriminal	20
CSP	Cybersecurity Professional	97
FSP	Financial Sector Professional	11
H	Hacker	4
ITP	IT Professional	4
J	Journalist	3
LE	Law Enforcement Agent	72
OO	International Organization Officer	6
P	Prosecutor	15
RDT	Redacted	5

establish online identities using nicknames, a foundational requirement before any cooperation can take place, while Chapter 5 investigates what mechanisms cybercriminals employ to enhance cooperation online. Chapter 6 explores why some cybercriminals seek to collaborate offline and how this might strengthen the industry. Chapter 7 assesses if there is a degree of offline governance aiding cybercriminal cooperation, whether provided by organized crime groups or otherwise.

2

From Lone Wolves to

Industrialization

THIS CHAPTER provides a history of profit-driven cybercrime. It charts the evolution from its origins to the present day. This has seen a move out of activity that was largely informal and focused on recreational and ideological concerns, and that was often not illegal in the early days of hacking, to the growth of a large, illicit, and somewhat professional industry, heavily driven by profit. It is largely a story of a shift from lone wolves to industrialization.

There is surprisingly little literature on the development of cybercrime. Even major social science texts provide scant background on how it has evolved.[1] While the history of hacking in the West has received some attention from scholars, journalists, and others, they have not shed much light on the related but distinct history of cybercrime.[2] Even those directly addressing cybercrime often deal broadly with the development of hacking, malware, and related activities, and give only secondary attention to profit-driven enterprises.[3] They have also tended to focus on the US and other western nations, devoting little space to those parts of the world that now house the engines of the cybercrime industry, such as countries in Eastern Europe. Additionally, much of their work covers the time period from the late 1950s to the turn of the millennium, tailing off at the very point at which profit-driven cybercrime began to flower. A small number of journalistic accounts do provide potted histories of this more commercial form of cybercrime.[4] But these are often truncated, as such popular books are primarily concerned with the specific stories they are telling. While useful, they do not offer comprehensive explorations of the evolution of financially motivated cybercrime.

This chapter, therefore, has to draw from sources beyond the limited accounts existing in the literature. Legal documents, whether publicly available or furnished to me directly, represent one source of relevant information (though in many cases, those that would provide fertile ground for research are sensitive and understandably held close by the relevant government agencies). Various digital footprints have been archived or published, such as elements of now defunct forums that played an important role in their day, and can be used for research purposes. Some cybercriminals have made public statements or written about certain issues, as well. These all provide important clues in tracing the evolution of profit-driven cybercrime. But even taken together, they are not enough to provide a rounded picture. As a result, a significant part of this chapter is also an oral history, drawn from interviews with those who directly participated in events and those who tracked them. Accordingly, some caution is required. While care has been taken to verify particular claims, given the paucity of other data, this is challenging at certain points. These oral sources provide a means to recount past events, but it should be clearly noted that human memory is fallible (especially on details like precise dates) and it is possible that certain individuals may give accounts that play up their own personal contributions or serve grudges they might have against old adversaries. Yet, until new data can be found to provide greater clarity, these sources remain the best starting point.

This chapter contains six main sections. The first section outlines a brief history of hacking, beginning with the early days when it did not involve illegality. The second section addresses the turn to illicit profit-making activities in the 1990s, and the third section recounts the rise of online cybercriminal trading forums and their Golden Age. The fourth section examines the specialization of forums that took place, while also addressing the fragmentation of the market that followed the end of the Golden Age. The fifth section is focused on the development of operational structures and groupings that carry out cybercriminal activities. The sixth section provides an account of the growth of essential cybercriminal "infrastructure" including virtual currencies and bulletproof hosting. The final section briefly assesses the current state of cybercrime and cybercriminals.

A Brief History of Hacking

While some locate the origins of hacking far back in human history, computer hacking by definition is a much more recent phenomenon. Its beginnings are conventionally traced to MIT in the late 1950s.[5] These first hackers were computer scientists, driven by intellectual curiosity, who began to experiment with the university's mainframes, the prototypical computers of the day. As Steven Levy recounts in his classic text *Hackers,* a "hacker ethic" soon emerged based on some foundational ideas that persist to the present day: that access to computers should be "unlimited and total"; that "information should be free"; that authority should be mistrusted; and that "hackers should be judged by their hacking" rather than by other considerations. These core principles were supplemented by some inspirational mantras such as: "You can create art and beauty on a computer" and "Computers can change your life for the better."[6] This hacking culture soon spread to other university computing centers, which was further assisted by the advent, in the late 1960s, of the Advanced Research Projects Agency Network. ARPANET was the first major network linking hundreds of universities, research institutes, and companies.[7] At this point, hacking did not involve any strong sense of maleficence; it was largely recreational and intellectual.

The other early activity often associated with computer hacking, but involving phone technology instead, was *phreaking.* This practice followed a similar timeline to early hacking but faded away with the introduction of digital phones. Nonetheless, it played an important role in the history of hacking and in the individual narratives of some who would become very well-known hackers, such as white hats like Steve Jobs and Steve Wozniak and black hats like Kevin Poulsen and Kevin Mitnick. Phreaking involved the manipulation of phone systems to make free calls by creating a 2600-Hz frequency tone through whistles or other means. While phreakers enjoyed some profit in the form of free calls, their main interest often appeared to be exploration and research into this new frontier.[8]

Beginning with the MIT hackers, and as the community expanded more widely in the decades leading up to the 1980s, the tradition was largely about intellectual curiosity. This was also before the introduction of relevant legislation banning computer intrusions and other activities. One pioneer of hacking in Europe, who operated in the 1980s, explained his motivations in this way: "I was about twenty-one, twenty-two, hacking for fun, not to gain any money, never did. Purely for fun, challenge of breaking into machines. Never really made any secret of it." Jeremy described his activities as not being "anything desperately clever," but being possible because "people left passwords where they shouldn't have done." His approach was also collegial, with regular online sharing within a network of other hackers, as well as offline meetups over casual meals to discuss their activities (WE-(F)H-1).

During the 1980s, matters started to become more serious, both in terms of the activities taking place and the increased legislation and enforcement that responded to them. By this time, personal computers had become more widely available and computer systems were increasingly networked, developing toward what would become the Internet. This meant there was a group of potential hackers much larger than just university students and others with access to institutional machines, and a much wider range of targets. Some in this period displayed darker motivations, causing significant damage and drawing the attention of authorities. In certain cases, it was "computer game-ish." Hackers, somewhat oblivious to the serious implications of their online actions, sometimes created a "giant oops factor." In other cases, there was a clearer mission to extract data or carry out malfeasance (US-(F)P-4). Perhaps the most famous black hats of the time were Kevin Poulsen and Kevin Mitnick. Poulsen began phreaking and hacking into ARPANET in the early 1980s. Later, as a fugitive from the law (from 1989 to 1991), he famously used his skills to rig a radio station call-in competition and win a Porsche.[9] Mitnick was involved in a number of serious intrusions against both government institutions and corporations, but profit never seemed to be his primary goal.[10]

At this point, a degree of organization also began to emerge and hacking groups developed. Some of the most famous of these are the Chaos Computer Club in Germany, the Cult of the Dead Cow in Texas, and other former groups like Legion of Doom and the Masters of Deception. Such groups blended traditional hacker ethics, centered on information sharing and open boundaries, with what might be regarded as early aspects of hacktivism.[11] They sometimes breached criminal codes in certain jurisdictions by infiltrating systems and engaging in other activities; certain members of Legion of Doom and Masters of Deception even faced prosecution for a range of offenses. Meanwhile, hackers with links to the Chaos Computer Club were caught penetrating US systems in the 1980s and selling the data to the KGB. Clifford Stoll's classic *The Cuckoo's Egg* recounts his personal hunt for one such intruder.[12]

Development of malware followed a course similar to hacking's evolution. In the 1980s, most viruses and worms were created out of intellectual curiosity or mischief. Perhaps the most famous example was the worm released in 1988 by Robert Morris, a graduate student at Cornell University. It wreaked havoc on computer systems, but that did not seem to be Morris's motivation. Once he realized what was happening, he tried to notify others of how to stop the worm.[13] By the 1990s and early 2000s, malware had become increasingly malicious and destructive, but the motivations still ostensibly centered on mischief, chaos, and cyber equivalents of vandalism, rather than on anything strongly profit-focused (UK-CSP-2).[14]

The Turn to Profit

The conventional history of hacking usually ends around the turn of the millennium. But it is at this point that profit-driven cybercrime begins in earnest. As echoed by others (HK(E)-CSP-1, UK-CSP-2, US-(F)LE-8), one retired senior US law enforcement official summarized the shift to this next phase of cybercrime:

> I think that it has evolved—I think that it has evolved to become organized. I think earlier on, it probably really starts where it can be measured in the late '90s. Before that, the connectivity and the commerce was not robust enough for it to be anything really profitable. I mean there was hacking—there has been hacking since the '80s, but the infrastructure and commerce didn't really take worldwide until the late '90s. And I think early on in the late '90s, the type of crime that was committed was more the equivalent of vandalism: people were defacing websites, there were denial of service attacks, there was absolutely state-sponsored intrusions back then, but not the level of criminal activity that we see now. Fast-forward twelve years later, fifteen years later, and you see, because of the way our economy has evolved and the way organizations have pushed data to the network, the value of the data is so great, it's inevitable that crime would migrate to the network, because that's where the money has migrated (US-(F)LE-2).

Two things distinguish the history of profit-driven cybercrime from that of hacking. First, as noted in the Introduction, cybercrime is not synonymous with hacking. There are many aspects of it that do not involve hackers or hacking. While some parts of the history of cybercrime derive from hackers shifting into criminal activities, there are also examples where that is not the case. There are many hackers who have no involvement at all in crime, and statements to the contrary can cause offense to this substantial group. Second, while the history of hacking has US roots, or rather is conventionally ascribed in such a way (rarely addressing developments elsewhere), the origins of profit-driven cybercrime have been found in a range of countries. In fact, it is more accurate to refer to multiple histories of cybercrime, with each geographical location producing its own brand of it. These various origin stories deserve attention, but there are too many to address comprehensively in the scope of this chapter and book (though some will be touched on in a later section and in the following chapter.) In any case, the general narrative remains similar. From the 1990s onwards, computers and access to the Internet become more widely available for users across the globe, just at the time when increasing amounts of data and commerce are being digitized and finding their way online. All across the world, an economic opportunity emerges to tempt both the technologically adept and those simply looking for new ways to make money.

A pattern emerges across many cases by which the development of local cybercrime takes place in phases. The first phase involves students and others who have access to new technologies, an eagerness to explore, and time on their hands. While some malfeasance might go on (for example, website defacements), at first, profit is not a major concern. This has been seen in examples as diverse as the United States, Russia, and China. At some point, a shift occurs leading to a second phase—and perhaps second generation— much more focused on financial gain. These groups may abandon some of the ethics, and even rules, of the earlier generation (US-(F)LE-2, RUS-ITP-1, CHN(E)-CSP-1). Andrey wrote about how this process worked growing up in the former Soviet Union:

> I think, it is important to understand, that our hobbies were in no way mixed with financial interest or any hopes to learn new specialty, we just liked it and were fond of it. However, once you learn, you apply your skills in the time of need, had this need arise. And this is just what happened. Everywhere (EE-(F)CC-2).

Russian IT professional Artyom talked of the people he knows from the "dark side" and how they are "highly professional." There is no romanticism anymore, he said, it is just about "money, money, money" (RUS-ITP-1). Lance also noted a similar process in the English-speaking forum scene. In the early days, many had an open mindset and were highly collaborative. But, over time, the dynamic shifted and little happens any longer without payment. As a result, Lance believed, there was less knowledge exchange and scams had become less innovative (NA-(F)CC-3). In places like Romania and Nigeria, the narrative of a movement from hobby to profit might not hold as strongly, since financial motivations were more present from the early days. Yet these places have still seen shifts toward professionalism and serious criminality. While Romanian cybercrime began with students, it became increasingly organized and sophisticated as time went on, and attracted the involvement of other criminal elements (ROM-(F)LE-1, ROM-LE-1, ROM-P-1). In Nigeria, cybercrime has likewise become increasingly technical, coordinated, professional, and capable of yielding serious earnings (NIG-ITP-1, NIG-(F)LE-1, US-LE-10).

The above discussion hints at the importance of geographical context in understanding cybercrime, a point to which we will return in the next chapter. As noted above, the scope of this chapter does not allow for a thorough examination of all the localized forms of cybercrime around the world. Instead, the remaining sections are concerned with the development of the global market for cybercrime, a virtual bridge for cybercriminals working in different geographical concentrations that allows them to conduct business together. It is open to actors from any country around the world, so long as they have some value to add to the community. This has led to the development of a distinct and flourishing transnational cybercrime industry.

The Golden Age of Forums

The birth of profit-driven cybercrime happened largely in the 1990s. Before this period, there were occasional cases of financially motivated attacks, such as the half-million dollar defrauding of the Internal Revenue Service in 1975 mentioned by Donn Parker.[15] But as time passed and new opportunities emerged, more scams came into existence. While a number of cases went unnoticed or unreported, some key investigations suggested what was to come. In 1994, St. Petersburg-based Vladimir Levin successfully penetrated Citibank in the United States, leading to the illicit transfer of over $10 million through a well-organized network of accomplices.[16] In 1997, Californian Carlos Salgado stole a large database of 100,000 credit card numbers and associated data by hacking into a major Internet company. Salgado attempted to sell the database for $260,000, but it was likely worth considerably more.[17]

As large as the potential damage was, the Salgado case is perhaps more important in illustrating the nature of financially motivated cybercrime during the 1990s. While individuals and small groups were starting to involve themselves in profit-driven criminal activity online, there was very little organization or sense of the industry that would evolve. In his excellent book *Kingpin*, Kevin Poulsen, a former black-hat hacker turned journalist, describes (somewhat derisively) how Salgado attempted to sell his wares online through the #carding Internet Relay Chat (IRC) channel under the nickname SMAK:

> It was like offering a 747 for sale at a flea market. At the time, the online credit card fraud underground was a depressing bog of kids and small timers who'd barely advanced beyond the previous generation of fraudsters fishing receipt carbons from the Dumpsters behind the mall. Their typical deals were in the single digits, and their advice to one another was tainted by myth and idiocy. Much of the conversation unfolded in an open channel where anyone in law-enforcement can log in and watch—the carders' only security was the fact that nobody would bother.[18]

The turn of the millennium brought this period of disorganization to a close. It was at this point that the true marketplaces for cybercrime began to emerge. In the early days, most trading between cybercriminals was done via IRC. Lance, a North American veteran of the carding scene and pioneer of the early forums, who has since left the business, explained the deficiencies involved with the IRC format:

> Before the forums, everything was done through IRC. The problem with IRC was, it was so quick that people could come and just say anything and it was really hard to conduct business. So what the forum purpose served was that you could see these posts going on and you had a record to refer back on, as far as what these people were talking about. With IRC you didn't really have that. Once a conversation was done, it was done. So the forums allowed that history and for users to look back and say, "okay this guy has been talking about this, this, this, and this." And to a point that allowed people to get a vibe for the seller or the buyer to see if they were able to do business, if they were able to trust them (NA-(F)CC-3).

Some scholars have argued that IRC marketplaces match the characteristics of a "market for lemons."[19] The most famous statement of this broad concept is found in George Akerlof's classic paper of the same name, which argued that buyer uncertainty over the quality of goods creates incentives for the sale of poor merchandise and could potentially lead to market failure. To avoid this outcome, various institutions—such as guarantees, brand names, and licensing—might serve to counteract quality uncertainty.[20]

The introduction of forums appeared to aid the development of such institutions and revolutionized the way business was done. This was the effective birth of the true cybercrime market and the increasingly professional industry that followed behind. Cybercriminal forums are not dissimilar to Internet forums on any other topic. They are a series of *boards* that have different topic areas where discussion threads can be posted and other users can respond. As Lance explained, this format crystalized these discussions and allowed them to be recorded for later viewing, rather than disappear into the online ether. This was essential for reputations and brands to form (US-LE-10), a point addressed in Chapter 4. In time, other functions emerged that facilitated more effective business dealings, such as product review systems and the provision of escrow services. These elements will be addressed in more detail in Chapter 5.

The history of forums is a little murky. The Ukrainian forum Carder-Planet has taken on a central status in the cybercrime narrative.[21] But while its impact was probably the greatest, because it provided a model for how future marketplaces would be run, it was not the first. That honor is shared by a set of forums that were either outright scam sites or that failed to flourish to the same degree as CarderPlanet did. Prior to the CarderPlanet period, Lance described getting conned by a scam forum where the administrator maintained multiple identities and posted positive reviews about himself back and forth (NA-(F)CC-3).

The first (known) genuine attempt to overcome these issues in English was a forum called Counterfeit Library (US-LE-3, US-(F)LE-8). While Counterfeit Library came to address this need in the market, it was hardly a "cybercrime forum" in its genesis. Founded in 2000 by a small number of fraudsters based in North America, who were not highly technical operators, it began as a place to complain about being ripped off, but evolved into a marketplace for the trade of fake documents, such as IDs, which are useful in conducting many types of fraud (NA-(F)CC-3). There are fewer details on the structure and operations of Counterfeit Library than on some other forums because the site closed down before it could be penetrated deeply by law enforcement (US-LE-3). Nonetheless, it seems that the key contribution that it made was to provide a credible meeting place online for various types of fraudsters and other criminals, along with a mechanism by which they could establish brands.[22] The nature of boards as opposed to the IRC format helped somewhat. But Lance claimed the site also offered an innovation: in order to sell products on the forum, the goods had to be reviewed by the administrator, which meant a physical copy had to be sent to him (NA-(F)CC-3). Merchants had to be vetted. It was an early version of what would later become common practice in many cybercrime forums: the verified vendor.

There is little doubt that Counterfeit Library predated CarderPlanet. But there were also prototypical developments happening in the Russian-speaking world. Script, the entrepreneurial Ukrainian cybercriminal who would go on to found CarderPlanet, described seeing another earlier website, www.carder.org, which inspired his efforts. He believed that this existing site was the first on the topic of carding, but that it had poor quality information among other problems. Script and his friends created a new website called www.carder.ru, intended to remedy its deficiencies. Although their site was short-lived, it was followed by the revolutionary creation of CarderPlanet.[23]

Beneath the surface of Script's account is perhaps a struggle to define the history of cybercrime. Thus far, CarderPlanet appears to have won this battle, with many writers accepting its dominant position with little challenge. But some actors do question this narrative, and significant further investigation is required to verify exactly what occurred in this period. In basic terms, it is important to note that CarderPlanet did not emerge from nowhere, but is rather a product of a slower evolution within Eastern European hacking and then cybercrime. The origins of the cybercriminal community appear to be tied to FidoNet, a computer network facilitating bulletin-board communication. This played an important role in the former Soviet Union in the 1990s, providing curious technologists with a means to interact and share before the Internet was widely accessible (RUS-CSP-5, RUS-CSP-6). Andrey wrote about his experiences in the 1990s with FidoNet:

> Since at the time, in Russia, Internet access was scarce and unbearably expensive, few people used it for personal or recreational purposes. BBS and FidoNet flourished and through my friends I became one of FidoNet happy users. "Fido" was way beyond just a network, it was community of friends, we have local and regional meetings, where we drank beer and discussed everything from personal problems to global issues, so basically everybody knew everybody. There was lots of moderated "echo conferences" dedicated to various topics, so you can subscribe and take part in conversations of your preference. Naturally, in those conferences leaders, knowledgeable, talented, and well respected persons emerged. Those conversations were barely governed by any law and ruleset except its own moderators and you can find whole lot of il-

legal subjects from phreaking, hacking, to illegal drugs, or even pornography in its extremes. From there I obtained first issues of "phrack" magazine, and basic concepts of hacking (EE-(F)CC-2).

He added that "in '97 in FidoNet echoconferences I first seen what might be precursors for carding, topics such as how to defraud online store or how to obtain freebie" (EE-(F)CC-2). But in his view, another powerful driver of interest in hacking came from the Russian magazine *Hacker* (Xakep). In his words, it was "pure revelation" and "a spark that set fire," openly covering fraud, mockery, pranks, social engineering, phreaking, carding, and more:

> Each issue contained examples (and still does) as of how different hacks were perpetrated and . . . featured everything from hacking Pentagon to AOL, to banks, ATMs, all stories are real, and later they even included CD with video. Of course, I tried myself, as did others and I liked what I seen. In fact, I remember topic on CarderPlanet, where we studied what way different persons came into hacking, and about 7 / 10 persons told that they became interested after reading "Xakep" (EE-(F)CC-2).

Once hooked, Andrey and his confreres went looking for others with similar interests. Some happened upon the Russian-language website called carder.org, which was founded by a user called VIP (EE-(F)CC-2; EE-(F) CC-4). This site filled the carding niche online, as but one of a number of Russian-language forums that existed around the turn of the millennium serving various grey and black desires (for example, hackzone.ru and asechka.ru).

Script's account indicates that carder.org served as a forerunner of his efforts to create CarderPlanet. But little is publicly known about how this occurred. Andrey suggested that carder.org was a community of skilled operators focused on financial fraud, a number of whom played a major role in cybercrime. It included some of the key figures, like BOA, who would help lead the CarderPlanet network. Another Eastern European former cybercriminal, Leonid, also believed that carder.org contained some of the "best carders" around (EE-(F)CC-4). Andrey noted that the "forum rules were strict, and it banned conversations on other than fraud-related topics, moderation was harsh. However, attitude was friendly and welcoming to the people who asked right questions and liked to learn, but completely intolerant to ignorance and arrogance" (EE-(F)CC-2). At a certain point, Script became known to the group as a vendor of stolen credit cards and was invited to join the forum. But afterwards, Andrey claimed, Script was effectively forced out. Following a damaging incident within the community, carder.org's administrator issued a decree that "reselling is 'right next to ripping' and pronounced that if somebody [wanted] to sell something, it should be goods they obtained by their own means and physically possess." In Andrey's recollection, Script argued against this approach and was banned from the forum. This then led him to found his own site—carder.ru—with the help of some others. This site was eventually shut down by its host, however, which ultimately led to the birth of CarderPlanet (EE-(F)CC-2).

Despite the more complex history of forums outside of the CarderPlanet narrative, there remains little doubt that CarderPlanet played a key role in popularizing cybercrime on a global scale (US-LE-3, US-(F)LE-8). When I probed whether other significant forums might have predated CarderPlanet, or been just as important as CarderPlanet at the time, interviewees generally did not present any strong evidence. Particularly among western cybercriminals, there was a clear sense that CarderPlanet was the first major Eastern European forum that had gone global and provided an entry point for dealing with cybercriminals in that region and beyond. In their minds, it was a foundational development.[24] Much of the mystique associated with the site is tied to its chief founder, Script. A somewhat legendary figure, he has the reputation in some quarters of being a technical mastermind. While some of my interviewees subscribed to this view, others suggested that this was an inaccurate picture (UKR-(F)LE-3, UKR-CSP-1, EE-(F)CC-2). In their view, Script was not a hacker in the true sense of the word and often relied on others to carry out his technical needs. His real abilities lay elsewhere: "he was talented manager, businessman, and somewhat politician, and on top of all he was very lucky to be at the right time in the right place" but also "brilliantly understood trends and tendencies," leading and organizing others to achieve great successes (EE-(F)CC-2). As former cybercriminal Leonid wrote, "Script's mind was more global" than others and he "made CP the best forum that times" (EE-(F)CC-4).

The origins of CarderPlanet have taken on somewhat mythical proportions because of evidence that the key players met in person and held a cybercrime "convention" in Odessa, Ukraine. But accounts differ on this point. Poulsen recounts a 2001 meeting where 150 Russian-speaking cybercriminals met for a summit at a restaurant in Odessa to discuss the launch of CarderPlanet.[25] He suggests they were spurred on by the success of Counterfeit Library, and that the conference attendees were eager to create a Russian-language site that would allow them to congregate online and do business. A short time after the summit, the International Carders Alliance was established, along with the website called CarderPlanet (although it is possible that these ideas had already been developed prior to the conference (EE-(F)CC-2)). Meanwhile, in his book *DarkMarket,* Misha Glenny describes a meeting in Odessa taking place in 2002. This was The First Worldwide Carders' Conference, marking the anniversary of CarderPlanet's birth. He suggests that the main meeting was held in the Odessa Hotel, with other, smaller, more exclusive gatherings taking place throughout the city. The meeting was not about the founding of the site, but rather about how to improve and expand the carding business.[26]

Rather than there being discrepancies between these accounts, it appears likely that both meetings took place, with a possibility that there were other major gatherings as well (UKR-(F)LE-3, US-LE-3). As will be discussed in Chapter 6, there were likely also smaller meetings drawing together key members of the network.[27] While individual memories on specific details are beginning to fade, law enforcement records can confirm some major points. One law enforcement document furnished to me confirms the 2001 meeting in Odessa, suggesting it included over 150 mostly Eastern European criminals and that it led to the establishment of both the CarderPlanet website and the International Carders Alliance. The other meeting in 2002 was also confirmed by a US law enforcement agent rechecking records, with the Odessa Hotel named as the location.

Leaving aside its origins, CarderPlanet's true impact was in creating the first genuine global marketplace for cybercrime. Poulsen views the site as a "reinvention" of Counterfeit Library for the former Soviet Union, but with a greater emphasis on being a "disciplined online bazaar" rather than a "freewheeling discussion board."[28] The other major difference was that Counterfeit Library initially focused on fake documents, while the central part of CarderPlanet's trade was compromised credit card details, which would become a mainstay for profit-driven cybercrime for many years. CarderPlanet also operated in Russian along with other languages to bring in a global membership (US-(F)LE-8). Overall, Andrey wrote about its contribution in these terms:

> Comparing to its progenitors, as well as earlier discussion boards, echo conferences, and chats, CarderPlanet underwent simple but extremely important change: it abandoned "geekish" cybersociety culture and cyberpunk values and adopted business common sense and values, and purely for profit model. It existed to make profit and to enable its members to do so, and all the business logic came with

it. It just happened that it promoted quick profit by absolutely illegal means (EE-(F)CC-2).

One Ukrainian security researcher with knowledge of this case even recalled
that coffee mugs had been made with the CarderPlanet logo on them, a form
of quasi-corporate memorabilia (UKR-CSP-1).

CarderPlanet would also become a model for future forums. First, it
introduced a strict hierarchy for the website, appropriating ranks from the
Sicilian Mafia, including the "Family," "Capo di Capi," and "Capo."[29] Inspired by *The Godfather,* Andrey described this as a good example of
Script's "Odessa touch," defined by a "knack for humor, commerce, argument resolution, and crime" (EE-(F)CC-2). Many subsequent forums
would employ a similar hierarchy, though often with less emotive titles.
There is some variation, but commonly each site has one or more administrators acting as leaders and supported by moderators. These latter officers enforce the rules coming from above and deal with day-to-day issues
in, for example, managing subforums. Below the moderators are ranks of
members with varying seniority and related privileges.[30] Second, and in a
similar way to Counterfeit Library, CarderPlanet required that vendors
pass through a review system before they could sell on the site. Whereas
Counterfeit Library vendors were reviewed directly by the administrator,
the CarderPlanet hierarchy provided for approved reviewers who could
perform this function, presumably freeing up time for its leadership.[31]
Third, CarderPlanet appears to have introduced a very important element
of governance into the burgeoning economy: a cybercriminal escrow
system.[32] This entailed the transfer of payment, and sometimes goods, between buyer and seller through a third party. This has since become a key
element of the cybercrime economy, especially among Eastern European
actors.

While CarderPlanet provided a viable model for cybercrime forums, this
in itself was not enough to ensure the development of an industry. In an
interview with *Hacker* magazine, Script explained that there are no such
things as "universal" carders and that any carder, at some point, will need
the services of another person. Part of Script's goal was to unite these specialties to allow the business to thrive:

> In reality, carders are like lone wolves, they do not gather in groups
> and do not create their own networks, they work for themselves. . . .
> So-called forums are like dens of wolves, they exchange informa-
> tion or observe who offers what in each field to find new solutions.[33]

But while Eastern European carders had significant expertise and a keenly entrepreneurial spirit, they lacked one key component in their business model. Many of their targets were in the West, which meant that the money from compromised credit cards and other scams often had to be cashed out there to avoid the suspicions of western financial institutions and banks. In many cases, purchases shipped directly to Eastern Europe would be blocked; sometimes shipping there was not even possible. Script and his colleagues needed a group of committed fraudsters in the West to carry out this aspect of the business. Lance argued that Counterfeit Library provided a near-perfect fit:

> Script and company have CarderPlanet open and it's strictly a Russian site. At the time, you've got all the information that's in Russia, but the Russians over there don't really have the ability to cash out. So stateside, it's Counterfeit Library at the time, and we're huge over in the states, but we don't have all this credit card information (NA-(F)CC-3).

In this purported narrative, the key moment was when a number of major Russian-speaking players, including Script, BOA, and BigBuyer, came over to Counterfeit Library and joined as vendors:

> Up to that point we were basically just identity theft and eBay scams, small time stuff like that. Script and all these guys bring the credit card information over there and like overnight we transition more from IDs into credit card thefts (NA-(F)CC-3).

A cross-germination took place. With the key CarderPlanet members vending on Counterfeit Library, CarderPlanet opened an English-language section allowing some members of Counterfeit Library to ply their trades there.

In contrast to Lance, the Russian speakers I interviewed were a little more circumspect, but still acknowledged the importance of this East–West interaction. Maintaining a sense of superiority, Leonid made clear that the vast majority of leading suppliers were from the former USSR, but that foreigners were "our main 'cash cow'" and provided a deep market for the considerable volume of credit data and other products made available (EE-(F)CC-4). Andrey wrote further about CarderPlanet's opening up to international operators and bringing in those who were behind Counterfeit Library and later ShadowCrew:

It was due to many factors, for one, Script, as talented manager invited Boa and other reliable vendors to CarderPlanet. In turn, Boa at the time had criminal enterprise of his own called boafactory.com and provided everything from bug detectors to fake passports through network of people he knew throughout the world. Boa was well known, respected, and prolific vendor, he advocated to attract "noobs," newcomers, and educate them, thus, we all were writing articles, from which new members were able to learn basics of fraud and carding. Then, as they advanced their criminal activities, they required more complex and sophisticated services, and thus they turned to us verified vendors and we gladly provided them with "cobs," "cvvs," "dumps," "plastic," etc. In turn, vendors such as Script or Boa, having no skills or ability to obtain goods they vending by themselves, tapped in large network of hackers and other enforcers, who always stayed in shadows (EE-(F)CC-2).

While not widely documented, this alliance likely provided some of the foundations for the development of a transnational cybercrime industry. Without the connection of the technical elements to the cashing-out elements, profiting from cybercrime is very difficult. This exchange of services between cybercriminals from the East and the West has remained fundamental to the structure of the cybercriminal economy ever since. Counterfeit Library and CarderPlanet largely originated the scene online. Whereas before, lone wolves operated, unable to easily find partners, buyers, sellers, and information, the establishment of the forum scene partly solved these problems and created an online community with its own norms and understandings.

The legacy of Counterfeit Library and CarderPlanet outlived the sites themselves. Both came to an end within a few years. The former ran into some practical difficulties and was shut down by its administrators (NA-(F)CC-3). CarderPlanet was also removed by its own leaders, in August 2004, after it attracted too much law enforcement attention.[34] Their concerns were probably justified. Roman Vega, aka BOA, had been arrested in February 2003 in Cyprus and extradited to the United States.[35] Dmitry Golubov, aka Script, was taken into custody by Ukrainian authorities in the summer of 2005. He was released only months later on the recommendation of some local Ukrainian politicians, and has now become a politician himself.[36] He founded the Internet Party of Ukraine in 2007.[37] Later, in 2014, he was elected to the Ukrainian parliament and, at the time of writing, Golubov serves as a member of the ruling Petro Poroshenko Bloc.[38]

The cybercrime industry would continue to grow after the fall of these sites. Just as the forum format developed by CarderPlanet became a model for future sites, the key players from CarderPlanet (and carder.org) formed the foundation of a network of talented actors who would be linked to a number of significant cybercriminal enterprises going forward (US-LE-3). Andrey acknowledged that a new generation has now emerged, but boasted that "we laid foundation to core principles and aspects of carding. Somehow, we were 'Escobars' of carding, so we did first, and the others followed" (EE-(F)CC-2). With CarderPlanet gone, many cybercriminals moved on to other forums and operated there. These groupings included Mazafaka, the International Association for the Advancement of Criminal Activity (IAACA), Carder's Army, and Carder's World, among others.[39] But, at the time, the most expansive global imitation of CarderPlanet was ShadowCrew. This was an English-language forum founded in August 2002, chiefly by Deck and Black Ops. These two figures were reminiscent of key CarderPlanet players. Following their convictions, Deck was revealed to be Andrew Mantovani, an Arizona business student in his early twenties who saw himself as the "spiritual leader" of the forum. Black Ops, like BOA, was the older partner. He was in his forties, with prior experience as a mortgage broker.[40] The scale of their achievement was impressive, with claims that ShadowCrew reached four thousand registered users and connected a diverse set of criminals from around the world, including Eastern Europe.[41]

Some of the central players from Counterfeit Library migrated over to this new forum, just as they were shutting down their own site. They brought that experience with them and contributed to the development of Shadow-Crew's review system, whereby approved vendors had to be vetted by endorsed reviewers (NA-(F)CC-3). While the site had a strong focus on carding, it also provided for a large range of other forms of criminality. These included broader cybercrime activities like the sale of DDoS attacks or fake documents (in the tradition of Counterfeit Library), but also activities that were not related at all, such as the sale of drugs. Child sexual abuse material was a rare banned product.[42] Such a prohibition is common in cybercriminal forums, but it probably had less to do with morals than with self-protection: fighting child sexual abuse has historically been the one cause that unites law enforcement cyber units across the world and benefits from strong political support and funding.

ShadowCrew was perhaps a victim of its own success. It soon attracted law enforcement attention and became the subject of a US Secret Service investigation. Albert Gonzalez (aka Cumbajohnny), a high-ranking member of the forum and a leading cybercriminal in his own right, was arrested in

2003 and turned informant. Following his cooperation, Operation Firewall was carried out on October 2004, leading to the arrest of some of the biggest players on ShadowCrew and the closing of the forum.[43] Although written to emphasize the gravity of the criminality involved, the indictment in the case also highlights the significant organization and governance involved in a major cybercrime forum:

> Administrators collectively controlled the direction of the organization, handling day-to-day management decisions as well as long-term strategic planning for its continued viability. Administrators determined which individuals were permitted to become and remain members of Shadowcrew; the functions, responsibilities, and levels of access to information for all members of the organization; and the rewards accorded members for their loyalty to Shadowcrew (e.g., elevated status within the organization) as well as the punishments meted out to members disloyal to the organization.[44]

With ShadowCrew gone, the forum scene was disrupted. Instead of one dominant successor forum emerging, several marketplaces competed for supremacy among the world's cybercriminals. Among these new English-speaking forums were Scandinavian Carding, the Vouched, TalkCash, DarkMarket, and CardersMarket. The latter two would eventually engage in the online war documented by Poulsen in *Kingpin*.[45] Former members of ShadowCrew were commonly involved in these later sites. JiLsi, aka Renukanth Subramaniam, a Sri Lankan immigrant to Britain, was one veteran of ShadowCrew who became a founding member and key administrator of DarkMarket.[46] Established in 2005, DarkMarket operated in a similar vein to ShadowCrew. Some liken it to a "Facebook for fraudsters,"[47] but as with other criminal forums, it was more akin to eBay in its trading function, though it was also a place where cybercriminals could congregate and build some sense of community, retaining a social component along with the purely business elements. It was perhaps the largest and most successful site of its kind at the time, at least in the English-speaking world, and provided a key hub for the trade of compromised credit cards, their associated goods and services, and a growing list of other cybercriminal wares (UK-LE-1, US-LE-2).

DarkMarket's central competitor in the carding business was CardersMarket, which was founded by Max Butler (aka Max Vision). Under the handle Iceman, Butler served as administrator of CardersMarket and displayed a rare skill set for someone in that position: he was an elite hacker. Carding administrators tend to be fraudsters, like JiLsi, rather than technical operators. This is logical given that, though some technical knowledge is required, overseeing a forum is largely an operational and managerial challenge. In contrast, Butler had a fearsome reputation as a hacker and his technical abilities continue to inspire reverence, or at least grudging respect, among some former cybercriminals I have interviewed (NA-(F)CC-2, EE-(F)CC-2).

Most famously, perhaps, this period saw the emergence of another well-known cybercriminal: Master Splyntr. With a reputation as a leading Polish spammer, Splyntr eventually rose to the rank of administrator on Dark-Market. But Splyntr's rise ultimately led to the downfall of DarkMarket in 2008, along with the demise of CardersMarket and the arrest of key cyber-criminal figures including Max Butler and JiLsi. Splyntr's real name was not Pavel Kaminski, as was widely believed, but Keith Mularski. Mularski was an undercover agent for the FBI, based in Pittsburgh, who had successfully fabricated an online persona that fooled major cybercriminals around the world.[48] While he wasn't the first such agent to infiltrate a major forum, Mu-larski can be seen as the cyber equivalent of Joseph Pistone, an undercover agent who worked his way into the Bonanno crime family in 1970s New York and was on his way to being a "made man" before the FBI extracted him.[49] Mularski's success can be viewed symbolically as the end of the period when just a few forums dominated the online scene. After this episode, a new environment developed. Numerous forums proliferated, with their status rising and falling over time, as new marketplaces came into existence and others went extinct (US-LE-10).

The Specialization and Fragmentation of the Market

While English-language carding forums have often attracted the most attention from writers and scholars, it is important to note that the cybercrime scene is a lot more varied than carding alone. In the early days, card fraud was one of the most lucrative activities available and so it became an immediate focus. But from CarderPlanet onwards, the carding sites themselves have incorporated other activities, even if card fraud remains their primary business. For instance, they have commonly offered other products and services, such as DDoS attacks, hacking tools, exploits, hacked eBay or Amazon accounts, databases of personal information, hardware, hosting services, spamming services, phishing services, malware, and botnet rental.[50] In recent years, some attention on those sites has shifted from carding to other increasingly profitable areas like online banking fraud.

Forums also emerged that specifically focused on other aspects of cybercrime. For instance, after its founding in 2008 and until its takedown in 2015, Darkode became perhaps the preeminent English-language forum on the more technical aspects of cybercrime, such as malware and botnets. Other forums have specialized in areas such as hacking and zero-day vulnerabilities.[51] Still more exist to support click fraud and spam.[52] Some forums focus on trade, while others center on discussion. Sites for generalists provide a broad range of subforums on various topics, while specialist boards emphasize core topics like spam. This splintering of focus might be an acknowledgment of the value of creating niche communities, but it may also be an attempt to limit law enforcement interest. An administrator might ban carding from a spam or click-fraud forum because the latter activities are sometimes viewed as legal grey areas, whereas carding is unequivocally criminal and would attract greater law enforcement attention and penalties. This is a similar approach to ShadowCrew's banning of child sexual abuse material and many carding forums' refusals to allow sales of drugs or firearms. Overall, forums are often classed as either primarily technical or more business-focused like the carding forums (NLD-(E)CSP-1).

Forums also developed to specialize not only by subject, but also by language. While they conduct business in many different tongues, from the beginning, the Russian-language forums have stood alongside English-language ones as the most significant for the global market (US-CSP-14, UKR-CSP-1, UKR-(F)LE-3). It is important to clarify, however, that these forums cater not specifically to Russian nationals, but to Russian speakers across the world and particularly those in the former Soviet Union. These forums can be thought of as the technical engine rooms of global cybercrime, hosting elite hackers and coders, and those representing them. As mentioned above, after the closing of CarderPlanet, many former members moved on to other forums. While some Russian speakers spent time on international boards like ShadowCrew, where they could access partners in other countries that could cash out their wares and provide other services, a number stayed with Russian-oriented forums. The most successful site in terms of reputation was Mazafaka, which continues, at the time of writing, to be one of the leading Russian-language marketplaces. Later Russian forums that emerged and became successful include Verified and Direct Connection, although there are a number of lower-level and "beginner" boards below this point as well (UKR-(F)LE-2).

Just as in the English-language scene, more technically-focused Russian sites also emerged. These appear to stem from a different line than the business-focused CarderPlanet. Perhaps the most famous of these forums has been anti-chat.ru, which originated in the same period and began as an irreverent "hackerish" discussion forum, later developing a commercialized section (RUS-CSP-5, RUS-CSP-6, UKR-CSP-3, EE-(F)CC-2).[53] The same basic trend also occurred in other technical sites. For instance, the software-cracking and reverse-engineering forum reversing.net had sections on topics like viruses, but also a section for commercial activity. These business sections allowed for the sale of products like exploit kits.[54] This trade led to an increasing specialization within the community, as actors did not need to be skilled in every discipline. Goods and services could simply be purchased from others with expertise in different areas (RUS-CSP-5, RUS-CSP-6).

After a time, some of these commercial sections developed into fully-fledged private forums, often charging an entry fee to keep out schoolchildren and low-paid security researchers. These marketplaces were increasingly specialized and often forbade activities like carding. Two Russian security researchers, Vladimir and Aleks, noted that there are many ways for cybercriminals to make money and the "smarter ones" generally try to stay off law enforcement's radar (RUS-CSP-5, RUS-CSP-6). Part of the shift toward private forums may have been in response to bans by some of the major discussion forums, like anti-chat.ru, of commercial activities on their platforms. Igor, a Ukrainian security researcher, suggested that a core of Russian-speaking cybercriminals used to come from anti-chat.ru, but that this is no longer the case. The site is now more for learning and sharing information, rather than being closely related to business. In a similar vein, Igor suggested that another important forum called webhack was closed entirely by its administrator, as he didn't want it morphing into a cybercriminal marketplace (UKR-CSP-3). In recent years, exploit.in has served as a particularly important Russian-speaking forum on the more technical side of cybercrime (UKR-CSP-3, UKR-(F)LE-2).

For some time, there has been a distinct schism between the English- and Russian-speaking forums. Eastern European cybercriminals are often viewed as less trusting than those from elsewhere, perhaps as an effect of their post-Soviet environment (RUS-FSP-3, RUS-CSP-10, RUS-CSP-11, US-LE-2). While all participants in the scene are considered somewhat suspect, mistrust is particularly directed at westerners. Part of this may be the lingering influence of Soviet-era propaganda, but more recent events also play a role. With the western law enforcement pressure facing CarderPlanet and the subsequent operation against ShadowCrew, which embroiled some major Russian-speaking players, it is not surprising that much of the ex-Soviet community retreated to Russian-speaking forums and became wary of those who did not speak the language. Mixed-language forums are now rarer, and a number of forums not only strongly vet potential members based on their reputations but even have entry tests that require knowledge of the Cyrillic alphabet or Soviet-era trivia to restrict membership to supposed insiders (RUS-CSP-3, RUS-(F)LE-1, RUS-CSP-5, RUS-CSP-6, US-LE-10). During the mid-2000s, when DarkMarket and CardersMarket were at their peak, the Russian scene was already largely separate. Mularski's deep infiltration into the English-language forums certainly wouldn't have helped repair the schism. In the face of law enforcement interventions, CarderPlanet's somewhat naive global vision seemed dead.

Nonetheless, some interaction between Eastern European cybercriminals and others remains. There is still money to be made in the global market, where the technical elite of the East can sell its wares to western and other criminals. For instance, the leading cybercriminal and supposed author of the Blackhole exploit kit, Paunch, was active on the English-language forum Darkode.[55] While new ways to monetize stolen data have emerged, cash-out specialists based in western countries are still a valuable part of the underground economy. Some forums like Carder.su were built around key Russian suppliers of credit card data or other products, with a market of buyers or partners from around the world. The interactions across geographical lines have become more cautious and guarded, however, than in the CarderPlanet and ShadowCrew era. For instance, while the leading Russian forum Mazafaka has had certain English-speaking members, perhaps claiming a Russian connection, these members cannot gain much trust from the community or go particularly far in terms of business (NA-(F)CC-2, UKR-(F)LE-2). Scott, a former North American cash-out expert who engaged in the activity full-time and at a high level, wrote about it this way:

> Mazafaka was supposed to be only for Russian-speaking people etc. I had been on it a lot but if you didn't speak Russian it was not really best place for English speakers. A lot of the serious Russians wanted to start dealing with only people that spoke fluent Russian because it was kind of a way for them to feel more comfortable that you were not a US law enforcement guy etc. (although that in no-way assures it). They could tell fakes trying to use Google translate etc. because they could never speak fluent Russian slang (NA-(F)CC-2).

The effect of law enforcement pressure on cybercriminal forums has not been limited to Russian-speaking cybercriminals. Since the operation against ShadowCrew that involved a Secret Service informant, and Dark-Market's eventually being run by an undercover FBI agent, cybercriminals have become very suspicious of major forums in general. The presence of undercover agents and informants has continued to be a major feature of these online marketplaces and their takedowns. Former cybercriminals I interviewed said they had been mindful that any partner could be a rat (NA-(F)CC-2, NA-(F)CC-3, NA-(F)CC-4, EE-(F)CC-2). Scott had been a member of forums since the CarderPlanet days but, due to these concerns, attempted to limit his involvement with them:

> Around the time the forums IAACA and DarkMarket (sting site) were around, I kinda fell off of the forums because I no longer needed them and felt like there was too much heat on them after the Shadowcrew bust in 2004. I had already made a bunch of contacts and didn't really have a need for the forums any longer, so I just chatted with the partners I already had on ICQ and IRC etc. I eventually got back involved with forums . . . later on when most of the people I had known for years eventually disappeared (busted, retired, etc.) and I needed some new contacts. There were still several people I had known for years that I talked to a lot, but most were scared to be on any forums anymore like I said so a lot of people were no longer participating in them. There were also other forums that they WERE on, and myself included, but it's probably best that I don't elaborate on that. They were more "elite" in general and more "closed" so I guess people felt they were more safe (NA-(F)CC-2).

Scott also homes in on the central purpose of forums within the cyber-criminal community. Rather than serving as the essence of the scene, they provide a place to network for those who do not have sufficient contacts. In the current environment, undercover law enforcement agents and security researchers are well entrenched in the major marketplaces. These meeting places now appear to be something of a necessary evil that one uses only when there is no other choice. This is a common view among former cybercriminals I have interviewed. Lance viewed forums with some suspicion, despite having been closely involved in establishing a number of them. While ShadowCrew was operating, Lance was making considerable income from other forms of fraud that didn't require online partners. At this point, word began to spread about law enforcement interest in Shadow-Crew and its members, so Lance took the opportunity to retire from the marketplace and gradually phased out much of his online presence elsewhere (NA-(F)CC-3).

Nonetheless, large forums have continued to operate in both the English- and Russian-language scenes. Examples have included the Russian stalwarts like Mazafaka and Direct Connection, and largely English-focused sites like Ghostmarket, Kurupt.su, Carder.su, Omerta, and Infraud (which was taken down in early 2018). Following the founding of Silk Road in 2011, there has also been an increase in so-called Darknet sites (or cryptomarkets, in the latest parlance) that make use of Tor or other anonymization tools. While these sites attract significant media attention and a growing amount of academic investigation, they are not a significant paradigm shift from an organizational perspective. First, for those participating on these "hidden" sites, they operate quite openly and in much the same way as traditional forums, albeit with perhaps an even greater bent toward business. Second, while some cybercriminal dealings, like trade in compromised credit cards, occur on sites like AlphaBay (taken down by law enforcement in July 2017), the emphasis of many cryptomarkets has been on drugs. Some believe these sites serve a lower level of cybercriminal actor and also offer lower-quality products and services, like card data (US-LE-10, NA-(F)CC-2).

It should be noted that a number of leading forums, including key Russian-speaking sites, do not operate yet as cryptomarkets (although some flirtation with the idea might be occurring in certain cases). One might hypothesize that more technical actors have other ways to protect their identities, beyond an off-the-shelf and rather slow solution like Tor, which might be better suited to drug buyers who lack a strong interest in technology and operational security. Foreign cybercriminals might also be suspicious of a software platform that was originally developed by the US government, or they might simply not need such protection, given that they feel safe from arrest in their local environment (a topic to be discussed further in Chapter 7). These points caution against conceptualizing a purely Darknet-centric underground. While there is some movement toward Tor, this instead often consists of sophisticated actors building the technology into the services that they provide (US-LE-10).

While certain Russian forums have operated for many years, English-language sites have generally faced greater pressure from law enforcement, often leading to arrests and website takedowns, and new marketplaces emerging over time. As a result of these threats, the preference among the connected now seems to be for smaller, more secure groupings. Scott elaborated a little further on what these groupings look like:

> As for the more "elite" closed forums, etc., there was really nothing different about them at the time other than it was just more secretive among the known people that were trusted for a while. Some were only known to people in their "inner circle." Some only were for Russians etc. . . . .
>
> As for the number of members on some of the other forums . . . I don't remember for sure but we are talking numbers in the 100's as opposed to 1000's. . . . I remember one hacking forum with as low as 80-something members, I think (and some of those are multiple logins from same people I'm sure) (NA-(F)CC-2).

The organization of profit-driven cybercrime has come almost full circle. Some cybercriminals have even reverted to small chat groups, which were originally in vogue before the rise of Counterfeit Library and CarderPlanet. At the time of this writing, Jabber is a particularly common platform being used by cybercriminals (US-LE-2, UDL-CSP-1, NLD(E)-CSP-1, US-(F)LE-1). One security researcher described the lengths to which some groups go to secure their communications, restricting membership to small numbers of trusted users who have been vouched in, and then using encryption, VPNs, and Jabber: "They tend to go ultra paranoid for those." He also noted the recent prominence of Telegram not only for communication but also for trade, which feels like "almost a step back to the more real time IRC days" (IRE-CSP-2).

The Development of Operational Structures

Of course, the history of profit-driven cybercrime is not only the history of marketplaces. While forums play an important role in the industry, they are far from the only organizational structure to have evolved. One should also consider groupings that go beyond simply engaging in trade to actively carry out aspects of cybercrime. Script may have envisaged forums as dens for lone wolves to meet, but it is not surprising that, once they met, wolf packs formed. In practical terms, one of the most common cybercriminal group structures is akin to a crew. Just like a bank robbery crew, a cybercrime crew involves a small number of individuals with particular roles.

Malware groups have had perhaps the most profound impact on the broader cybercrime economy. The year 2007 brought the archetypal Zeus Trojan horse.[56] With that, a new era of cybercrime emerged in which malware was widely used for profit-driven activities and became a valuable product in itself. Zeus has been linked to widespread malfeasance, including the compromise of bank account credentials. Other families of malware followed, including SpyEye, Gozi, and Gameover Zeus. The latter is a variant of the original, and has been linked with the impactful CryptoLocker ransomware campaign that began in 2013.[57] This was not the first form of ransomware, but the scale of the attack captured public attention and caused substantial losses. The threat of ransomware has hardly receded, as evidenced by the 2017 WannaCry campaign that made headlines around the globe.[58]

But what do the groups behind these pieces of malware look like? Rikard, a security researcher with a strong knowledge of the malware scene, described teams of typically three to eight people, with eight usually being the limit (UDL-CSP-1). This rough assessment was echoed by other participants (UK-CSP-2, UKR-CSP-1). Maksym, who monitors the Russian-speaking underground, stressed that there is no one-size-fits-all model, but sketched the structure of a malware production group (Figure 1). In his illustration, there is a boss who is likely the original author of a piece of code and its owner. The boss may hire a software developer to work on aspects of the code, in the same way that legitimate coders sometimes engage others due to time restrictions, the amount of work involved, or the specialist nature of the programming required. This developer is kept on salary. The boss and the developer bring the malware to fruition, and then the boss hires two or so sellers to take the product to market. These sellers are usually on a salary, but may also earn commissions on sales. Maksym believed such groups could work successfully over a time span of months, but that a year was usually the longest they could hold together before various "disruptions" occurred (UKR-CSP-1).

Certain crews may also operate together in an offline capacity, having met in the first instance on forums, in their local communities, or through mutual acquaintances. Moving beyond malware, Albert Gonzalez, one of the most infamous and highest-earning American cybercriminals of all time, operated with a number of associates. Together they engaged in "war driving," cruising past the Wi-Fi signals of major "big box" stores to find

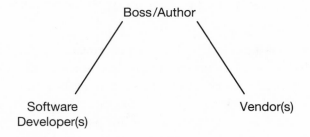

Boss/Author

Software
Developer(s)

Vendor(s)

Figure 1   Malware Production Group

and access networks from which they could steal credit card information.[59] But perhaps the most prevalent offline structure that has evolved is the cash-out crew. These groups are responsible for turning digital gains into cash or valuable items. Given the nature of the work, which usually requires in-store purchases or ATM withdrawals, it is logical that many of these offenders are personally acquainted with one another (NA-(F)CC-2). While there are examples to the contrary, the organizer of each crew often recruits people known to him or to others he trusts, some of whom might come from a broader background of criminality (WE-(F)CC-1, NA-(F)CC-2, UKR-CSP-3).

Some examples move beyond crews toward larger entities that mimic legitimate businesses. In 2012, Russian authorities moved against a Moscow-based criminal group that had stolen tens of millions of rubles from online bank accounts using Carberp malware. Among those arrested were two brothers, who had leased office space and given their enterprise the external appearance of a tech company.[60] When Brian Krebs profiled some of the leading spam operations of recent years in Russia, he provided great detail on how business-like they can be, with official places of business, hierarchies, and employed staff.[61] It should be noted that spamming operations fall into different legal categories depending on the jurisdiction, but in Eastern Europe they are generally regarded as being in a fringe area of legality, allowing some grey enterprises to function. Overall, it is clear that operational structures have evolved alongside the development of the broader industry. In fact, all these groupings relate closely to the concept of firms, which will be discussed more directly in the next chapter.

The Growth of Cybercriminal "Infrastructure"

Another important facet of the evolution of profit-driven cybercrime has been the growth of what might be called economic infrastructure. For instance, this has included the development of virtual currencies, and the hosting of illegal content and operations. The advent of virtual currencies has been vital to the expansion of profit-driven cybercrime. Without a functioning monetary system, widespread trade and online payments would have been very difficult to facilitate. In the early days, the Russian company WebMoney offered a solution to this problem. Founded in 1998, it began operating just at the time when the nascent cybercrime industry was itself emerging and was widely used for online payments on CarderPlanet.[62] Security researchers Vladimir and Aleks described the importance of WebMoney to cybercrime by comparing it to *hawala,* the money-transfer system that facilitated trade out of the Islamic world in the medieval period (RUS-CSP-5, RUS-CSP-6).

Other virtual currencies also have been adopted by cybercriminals. These have included E-gold, Liberty Reserve, and Perfect Money. The attraction of these currencies is that they often operate out of nonwestern jurisdictions, ostensibly beyond the reach of western regulators or law enforcement who might try to interfere with them. Equally important is that, being loosely regulated and requiring little if any information that would identify their users, they allow pseudonymous transfers. The Costa Rica–based Liberty Reserve, founded in 2006, was a good example of such practices. It became perhaps the leading cybercriminal currency before being shut down in 2013 by a multi-country investigation involving the US Secret Service.[63] In the wake of Liberty Reserve's demise, Bitcoin arose as an increasingly important currency among cybercriminals. Like other virtual currencies, it allows its users to maintain anonymity, while offering the added advantage of being decentralized (US-LE-8). Within more recent times, there are claims that cybercriminals are increasingly exploring the use cryptocurrencies other than Bitcoin.[64]

The evolution of cybercrime also owes much to another facet of infrastructure: bulletproof hosting. A bulletproof host is quite similar to a standard Internet service provider (ISP), but specializes in hosting activities and businesses that would be deemed illegal in a number of jurisdictions. Bulletproof hosts refuse requests to shut down the offending sites.[65] The most famous of these enterprises was the Russian Business Network (RBN), which was perceived as a cyber bogeyman for a number of years, and a usual suspect in much cybercriminal activity, even when its involvement was unlikely.

The history of RBN is shadowy, partly because some researchers and writers choose not to comment publicly on it for fear of reprisals (US-CSP-14; UK-CSP-2). This appears to stem from beliefs that the group was connected to the Russian Mafia, but the validity of that concern remains equally unclear given the lack of published material on the subject. The commonly agreed facts have been that RBN's primary business was to provide bulletproof hosting and that it operated out of a hub in St. Petersburg.[66] RBN played a very extensive role in the market and was regularly implicated in supporting a large number of cybercriminal enterprises.[67]

Drawing on Russian-language sources, Krebs provides rare details on the history of RBN. He traces the group's origins to Minsk in the early 2000s and in particular to a young Belarusian named Alexander Rubatsky, whose father was a high-ranking police officer. Rubatsky was a talented technologist and quickly became associated with local organized crime groups, assisting them with various money-making schemes that required his skills. But he got his real start when he chose to specialize in payment processing for sites selling child sexual abuse material. In 2004, he fled to St. Petersburg after his organized crime associates were arrested for kidnapping a rival who was moving into the same business. After a failed attempt at a new payment processing enterprise, Rubatsky shifted into hosting instead, partnering with a Russian ISP called Eltel. According to Krebs's account, the company had previously hosted child sexual abuse material and was under the protection of certain Russian law enforcement agents. Rubatsky's contribution was to establish a direct link to major Tier 1 Internet backbone providers, making Eltel less susceptible to being shut down by intermediary ISPs. They called this Internet pipeline the Russian Business Network and placed a young hacker known as Flyman in charge of it.[68] Flyman would become an infamous name in relation to RBN and is suspected of having his own strong political connections through his father, "who occupies a position of influence at a key Russian ministry."[69]

RBN would eventually disintegrate after gaining too much public attention and facing difficulties from upstream providers. It officially dissolved in late 2007.[70] Certain members of RBN are said to still operate in the same market or be involved in other forms of cybercrime, while others have moved into legitimate companies (US-CSP-14). Bulletproof hosting did not cease to exist at this point, of course, but merely became less brazen and more likely to be handled by smaller, less centralized enterprises. Some companies that have emerged include Atrivo, McColo, and 3FN. While such enterprises can be based in Eastern Europe or run by Eastern Europeans, bulletproof hosting is not limited to this region.

The Current State of Cybercrime and Cybercriminals

Cybercrime is an amorphous and constantly changing phenomenon. As new technologies emerge, new attack vectors and scams become available. Thus far, some of the major forms of cybercrime have included credit card fraud, banking fraud, the theft of data and money, extortion of companies by threatening their online business portals, confidence scams of varying types, and illegal marketing in the form of spam. As noted in the Introduction, cybercrime is not something fundamentally new, but rather leverages new technologies to carry out long-established forms of crime. The difference is in the expression of those crimes, through new methods and perhaps carried out by novel actors, rather than in the crime types themselves. With so many opportunities available, and technology evolving quickly, it is almost impossible to develop a taxonomy of the subtypes of cybercrime that have emerged. It is a near limitless terrain. If there is money to be made, someone will devise a way to make it (NA-(F)CC-1). Dave, a hacker who was previously involved in a boutique "niche fetish porn" spam enterprise, illustrates this point perfectly:

> Do you know what my biggest spinner was? It's called balloon pop pornography. It's basically a girl, she's fully clothed—Japanese, it has to be Japanese—she's wearing an office uniform, white blouse, pencil pleat skirt, pantyhose, she's sitting on a balloon. And you see a hand with a pin. It gets closer and draws away. Then it gets closer . . . pop! That was it. So what I did was I hacked all the sites that did this, like all of them, and I got all their customer [data]bases. I started spamming just one of them from all of them. I got 33 percent of people to sign up to it. 33 percent return on spam is fucking insane . . . because it's so niche, so fetish. Japanese businessmen (SEA(E)-(F)CC-1).

Of course, the whole business was a scam and the pornographic product being advertised was never supplied.

Instead of providing a taxonomy of contemporary cybercrime, a broader view of the overall system might be useful. There is almost universal agreement among subjects I have interviewed that cybercrime has been growing more organized and sophisticated. It is now extremely business-like in its operation and has developed into a bona fide industry. Carter, a US law enforcement agent with considerable experience in the cyber underground, summarized developments in this way:

It's more sophisticated, for one. With every law enforcement action, the criminals they adjust. So it's very sophisticated. I think some of the money they are dealing with is staggering. I think more of it now is malware-based cybercrime. Whereas before it wasn't as much. It is very malware-based and very highly sophisticated, you know, with the different types of obfuscation techniques you could utilize. I guess probably one of the best ways I could describe it is, more automated. There is, for example, in 2005, if you were going to be doing infections, you would have a zero day vulnerability, you would have one and take advantage of that. Now you can go out and buy an exploit kit that has twelve vulnerabilities in there and you would just drive traffic to the site and it infects people. Whereas before you would maybe have to have an executable and have them click on it to get infections. And you would have to know how to script all that stuff. Now I just buy the kit and drive traffic to it. Now I just buy the malware. I don't even need to buy the malware—I can buy the malware as a service right now and say, hey, I am going to pay 300 dollars a month to have access to it, kind of like, lease it. Everything I think is more automated. Even right down to vendings, they have these automated vending carts—so, like, for selling compromised credentials, like credit cards or bank logins or things like that. Whereas in the past, I would have to reach out to you and do business with you personally on instant messaging, and I would pay you. But now they kind of have like store fronts, kind of like buying a pair of shoes online. You visit the website, you set up an account with an email address, and it's a drop down menu, you go through the checkout process and it's automated payment—where I would never even talk to you or know who is even behind it. Very automated (US-LE-2).

The profiles of contemporary cybercriminals are also suggestive of this shift toward sophistication and specialization—and ultimately, corporatization. In the early days of cybercrime, before large-scale, profit-driven activities truly existed, the scene was made up of hackers and "phreakers" who had some technical skills. Some were quite young, particularly those that had run-ins with the law. But in an industry centered on profit, hackers and coders are now only one facet of a system also populated by conventional criminals of various stripes and new breeds of fraudster. Tom, a UK law enforcement agent, indicated it was time to dispense with the old "stereotype of a fifteen-year-old sitting in a darkened room." In his experience, cybercrime offenders reflect a cross section of society (UK-LE-1). Recall that Carter came to a similar conclusion based on his experience in the field: "About the only profile that I can probably say is that they're male" (US-LE-2).

The final point to note is a tangential one. Amidst this process of growing sophistication, organization, and automation within the sphere of profit-driven cybercrime, the relevance of state actors has grown. To explore this development is beyond the scope of this book, particularly because it involves motivations that are largely ideological or geopolitical, rather than financial.[71] Nonetheless, there is some blurring that should be noted. For instance, states might outsource activities to professional cybercriminals operating as freelance proxies, to offer a layer of deniability. Even more relevantly, we are possibly now seeing the encroachment of state actors themselves into profit-driven cybercrime. China has attracted considerable attention in recent years for the involvement of government units in large-scale thefts of intellectual property from not only foreign governments, but also private companies within those jurisdictions.[72] Then NSA director General Keith Alexander called such corporate espionage the "greatest transfer of wealth in history."[73] China is not the only state seeking financial gain. Some have claimed that North Korea was behind the widely destructive WannaCry attacks of 2017, an extortion campaign.[74] If so, the profit motive wasn't about strengthening national industries, but purely generating cash for a bankrupt state.[75] I merely note this state dimension here, which is somewhat speculative and based on public reports rather than my own data, as I did not pursue this line of inquiry directly. This subject would easily justify a separate major study, though it carries much greater risks for any intrepid scholars who might want to carry out the necessary fieldwork.

Conclusion

This chapter has charted the evolution of profit-driven cybercrime. It outlined the early history of hacking from the late 1950s onwards, from which some key aspects of cybercrime emerged, and then focused on the turn toward profit-making activities in the 1990s. Tracing the evolution of forums from their birth and Golden Age in the 2000s through to their increasing specialization and fragmentation, the chapter then drew attention to the development of other aspects of the industry such as operational groupings and the cybercriminal "infrastructure" that underpins the economy, including virtual currencies and bulletproof hosting. The last section addressed the current state of cybercrime and cybercriminals. Figure 2

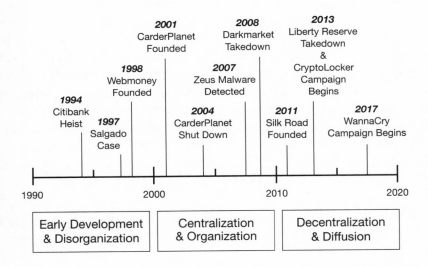

Figure 2   Key Moments of Profit-Driven Cybercrime Timeline

presents a timeline of some significant moments in the evolution of profit-driven cybercrime.

In a number of ways, the development of cybercrime is reminiscent of broader trends in organized crime. In contrast to cybercrime, the literature on organized crime is established and rich. One focus of such studies is the central financial motivation of organized crime groups, and all the entrepreneurial energy, professionalism, and business-like structures that can come with that focus.[76] For many, illicit business of one kind or another lies at the heart of this subsection of the criminal world.[77] Given this core financial motivation, many different forms of organized crime have been subjected to economic analyses. Some studies have addressed the role of mafias in criminal markets.[78] Others have examined the economics of the drug trade or related street gangs.[79] Still others have looked into fraud schemes and other activities such as gambling and loan sharking.[80] As such, cybercrime is not an outlier or unusual case, but fits into the spectrum of what is already known about the corporatized nature of traditional and transnational organized crime groups.

The above discussion of history has elucidated a central feature of contemporary cybercrime: it is industrialized. This is the subject of the next chapter, which takes a more analytical focus, framing cybercrime in terms of industrial organization. But it is already clear from this chapter that, like many aspects of licit and illicit commerce, cybercrime relies on a competitive market where individuals and firms seek profits by specializing in valuable aspects of the business. From the beginning, there has been a fusion of technical and criminal minds. As noted above, where money is to be made, a new expression of cybercrime will likely emerge. Old firms will evolve and new firms will spring up to meet different demands. Given that a considerable part of this industry's activity takes place online and outside licit channels, there will likely always be a certain amount of flux within the market. Chapters 4 through 7 will explore aspects of how cybercriminals manage these challenges and their inherent instability. While the market will never function perfectly, it certainly provides a suitable den for wolves, so they no longer need to be alone.

3

Making Sense of
the Cybercrime Industry

THE PREVIOUS CHAPTER outlined the industrialization of cybercrime in a historical sense. In light of certain issues that emerged from that account, the present chapter approaches matters from an analytical perspective. By now, it should be clear that cybercrime constitutes an industry, given that there are multiple (illicit) businesses operating for much the same effect and in similar ways. As Ukrainian security researcher Maksym put it, it's just "business, criminal business" (UKR-CSP-1). This chapter takes matters one step further by making sense of central aspects of cybercrime and how they work together within a framework of commercial behavior. It achieves this by applying some fundamental ideas from economics, chiefly pertaining to industrial organization, which is concerned with the operations of firms and markets.[1] As part of this application, this chapter also seeks to illuminate some core aspects of cybercrime that have not been well understood up to this point. The first section addresses its specialization, and is followed by a section analyzing its professionalization. The remaining two sections examine cybercriminal markets and provide wider firms, respectively.

Not directly discussed in this chapter, or the book more broadly, is the topic of social networks. This is not to downplay the importance of social network analysis. In fact, the developing work in this area suggests this may be a very fruitful approach to studying cybercrime.[2] There is also a wider social science literature pointing to the importance of social networks for cooperation.[3] While it is beyond the scope of this book to delve into the intricacies of networks, it is also true that social networks encompass almost everything contained in this work. I adopt a broad view consistent with

Mark Granovetter's influential statement that "most behavior is closely embedded in networks."[4] In my view, while some of the core concepts discussed in this book are organizational structures like markets and firms, these fall firmly within the concept of social networks. A market often relies on an intricate network of social ties among buyers and sellers and can be studied as such. Firms feature in networks on two levels: there are the connections and interactions of individuals within them; and firms and their people are connected to external individuals and firms through markets and other means. The broad organizational structures outlined in this chapter and book are meant to serve as a rough foundation for further work which should include social network analysis.

Specialization

Among cybercriminals, there is an evident division of labor. This concept, foundational to economic thought, holds that when specific tasks in a production process can be separated from each other, roles can be specialized. This then dovetails into the formation of firms and trading within markets, as individuals can benefit from the skills and goods that other specialized workers can provide. Specialization also generally leads to increases in productivity. Famously, Adam Smith used his observation of pin-making in eighteenth-century England to explain the process:

> in the way in which this business is now carried on, not only the whole work is a peculiar trade, but it is divided into a number of branches, of which the greater part are likewise peculiar trades. One man draws out the wire; another straights it; a third cuts it; a fourth points it; a fifth grinds it at the top for receiving the head; to make the head requires two or three distinct operations; to put it on is a peculiar business; to whiten the pins is another; it is even a trade by itself to put them into the paper; and the important business of making a pin is, in this manner, divided into about eighteen distinct operations, which, in some manufactories, are all performed by distinct hands, though in others the same man will sometimes perform two or three of them.

Smith goes on to describe a small factory in which ten men were able to produce over forty-eight thousand pins in a day, well above what they would be capable of producing without specialization:

Each person, therefore, making a tenth part of forty-eight thousand pins, might be considered as making four thousand eight hundred pins in a day. But if they had all wrought separately and independently, and without any of them having been educated to this peculiar business, they certainly could not each of them have made twenty, perhaps not one pin in a day; that is, certainly, not the two hundred and fortieth, perhaps not the four thousand eight hundredth, part of what they are at present capable of performing, in consequence of a proper division and combination of their different operations.[5]

The last chapter outlined how cybercrime evolved to mirror this process. Cybercriminals moved from operating largely as lone wolves, to trading and forming groupings, which expanded their productivity on a large scale. A core part of this process was specialization, although it can be difficult to determine whether the development of marketplaces drove specialization, the other way around, or both. However this process occurred, there is now a demand for a variety of goods and services that require very particular skills, which in turn is driving productivity (UDL-CSP-1, US-(F)LE-2). US law enforcement agent Terry used the analogy of animals stripping down a carcass in the wild: cybercriminals have found ways of extracting value from every piece of data and every specialist role (US-LE-10). An actor might purchase malware from skilled coders, and hire others who are experienced at infecting computers. Among other capabilities, his plan could require social engineering skills or the help of professional translators to produce compelling emails to send to foreign victims. The actor may also need a transfer team to move money out of compromised bank accounts and even hire a professional social engineer to convince the relevant card issuer or bank that the transfers are legitimate.[6] A cash-out crew would then be required to extract the money and return the proceeds to the organizer. At this point, money launderers could also play a role. In an overview of the malware ecosystem alone, the Eastern European former cybercriminal Ivan outlined more than fifteen roles that individuals or groups can play, which itself is probably not an exhaustive list (EE-(F)CC-3). Within all these specializations are also subspecialties. For instance, coders specialize in certain programming languages or different components of the malware they are writing. Even in cashing out, there are different roles within a group (NA-(F)CC-2). Various subspecialties also can be incorporated within certain firms to achieve better products and services, a subject that will be taken up in a later section.[7]

At a minimum, successful cybercrime requires the fusing of technical and business skills, essentially accounting for both the "cyber" and the "crime." I encountered only rare cases where these two skill sets were present in the same individual. Sean, who not only hacked bank accounts but also organized his own network of money mules, was one such exception (WE-(F) CC-1). In simple operations, two people can chiefly fill the complementary roles (US-(F)LE-8). Other operations require more partners. Script, it was said, had a strong business brain but needed to rely on the technical talents of others in the CarderPlanet network. Likewise, it can make sense for more technical actors to sell their products through forums and other markets precisely because they don't have the inherent ability, or a partner, to carry out the complex organizational work of exploiting the product (EE-(F)CC-3). Ivan wrote this about his malware, and his decision to sell it rather than use it himself:

> I had no money to use it by myself. You have to spend some money of infrastructure. You have to have servers, traffic, exploit pack at bare minimum. And you have to spend time. And all of this with absolutely no guarantees that you will have a profit in the end. It was just too stressful for me, I had no experience in building up a botnets and stealing money (EE-(F)CC-3).

In the case of Western European former cybercriminal Jonas, even the trading function was not provided by the technical actor. While Jonas wrote the software and managed the updates on it, he allied with a partner he met online who was chiefly responsible for marketing and selling the product at high volume, along with coordinating the team of people required to do this. For a cut of the profits, this entailed building a website and developing promotional materials, as well as hiring a software support team and people to receive payments. Jonas was very impressed with what his partner achieved, stating that, from the point they joined forces, all he saw was "money, money, money" (WE-(F)CC-3).

GEOGRAPHICAL SPECIALIZATION

Specialization can also occur geographically. In meta-histories of economic development, such specialization occurs following the development of long-distance trade.[8] A similar process appears to apply to cybercrime. The expansion of trade through access to online marketplaces allows cyber-criminals to benefit from the skills of others. Such trade favors those who invest in developing particular forms of expertise which are highly valued.

The fact that the cybercriminal industry is global and that actors from different countries can collaborate and trade online means that this specialization also takes on a regional character. Looking across the varied forms of expertise that specific nationalities have developed, it would appear that prevailing socioeconomic and cultural conditions drive some of the differences. After all, every cybercriminal physically exists in a certain location. As much as actors adapt to the market, the market also adapts to them. Ignoring this geographical dimension of cybercrime would mean failing to see the particular factors playing into the structure of cybercrime operations within countries, the nature of local participants, and the specific ways they contribute to the overall industry.

For instance, it is not random that Eastern Europe provides much of the technical engine of global cybercrime. Since the early CarderPlanet days, the leaders driving innovation in the carding business have been concentrated in this region. In recent years, some of the foremost pieces of malware have been created and written by Eastern Europeans. It is these skills that they are known for in the industry and can offer in exchange (NA-(F)CC-2, UK-LE-3). This specialization appears to be tied to the socioeconomic context across much of the former Soviet Union and other former communist states in the region (US(E)-CSP-1). In these places, there was a strong interest and investment in science and technology—it was a matter of official policy originating with Vladimir Lenin himself. As a result, education in STEM disciplines was at a very high standard, with top universities in these areas producing a large supply of good quality graduates.[9] As Eastern European former cybercriminal Andrey wrote:

> It worth mention that I wasn't alone in my computer hobbies in ex-Soviet Union, and lots of my peers did just the same. With all the problems Soviet Union had, you have to give credit to their educational system, and most of us graduated from high school with very good basics, and even way beyond this. With all the problems post-Soviet space had, neither me nor my peers had any serious problems learning computer-related skills. Even if their families were unable to buy them computers, they used ones of their friends, schools, etc. (EE-(F)CC-2).

A second interesting element of recent Eastern European history is that, because of trade limitations during the communist period, western technology was often out of reach. As a result, substantial efforts were made to replicate those technologies that had not been developed locally. For instance, in Romania, Nicolae Ceaușescu oversaw the reverse-engineering of foreign computers so that a local version could be produced. During my fieldwork in the country, it became apparent that these technical achievements were a national badge of honor for some locals. Cracking and pirating commercial software also became prevalent across the region, as it has in large parts of the world. One might view such activity negatively, but in some cases it appears these efforts were originally undertaken because the relevant software could not practically be obtained. This was usually either because the software was not marketed in that country or because the low local wages made it unaffordable (UK-CSP-4, RUS-CSP-5, RUS-CSP-6). Eventually a tradition developed and a community of crackers emerged with a true skill for reverse-engineering. This is precisely the skill set required for success in a number of technical aspects of cybercrime.

While a large talent pool of technically educated graduates, alongside a tradition of cracking and reverse-engineering, provides a supply of people who *could* engage in cybercrime, it would be presumptuous, and offensive, to conclude they will invariably do so. Individual personalities and backgrounds likely play important roles. But the shortage of well-paying jobs in technology sectors and, in general, across other sectors in Eastern Europe provides an extra push for people to involve themselves in cybercrime. This was a point I heard many times from interview subjects across the region, and, for that matter, around the globe (RUS-CSP-5, RUS-CSP-6, UKR-(F)LE-2, UKR-LE-2, US-(E)CSP-1). Some knowingly take part in cybercrime on a full-time or part-time basis to earn income. Others are unemployed (or underemployed) programmers who simply respond to online advertisements seeking help. As they are hired and begin working, they might fail to realize that the projects are illegal, choose not to confront that suspicion, or decide they are happy to be involved nonetheless (RUS-CSP-13).

As a contrasting view, it is important to note that some working within local tech sectors believed that there were enough high-paying jobs to be found and that the labor-market situation in Eastern Europe compared relatively favorably to other parts of Europe, especially factoring in the local cost of living (UKR-CSP-2). These views were in the minority, however, and perhaps reflect the perspective of those who have managed to gain good legitimate employment, are willing to work hard, and find criminal activity morally unacceptable. Furthermore, while salaries on offer might allow one to make a living or even a good wage in a country like Ukraine, they often cannot match the incomes one could earn in the American technology industry or as a high-earning cybercriminal.

In essence, cybercrime is an aspirational endeavor. In many cases, offenders have some amount of education and access to technology, and are not driven by desperation to maintain survival. Although they can be relatively poor, some dream of going beyond making a decent living to earn the kind of fortune people associate with Silicon Valley entrepreneurs. Vasily, a Russian former law enforcement agent, made this point. He observed that there wasn't much space for tech entrepreneurs and start-ups in the Russian economy. The private sector is dominated by a small number of large companies, in contrast to the situation in the United States where small creative companies abound. There is also a local population that has a strong supply of educated, highly skilled, technical talent and easy access to online information about committing cybercrime. As many young people of limited financial resources fail to find positions in large companies, some are tempted by the dark side (RUS-(F)LE-1). In certain ways, the talent created by the region's communist heritage may also be stifled by it, in the form of a less-than-dynamic economy encumbered by government and oligarchical interests. Those with the energy and instincts for new business creation are effectively steered toward creating cybercriminal ventures instead. They are a new breed of entrepreneurs.

The final piece of the Eastern European puzzle is a factor common to many parts of the globe: corruption. Corruption is rampant across the region and was a regular topic of discussion in interviews, including with those from law enforcement backgrounds (ROM-(F)LE-1, UKR-(F)LE-2). Subjects made it clear to me that the identities of some major cybercriminals are likely known to various law enforcement and private sector investigators (UKR-(F)LE-2, US-LE-10). Yet these individuals are only sporadically arrested. It cannot be forgotten that Eastern European cybercriminals function in often-corrupt environments. This partly explains how they can operate with virtual impunity, assuming they navigate the system correctly. But it might also help to explain their career choices. They might perceive government as just as compromised as the cybercrime scene, and that trying to engage in legal business likewise risks moral compromises (for example, in the form of bribes and kickbacks). Kirill, a Ukrainian government agent, even suggested that some of those involved in cybercrime might view their criminal collaborators as relatively trustworthy and rule-abiding in the context of a fundamentally broken state (UKR-LE-2).

This environment often connects with a mentality that cybercrime against rich foreign targets is not really a crime. In a certain sense, the victims deserve it. Some saw this activity as a quasi-patriotic service in support of the former Soviet states against their old enemies, which goes hand in hand with a regional blurring of business, government, and crime (US(E)-CSP-1, UKR-CSP-1). It is also common to hear claims that large, well-insulated financial institutions, rather than individuals and their families, are the true victims of cybercrime. In this view, cybercrime is not shameful (EE-(F)CC-3, US-(F)LE-8). Andrey summed up this mentality, writing that the "spark became flame in Eastern European cyber society" because it was not only easy to obtain things of value, but also to feel "at peace with conscience" since the fraud was against the "fat, stupid, lazy, arrogant" West:

> Thus, emerging "carders" perceived themselves as Robin Hoods of sorts, taking from rich western banks and corporations and giving to the poor Eastern European people by spending it. The emerging culture also claimed right to perpetrate fraud . . . since, according to people taking part in discussion, it was that western society destroyed Soviet Union, and, therefore, left Soviet people to their own sorts and devices, so they have to struggle and survive as they could, and, therefore, they now taking money from "westerners" by the means of Internet. Those ideas were common and popular across forums (EE-(F)CC-2).

This mentality might have contributed to a norm against targeting victims in the former Soviet Union. As Sergey Pavlovich, the Belarusian cyber-criminal, wrote in his memoirs:

> we made a point of staying away from citizens of former Soviet countries. Why? We felt bad for them. In the States they have insurance for bank deposits, but in Russia and Eastern Europe they won't leave you alone until they make sure you didn't steal the money from yourself. There are enough well-off westerners to go by. Call it being patriotic, if you will. I don't remember when we adopted the rule, but it was a rule everyone respected: never steal from your people.[10]

Avoiding the attention of local law enforcement also likely contributed to this norm. It is only in recent years that this custom has begun to break down, as some cybercriminals in the new generation appear more willing to take on greater risks and strike at home. Political events such as the war in Ukraine have also produced ideological disputes among cybercriminals from different countries that have led to online "flame wars" and threatened to disrupt some of the brotherhood that has existed among actors from former Soviet states (UKR-CSP-1, UKR-(F)LE-2).

This discussion is illustrative of how important it is to consider geographical context in understanding regional specialization. But it would be wrong to see Eastern Europe as a monolith without any variation in the way that cybercrime presents. Before, during, and after the fall of the Soviet Union, the socioeconomic conditions inside that bloc have not been uniform. Since the breakup, nations have taken divergent paths in democratization, development, trade, EU membership, and more. This study largely focuses on the situations in Russia and Ukraine, the countries most commonly identified throughout the research as cybercrime hubs in the region. While there is good evidence to suggest that other countries (such as Belarus or the Baltic states) have played their roles, further investigation would be required to determine just how much cybercrime exists in those places and whether their local brands of cybercrime are differentiated in significant ways.

Of course, other Eastern European states were never members of the Soviet Union and one might, yet again, expect to find different socioeconomic conditions and resulting forms of cybercrime. For instance, Romania provides a compelling counterpoint to the nature of cybercrime elsewhere in the region. It benefits in both infrastructure and human terms from its communist heritage of heavy investment in technology. It continues to be ranked toward the top of global Internet connectivity and speed rankings.[11] And it also heads global lists as a hotbed of cybercrime. But the local form is quite different from cybercrime in other parts of Eastern Europe. Often far less technical, its practitioners focus much more on social-engineering scams, such as selling fictional goods on eBay and similar sites—a crime known as online auction fraud (ROM-(F)LE-1, US-LE-3). ATM fraud is also a popular local specialty. Like its Eastern European neighbors, Romania has a technical talent pool, a history of cracking and reverse-engineering, and endemic (though perhaps lessening) corruption. But it also has a thriving tech sector and access to the rest of the EU job market, and these appear to be reducing its involvement in the more technical aspects of cybercrime.[12] The Romanian scene is more about fraudsters gaining access to the Internet than it is about an oversupply of technical talent and a lack of suitable employment opportunities. Background discussions indicated that there may still be an unemployment problem in parts of Romania that contributes to cybercrime, but this is a broader problem that cannot be solved with tech sector jobs alone.

The above discussion notwithstanding, it is important to remember that cybercrime is a global phenomenon, not just an Eastern European one—as can be forcefully pointed out by some in that region (RUS-CSP-2). The larger point is that the flavor of cybercrime differs depending on local conditions and variations can be expected around the world. The Nigerian case may have something in common with Romania, at least on the fraud side. The poor economy, relatively reliable and accessible Internet, and prevailing corruption may combine to create a breeding ground for online crime. In this case, there is not a technology sector at the same level as Romania's, but there is also not a supply of technical talent on an equivalent scale. Given that Nigeria lacks the large pool of programmers and hackers present in other countries, it is not surprising to see a greater proportion of low-tech scams and greater reliance on foreign actors for technical assistance (NIG-(F)LE-1). There appears to be a direct connection between the email scams that emerged at the turn of the century, known as *advance fee fraud,* and previously existing paper-letter campaigns to the same effect (NIG-ITP-1, NIG-(F)LE-1, NIG-CSP-1, US-LE-9). This suggests that cybercrime in Nigeria largely grew out of a community of fraudsters rather than hackers or other more technical actors. In recent years, Nigerian scams have become more technically sophisticated (NIG-CSP-1, NIG-(F)LE-1), but they are still often centered on advance fee fraud, along with other frauds such as *business email compromise* or *change of account details fraud,* which usually involves the impersonation of a business officer to request the payment of funds from a company into an account controlled by the fraudsters (MY-LE-3, US-LE-10).

Meanwhile, China provides a still different example of cybercrime. China gains attention for hacking and government-endorsed cyber-espionage, but little attention is paid to specific cases of cybercrime.[13] Surprisingly, given the oft-expressed, vague fears of Chinese cybercrime, local conditions have meant that up until the present, profit-driven cybercrime has not been a major concern. Internally, the theft of online gaming credits or items is one of the main problems, and there is only limited engagement with the global cybercrime scene (CHN(E)-CSP-1). With that said, there is a regional dimension to Chinese cybercrime, as those in nearby countries like South Korea and Vietnam do report criminal attacks from Chinese actors. For instance, many online games are made by South Korean companies and enjoyed by citizens in that country, as well. As a result, South Koreans are major victims in this curious form of Chinese cybercrime (KOR- CSP-1; KOR-CSP-2). But there are more traditional online fraud operations that target both South Korean and Vietnamese citizens. In these cases, a critical element appears to be the involvement of Korean and Vietnamese speakers, who themselves may be living in China. They allow the scams to cross geographical and linguistic boundaries (KOR-LE-1, VN-CSP-4, VN-CSP-5, VN-CSP-6). Similar activity may also be taking place in other countries, such as Malaysia (MY-LE-3).

A more focused study on why Chinese cybercrime has operated on such a limited scale could be fruitful. One hypothesis might attribute the paucity of local cybercrime to strong patriotism among Chinese hackers.[14] This would suggest a counterpoint to the common perception, at least in the West, that hackers are strongly antiauthoritarian and countercultural. Other possible explanations might relate to the Chinese government's close monitoring of the Internet, or to the fact that Chinese e-commerce is still in its infancy, so that credit cards and online banking are not widely used. As to why Chinese cybercrime is largely focused on local and regional targets, it may be that language barriers and difficulties in cashing out from vastly different financial systems are limiting cybercrime activities against foreign targets (CHN-CSP-1, CHN(E)-CSP-1). As e-commerce continues to take hold, foreign language skills improve, and other shifts take place, it is possible the situation may change over time.

As odd as it sounds, a cybercrime scene that bears similarities to the Chinese setting is Brazil's. It is also highly localized, appearing to consist of a relatively large number of offenders who are interested in hacking and malware, but who are not always highly skilled or educated. Brazil's and China's situations suggest that a country's language may be instrumental in whether its cybercriminals operate globally or mainly locally. A number of participants noted that Brazil is the only Portuguese-speaking country in South America (BRA-CSP-2, BRA-CSP-7), with one describing it as an "island" among Spanish-speaking neighbors (BRA-CSP-3). One security researcher took pains to differentiate between the perceived low skill of Brazilian cybercriminals and their highly skilled confreres in Eastern Europe. When I asked this researcher whether cybercriminals in the country speak English, the retort was that they barely speak Portuguese (BRA-CSP-3). Unlike in China, the central focus of Brazilian cybercrime has been on credit card fraud and banking fraud. But the (indirect) targets are almost always Brazilian banks, which as a result have significantly hardened their defenses to respond to countless variants of local malware and ceaseless attempts to steal their customers' credit card data and online banking credentials. In this internal game of cat and mouse, many participants believed that the banks were leading the world in security and were holding the cybercriminal horde at bay (BRA-CSP-2, BRA-CSP-3, BRA-CSP-7). With much of the cyber talent employed by a growing technology sector, the attackers were extremely persistent (perhaps even desperate) but not up to the challenge (SA-(F)CC-1). Many of the participants in this study dismissed Brazilian cybercrime as a pervasive but low-impact problem, especially in a country where widespread threats of violent crime attract greater attention.

Finally, one cannot leave the West out of this discussion. While the West has produced a significant number of elite hackers, such as Max Butler, many who could engage in cybercrime are seemingly deterred by law enforcement and enter the technology sector or government, where opportunities now abound. Anecdotally, the typical western cybercriminal seems to have a quite different profile from his Eastern European counterpart, starting with a lower likelihood of tertiary education (WE-(F)CC-1, SEA(E)-(F)CC-1, NA-(F)CC-2). The core of western cybercrime is made up of people who can handle the money side of the business. As was noted in the previous chapter, these individuals have been some of the key players involved in cashing out in the United States and elsewhere. They are also many of the key buyers of services from Eastern Europe's major suppliers (EE-(F)CC-2). Even some western cybercriminals who have technical abilities, like Scott, conclude that they can make more money specializing in cashing out (NA-(F)CC-2).

While the East provides the technical engine of cybercrime, the West provides much of the fuel by facilitating a large part of the money side. In the carding business, Eastern Europeans procured credit card data which were often passed to western cybercriminals to purchase goods or make cash withdrawals. In more recent times, those in the former Soviet Union have driven the development of malware, and westerners have bought these products, while also retaining their role on the cash-out side of the business. These two hubs are a perfect match for exchange: suppliers and buyers. Although the relationship has ebbed and flowed over time, it remains intact. Without western cybercriminals, the industry would likely be far smaller and less successful.

This symbiotic relationship is a perfect illustration of the geographical specialization one would expect in broader economic development. But it was only possible because forums and other channels facilitated communication and networking between these physically distant concentrations of talent. And, while the point is made that there are geographical hubs within cybercrime, the exchange between Russian-speaking cybercriminals and the West demonstrates that these hubs can still work together on different schemes. Along the same lines, I also found evidence of Nigerians

Table 4

GEOGRAPHICAL SPECIALIZATION

Former Soviet Union	Malware production and distribution
	Other technical criminal endeavors (*for example, spam and bulletproof hosting*)
Nigeria	Advance fee fraud
	Other confidence scams (*for example, email compromise and impersonation*)
Romania	Online auction fraud ATM fraud
China	Online gaming theft Intellectual property theft (*state affiliated*)
Brazil	Credit card fraud Banking fraud
The West	Cashing out and money mules Some hacking and malware exploitation

doing business with Russian-speaking cybercriminals, and with Romanians, among other cross-border examples (UK-LE-3, US-LE-9).

Table 4 summarizes the geographical specialization observable in cyber-crime. It illustrates that cybercrime is not a monolith, but the varied product of socioeconomic forces in particular locations producing specific expressions of the phenomenon. There is a strong geographical and local-ized dimension. But one should not read this table too simplistically. It does not imply that other, unlisted types of cybercrime are not also carried out in these locations. By the same token, it does not imply that the listed types of cybercrime cannot also be carried out in other places, including ones not mentioned in the table. These are simply the cybercrimes with which these locations have traditionally been associated and for which they are somewhat famous. It is also important to note that some types of cybercrime are not even represented on this table because no place has a special claim on them. For instance, during fieldwork, evidence suggested that phishing attacks were common across all these jurisdictions, sometimes connected to the listed cybercrime types but other times not. While early Eastern European carders pioneered the phishing of credit cards, Romanians, Nige-rians, and Brazilians have also embraced this technique. It was also present in other jurisdictions around the world, though it was not always clear if the perpetrators were local or offshore.[15] Finally, this table likely does not capture the full complexity of the geographical story. It is possible, for example, that there is further geographical specialization within the countries of the former Soviet Union, and also regionally within Romania, which appears to have some centers that are well known for online auction fraud and others known for ATM fraud (ROM-(F)LE-1, ROM-LE-1).

Professionalization

The process of specialization is mirrored by a process of professionalization.[16] Some amateurish dabbling still occurs, but in a number of contexts, many cybercriminals approach their trade as a full-time job or at least a serious source of income (RUS-CSP-13, NA-(F)CC-2, EE-(F)CC-2, UKR-CSP-1). There was a clear division in my sample between those who relied on cybercrime to make their livings and those who engaged in it as a secondary activity. This appeared to be tied very closely to age, with the mid-twenties as the peak age range for involvement in serious criminality. Those former cybercriminals I interviewed who had never been arrested had generally gravitated away from cybercrime as other life opportunities took hold, whether to pursue undergraduate education or shift to legitimate full-time employment. As they began to settle down in their lives, it simply stopped being practical for some to engage in cybercrime. In at least one case, one of the driving factors for quitting was potential shame:

> When I was doing illegal things I always freaked out, mostly because I was a kid, but I always thought I was going to get busted. My parents are going to be so disappointed, I'm going to go to jail. Everything they said is going to come true. So it's good to be legit (SEA(E)-(F)CC-1).

For those who had been arrested, factors outside their control removed them from cybercrime. As a result, it is not possible to know when, if ever, they might have retired from the business on their own. But there appeared to be a clear choice. Either one largely left the business and attempted to find a suitable job in the legitimate sector, or one became a professional cybercriminal and pursued that business as a primary job.

Within geographical contexts where arrest is a far lesser threat and engagement in cybercrime may be viewed as less shameful, there is a lower incentive to leave cybercrime as one enters adulthood. The employment situation also functions differently in various regions. In Eastern Europe, for example, where incomes are lower, a job might act as an alternative to cybercrime but also as a cover for illicit activities. Sometimes this cover story is somewhat informal, as in the case of "freelance programmers" or those who "run their own businesses," but in other cases cybercriminals hold steady jobs in licit companies (RUS-CSP-8, UKR-CSP-1). It was even suggested to me that some of the leading criminal coders behind high-level malware, who have been involved in the scene from the early days, continue their involvement despite being middle-aged men with families, and working legitimate jobs. Claims like this contribute to the overall perception that the Russian-speaking scene is more serious and business-like than its English-speaking counterpart (EE-(F)CC-2, US-LE-2).

It is clear that cybercrime is not attracting the dregs of society but includes intelligent, educated, and able offenders. Some might downplay the technical ability of cybercriminals relative to programmers working in the legitimate sector. There are arguments to be made on both sides of the debate, but the more important comparison to make regarding intellectual abilities is between cybercriminals and more conventional criminals. There is no better illustration of this difference than in the Eastern European context, where my data suggest that cybercriminals quite regularly are university educated and display significant intelligence and professionalism. On the technical side, there are unemployed, underemployed, and underpaid coders who become part of the illicit industry for short or long periods. If they share similarities with coders who have gained legitimate employment, it is because some of them are the same people (RUS-CSP-13, UKR-LE-2). There is also a class of cybercriminal entrepreneurs and managers creating their own illicit start-ups when legitimate moneymaking avenues on that scale are less available. One such individual I spoke to, Andrey, had a good general education and was very well read, regularly making references to famous political thinkers and literary figures in our discussions (EE-(F)CC-2). Romanian law enforcement also noted in discussions with me that some of the fraudsters in the hub of Râmnicu Vâlcea, who are generally involved in less technical enterprises, are "smart guys" who often have university educations but poor job prospects in the area.

In the West, the situation is slightly different. The combination of greater enforcement and increased employment opportunities in the technology and other sectors makes it more likely that university-educated hackers (and even some without degrees) will find legitimate and appealing jobs. As a result, it appears to be relatively rare for western cybercriminals to be university educated, although there are cases of this. Among the cybercriminals with western backgrounds I interviewed, only two had attended university.

One quit his involvement in illegal activities during his studies. I met with one Russian security researcher who thought this lack of education was a serious flaw (RUS-CSP-8). Perhaps the real concern is the large number of Eastern European cybercriminals who have not been successfully channeled into productive occupations—not the fact that western cybercriminals could be better educated and more skilled!

While some western cybercriminals lack university degrees, they do not necessarily lack intelligence. I interviewed individuals with impressive hacking and coding skills, and some of them had found good jobs in the technology sector. Among those who had some hacking background, a number demonstrated keen intelligence, exhibiting the hacker mindset discussed earlier. Many showed real enthusiasm for the intellectual challenge of hacking, rather than only the financial payoff. In the words of one:

> There is challenge, respect, the thrill of it, out of doing it. The respect you get from it. How well you can do it, how quickly. There are so many different aspects. I don't ever recall saying to myself oh my god I just made 2 grand in one day. It was usually a case of oh my god I've just managed to get 20,000 cards or 2 grands worth of equipment in one day. It was never I've got this amount of money in my hand. The money was almost a byproduct from it, I was always more proud about what I had managed to physically manifest from it rather than the money that came out of it (WE-(F) CC-1).

While he specialized in cashing out, Scott also demonstrated hacking traits and had an interest in the problem-solving component of cybercrime. This is his vivid account of why his activities were about more than only money:

> When I was hacking or phishing I used to love tweaking my methods and getting better and better at it to increase the results. The increased results to me were not really about dollar signs in my head but how good I could do at it and how many accounts or whatever I could obtain. I guess how well I could "beat the system" (Look what I can do!! sorta thing ha). I used to do allot of drugs, and I would say that all of this stuff was way more addicting than any of them. Back in the day when me and my partners were first playing around with generating tracks from phished accounts to cash at

ATM, we had several trial and error periods, and the first time I actually heard the ATM clicking sound come on a money spit out (first successful trip) is a memory that I never will forget. This part sounds really sick, I still have dreams of going to the ATM to this day sometimes. Just the click sound and the money coming out. . . . reminds me of that scene in Terminator 2 lol. I guess you could say that eventually the money became also addicting (and the just general ease of getting it) but overall I would say it's the "game" more than anything (NA-(F)CC-2).

While this sense of challenge is important to western cybercriminals, it is also relevant to others around the world. Thiago, the South American former cybercriminal, described feeling "nice" and "strong" when he gained access to a target, on top of any monetary success that would follow. For him, it was the challenge and chance to demonstrate his skill and knowledge that initially drove his behavior (SA-(F)CC-1).

The preceding discussion indicates the increasingly professional nature of cybercrime offenders. But this professionalization is also reflected in the way the business is carried out. As noted in Chapter 2, cybercrime has also been growing in sophistication. US law enforcement agent Carter pointed out the increasing levels of automation, which have even led to user experiences not dissimilar to shopping with legitimate enterprises (US-LE-2). Cybercriminals like Roman Seleznev, mentioned in the Introduction, run virtual shop fronts where stolen credit card details (among other goods) can be purchased in the same way one might buy shoes or clothing online. Buyers simply enter the number of each product to be purchased and then check out, making payment in an acceptable currency like Bitcoin. No human interaction is required.[17]

Cybercriminals have also adopted other practices common in legitimate business. Krebs outlines the surprisingly positive experiences some buyers have in purchasing pharmaceuticals advertised through spam.[18] For instance, if a customer complaint is made, a refund is often promptly provided to avoid a chargeback from the bank in question. The malware business has also become increasingly advanced. As noted by Carter, one need not even sell or buy malware outright, but it can instead effectively be rented (US-LE-2). This is because some malware firms manage their businesses just like legitimate software companies. Instead of selling a product, they might license it to customers and build into the code a restriction that allows it to be used only for a certain time period. Along with quasi marketing departments to boost sales, some even have customer support functions that can be contacted if users need help deploying products (GER-CSP-1). Jonas and his partner used Google Analytics to track sales of their product and took action when the numbers were down. Jonas also added in protections to the code so that the software couldn't be easily cracked and appropriated without payment (WE-(F)CC-3).

A variety of other standard commercial practices have been adopted by cybercriminals. These include outsourcing, offering different pricing according to the quality of products or the nature of the buyers, issuing replacements or refunds if credit cards or other products don't work, and making distinctions between wholesalers and resellers (UK-CSP-2, SEA-(F)CC-2). Law enforcement agent Terry argued that "they are businessmen." When he speaks to arrested suspects, they refer to their businesses, and it is clear that they invest in infrastructure, provide weekly salaries and employee benefits, use accounting and task-tracking software, keep records, split the proceeds in very specific ways, sometimes operate out of offices, and generally run things as "illegal corporations" (US-LE-10).

Markets

Markets are central to the successful functioning of industries and a focus of economic studies on industrial organization. Marketplaces are distinct from markets, in that *market* denotes exchange rather than a specific place to trade.[19] Markets are "institutions that exist to facilitate exchange."[20] It should be clear from the previous chapter that marketplaces have played a vital role in the evolution of profit-driven cybercrime. They continue to play a key function today.

Forums are highly visible and much literature focuses on them.[21] Whole books, in fact, have focused on the stories of specific forums or those who administer them.[22] This can create the impression that large online marketplaces are the cybercriminal organizational structure *par excellence*. It is important, however, not to overemphasize the importance of these sites in the cybercriminal economy. Markets are the bigger story. Forums perform a significant role by providing a meeting place for those looking for partners to do business with. They also provide a level of governance that improves the quality of that business. But there are downsides to involvement in these marketplaces, as well, including greater exposure to undercover agents and, even with protections in place, to being scammed by strangers. Law enforcement interventions have also weakened the effectiveness of these marketplaces and driven many of the more advanced and networked cyber-criminals further underground (US-LE-10). This in turn can retard trade, as some users become hyper-cautious. Maksym, an experienced Ukrainian security researcher, believed that mid-tier forums often have the most activity because their relatively experienced users operate more openly than those in elite settings (UKR-CSP-1). More elite forums might also strongly restrict membership, resulting in less "new blood" and fewer buyers (RUS-CSP-5, RUS-CSP-6).

The cybercrime industry is much more complex than forums alone. The fact that there are cybercriminals who do not involve themselves in major forums, but who are still able to operate and trade in other ways, makes clear that a more nuanced understanding of marketplaces is required, viewing them as networking hubs within a much broader market and industry. As discussed in the previous chapter, some cybercriminals began to steer clear of major forums once law enforcement turned up the heat. In some ways this trend has continued, and smaller, more trusted groupings have become popular. Chat groups are now making a comeback of sorts.

It is important to note that some actors have not moved away from fo-rums, but were never involved in large forums in the first place. Eschewing the major marketplaces, some still managed to achieve success in their cyber-criminal careers and make a good deal of money. For instance, Sean, who stole hundreds of thousands of dollars over the course of his career, explained it this way:

> I never got involved in the ShadowCrew side of things. I found that to be . . . there was more structure and business behind it. I didn't like it very much. That was more for the lower level carders. Whereas I was in a completely sort of different realm to them. So I didn't get involved in that . . . (WE-(F)CC-1).

Dave, a talented hacker who now works legitimately as a pentester (that is, an ethical hacker hired by organizations to test their security) but who used to be involved in a spam operation, saw things in a similar way. Part of his resistance to joining major forums was that he feared law enforcement stings. In addition to that, he preferred not to make connections with strangers on a forum:

> They wouldn't have the connections, which means they don't have the reputation, which means they haven't impressed someone. So it's pretty easy in the Internet, when you start getting good at

anything in an illegal field, you start making friends and you im-
press people then get into those circles . . . .

So I worked always with someone who came from a mutual recommendation, so someone else recommended them, "this guy's
good." So to meet some guy random on the Internet, "I don't know
you from a bar of soap. So, no way" (SEA(E)-(F)CC-1).

There is a clear sense of superiority in these statements. In general, there
seems to be a hierarchy of the types of marketplaces and other groupings
that have evolved. It appears that carding forums and others that are focused
more on the trade, cashing out, and less technical aspects of cybercrime
are "below" the more technical groupings focused on hacking or malware
(RUS-CSP-5, RUS-CSP-6). These more technical forums might also have a
stronger element of discussion, as opposed to a pure business focus. Scott,
a North American former cash-out expert, saw it this way. He was a relatively proficient hacker himself but eventually saw that his interests would
be best served by specializing on the money side, and shifted to a full-time
focus on that activity. This is his outline of the unofficial hierarchy of forums: "The more 'elite' forums that I was on at that time were more of the
hacking / malware / blackhat forums that mostly had a lot of the people
'above' the people on [redacted] and other carding forums at the time (they
were suppliers to lower vendors, etc. on the carding forums)" (NA-(F)CC-
2). While some of the more technical actors did not involve themselves in
carding forums, it seems that "grey" discussion forums were a prime location where some more business-minded cybercriminals might locate technical talent (WE-(F)CC-3).

Both Sean and Dave are instructive in showing how cybercriminals can
successfully operate in an ecosystem not directly connected to the big
marketplaces. Both were hackers on the technical end of cybercrime and
deeply interested in hacking in its own right. Whereas large forums are often
more business focused, these two, as true hackers, primarily operated in chat
groups on various platforms. Dave referred to these as "social bubbles"
(SEA(E)-(F)CC-1). Sean described the hacking groups with which he was
involved in this way:

Because it's just an open chat room it can mix between collaboration between projects—one of you is working on something and the
other person sees and joins in. So it's very much open, there's no
structure to it at all. You just do whatever the fuck you want whenever you want . . . (WE-(F)CC-1).

Despite not belonging to major trading platforms, these two hackers had no shortage of collaborators who could help them make money when they wanted to move in that direction. Other opportunities for exchange were available to them. Dave usually relied on a mutual acquaintance to make an introduction online (SEA(E)-(F)CC-1), whereas Sean was unusually self-sufficient. He sometimes partnered directly with his online acquaintances in formal business relationships but, more often, they served as a collaborative technical support network. Although he specialized in taking over victims' bank accounts, Sean never required the services of a cash-out expert. He performed this role himself, recruiting women in the local drug community (who were known to him because he was an addict himself at the time) to act as "drop girls" who would receive goods purchased with stolen funds (WE-(F)CC-1).

The cases of Dave and Sean illustrate that cybercriminals can carry out exchange through less structured and visible channels. Combine this with the historical shift away from major forums outlined in the previous chapter, and what role do large marketplaces actually play in the underground economy? It appears that the key function of forums is to provide a highly visible focal point for networking. In fact, even those who use forums often conduct their deals through private channels rather than on the site itself (US-LE-2). As noted by Script in the previous chapter, forums offer locations for cybercriminals to come together and meet others with specialties different from their own. They also offer places for information sharing and learning. Andrey, who was a member of CarderPlanet, noted that Script actually required the site's more senior members to actively educate the more junior cybercriminals in the ranks (EE-(F)CC-2).

The networking function of forums is apparent, from those who participated in the marketplaces as much as from those who didn't. The above stories of Sean and Dave illustrate that if networking can be achieved by other means, whether through existing contacts, chat rooms, niche forums, or offline contacts, then the major marketplaces are not essential for exchange. Scott suggested that many active forum users might happily recede from the marketplaces if they gained sufficient partners, and only return if their existing contacts disappeared (NA-(F)CC-2). Of course, in such cases, the forums are still important as the original source of contact for many of those who work together. CarderPlanet was influential not only because it was the first cybercriminal marketplace successful on a wide scale, but also because it created a leading network of cybercriminals. This cohort continued to maintain ties after the death of that site and its members have been implicated in numerous high-level attacks and schemes around the world (EE-(F)CC-2). Online marketplaces should therefore be recognized as a significant aspect of the overall cybercriminal market. But to characterize these marketplaces as the sole available means of exchange would be far too simplistic.

Firms

Cybercriminal forums are not organizations that orchestrate the activities of their members in a direct sense. They are, more properly, marketplaces. It is important to state this, as it runs counter to the view put forward by those law enforcement agencies who paint these marketplaces as organizations with clear focus and direction. For instance, the 2012 indictment of members of the Carder.su forum described matters in this way:

> the defendants herein, and others known and unknown, are members of, employed by, and associates of a criminal organization, hereafter referred to as "the Carder.su organization," whose members engage in acts of identity theft and financial fraud, including, but not limited to, acts involving trafficking in stolen means of identification; trafficking in, production and use of counterfeit identification documents; identity theft; trafficking in, production and use of unauthorized and counterfeit access devices; and bank fraud; and whose members interfere with interstate and foreign commerce through acts of identity theft and financial fraud. Members and associates of the Carder.su organization operate principally in Las Vegas, Nevada, and elsewhere.[23]

Given the difficulties in charging certain offenders, it is not surprising that the US authorities took such an approach in this case, even ascribing a geographical hub, Las Vegas, to a community that was spread across the globe. Classifying forums in such a way not only gives a sense of heightened harm, it also makes them susceptible to prosecution under the Racketeer Influenced and Corrupt Organizations Act (RICO). This act has conventionally been applied to traditional organized crime groups and allows for more severe penalties for members of an ongoing criminal organization.

But leaving aside legal imperatives, in organizational terms, the activities of a forum's members are often quite distinct from the marketplace itself (US-LE-2). While some forum officers may be held in high regard and may run successful moneymaking operations, this is separate from their activities managing the marketplace. There are also many others on these sites carrying out various cybercriminal scams. Most of these actors never serve as administrators, as moderators, or in other positions—and some seem to avoid such roles as they may bring increased responsibilities in return for what they see as little gain, and the risk of unwanted attention from authorities (NA-(F)CC-2). Many members, sometimes numbering in the thousands, have not interacted directly with each other and often have little to no knowledge of others' schemes. Rather than joining to serve a well-structured criminal organization with a clear goal, the interest of forum members begins and ends with a desire to network, trade, and engage in their own enterprises.

It is at this point that the concept of a firm becomes important. A firm is a business: a profit-making entity that supplies goods or services.[24] Ronald Coase famously argues that firms emerge because of the desire to avoid the transaction costs associated with markets, including the costs of obtaining goods, information costs, bargaining costs, and costs associated with enforcement and trade secrets.[25] In certain cases, production efficiency may be enhanced within a firm structure. As Eastern European former cybercriminal Ivan wrote:

> Yes, forums enhance trust and cooperation between cybercriminals. You can analyze history of posts of a person to understand what he is doing, what kind of disputes he had and so on. So, basically, you can view history of his messages etc. At the same time, if you already know reliable people (i.e. have a "private team"), you can easily move to IM and PGP type of communication with them, without ever bothering to visit a forum whatsoever—why bother if you are already making decent money? (EE-(F)CC-3).

Former agent Landon explained the other side of the equation:

> It's a business. And in a business you have to have suppliers. You have to have vendors that provide products that are not within the business. You don't always want to own the whole vertical of the business (US-(F)LE-8).

Cybercriminal organizational structures are diverse, go well beyond forums alone, and include operational groupings that appear to approximate firms.

The concept of a firm is what has been missing from much of the literature on cybercrime. Even though similar analyses have been applied to other forms of crime, in cybercrime studies there has been too much focus on marketplaces rather than on those groups that actually carry out cyber-criminal acts.[26] These firms essentially manage production rather than simply trading their loot. In fact, trade could hardly occur without this production.

At the helm of each firm is a boss, who is the equivalent of a criminal technology entrepreneur, with the resources and organizational ability to employ the relevant talent. These leaders do not need to be technical specialists (RUS-(F)LE-1), as they are supported by others in specialized roles. But the structure of a firm and roles within it will depend on the focus of the group. For instance, a firm focused on deploying rather than developing malware would be set up differently than the model sketched by Maksym in the previous chapter. In the case of a scheme involving a Trojan horse to steal online banking credentials, the boss would need to acquire the relevant malware (assuming he is not the original author or owner) and hire and coordinate a team of specialists in infecting computers. Then he would need to arrange for the money to be transferred out of victims' accounts into accounts controlled by the firm. After that, the funds would need to be cashed out in some form, severing the money trail back to the criminals. The boss might employ people to carry out these latter functions, outsource them to other firms specializing in these areas, or simply sell the compromised banking logins as products to others (UDL-CSP-1, UKR-CSP-1, UKR-CSP-3, US-LE-2).

These online groupings tend to be small and look something like crews specializing in conventional forms of crime, such as bank robbery. Each member of the group is brought in to perform a specific role, which one participant compared to a *Mission Impossible*–type breakdown of specialties (US-(F)LE-8). This group structure is represented in Figure 3. The dotted and black lines indicate that, depending on the case, it is possible for those elements to be parts of the overall firm or distinct groups that are merely trading partners of the central firm. The "Boss" may also be more than one person or have assistants that aid in coordination or the management of technical infrastructure.

Other firms appear to have a strong offline component. In the last chapter, this was discussed in the context of cash-out crews, among other groupings. There was also evidence of "teams" built around geographical hubs in Eastern Europe, with a degree of longevity and involvement in multiple schemes over time (EE-(F)CC-2). These types of operational groupings appear to

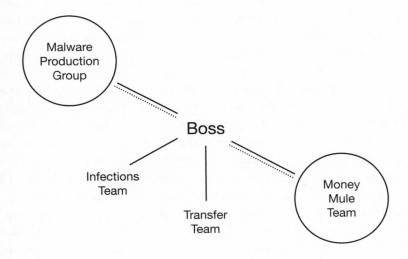

Figure 3   Malware Deployment Group

move beyond the idea of crews into something more substantial. Andrey, an Eastern European former cybercriminal who operated at the highest levels, described such a team as being built around some key founders and a common geographical location. Examples included the Odessa team, the Moscow team, the Donetsk team, and the Sebastopol team. From Andrey's descriptions, it appeared that some of associates of these teams might have changed, but in each case, the firm itself lasted for many years (EE-(F)CC-2).

Some offline firms are very sophisticated in structure, appearing to move beyond crews to larger-scale enterprises that approximate legitimate businesses. The Carberp example discussed in the last chapter demonstrated how cybercriminals sometimes operate out of physical office space.[27] On an even grander scale are enterprises like the Russian Business Network, which are effectively technology companies. They simply have more sinister missions. As noted, RBN was an Internet service provider. Based in St. Petersburg, it had an office and employees. It just so happened that its core clientele consisted of criminals, and it would refuse to shut down their hosting in return for a lucrative fee structure.[28] In Costa Rica, Liberty Reserve operated its virtual currency business in a way similar to other businesses, again with the exception that many of its customers were criminals.[29] Spam outfits based in Russia are ostensibly online marketing companies that engage in nefarious business practices to promote counterfeit pharmaceuticals, among other products.[30] Some of these enterprises can operate relatively openly because they often fall within grey areas of the law within their country of operation. They often also make use of corrupt government agents and officials to shield their business operations for as long as they can (as will be explored in Chapter 7).

There is ultimately no one, universal group structure in cybercrime. There are numerous forms of cybercrime and the group structures are tailored to the activities in question. The purpose of this discussion has been to differentiate between what is the market for exchange between partners and what is the structure of groups that actually carry out various forms of cybercrime. It seems clear that some groups might be considered to be firms, given the role they play. But in certain cases, it may be difficult empirically to distinguish between very long-term trading partners and members of the same firm. Conversely, some firms may be fragile and short-lived, especially when they exist solely online. In some cases, these may resemble "projects" more than entrenched organizational structures. In yet other examples, like that of South American former cybercriminal Thiago, there are further grey areas. In his case, there was clear evidence of multiple actors working collaboratively as a team, but not necessarily a tight hierarchy with a clear leader (SA-(F)CC-1).

While firms have become common, not every cybercriminal need be part of one. It is also the case that lone wolves persist, whose only form of interaction with other criminals is trade. Eastern European former cybercriminal Ivan was the author of a significant piece of malware, but he did not consider himself part of a firm. He used freelancers to assist with smaller coding jobs or to help promote his product online, such as through the creation of ad banners. He also vended the product himself in forums. Ivan drew a distinction: those who were given a regular percentage cut of an enterprise's profits were part of a "private team" (a firm), but those who were paid in lump sums per transaction were not (EE-(F)CC-3).

Ivan is not the only sole trader around. It appears that leading coders who have been in the game for quite some time may simply write code on their own and, beyond selling the product (perhaps not even through forums), may not be involved with collaborators in significant ways. These are some of the most cautious actors in the industry (UKR-CSP-1). These sole traders must feel that their interests are better served by not joining firms. Sole traders also appear in other geographical contexts. In Southeast Asia, former cybercriminal Tan largely operated independently and hired freelancers to perform various technical and design functions. Some of these people were

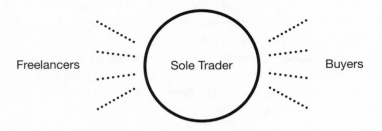

Figure 4 Structure of Sole Trader Operations

hired through legitimate channels and were not aware of the real "business" he was conducting (SEA-(F)CC-2). Figure 4 illustrates the structure of sole trader operations.

Conclusion

This chapter has continued the argument that cybercrime is now a bona fide industry. In analytical terms, it operates according to the foundational elements of industrial organization regularly observed in other settings. There is a clear division of labor, with strongly specialized individuals performing distinct functions. It has also become increasingly professional, both in terms of the cybercriminals themselves and in the way they conduct their business. Additionally, there is clear evidence of competitive markets. Large marketplaces play an essential role as focal points for networking and trade, even as many other opportunities for exchange also exist. Finally, while often overlooked, there is strong support for the existence of cybercriminal firms. These groups serve as the primary drivers of production in the underground economy and are the lifeblood of the industry.

Thematically, there are two important issues that cut across these points. First, there is a significant, perhaps unexpected, offline dimension to cybercrime. Exchange is not restricted to an online environment, but can also be conducted through offline networks. Some firms are also rooted in the "real world." In fact, this appears to be the case for the largest and most sophisticated firms, which begin to rival the size and structure of some large, licit enterprises. The importance of this offline dimension will be discussed further in Chapter 6. Second, geography is also very important to the cybercrime industry. This is notably true regarding specialization, but it affects how the industry functions more generally, whether in relation to professionalization, markets, or firms. Cybercrime is not a monolithic enterprise. The geographical background of offenders matters a great deal to who they are, how they operate, and even why they enter the industry in the first place. This is a point that does not need to be specifically addressed again in this book, but will underpin many discussions and should not be forgotten.

4

Nicknames and Identity

SO FAR, WE HAVE examined how cybercrime developed into a sophisticated, profit-making industry. The focus in this and the next three chapters is on how this development has been achieved given the challenges faced by cybercriminals operating anonymously. How have they managed to collaborate, cooperate, and organize to such a degree when they exist in a fundamentally distrustful environment? The subject of this chapter is a foundational problem for online criminals: identity. Already outlined at a theoretical level in the Introduction was the significance of trust and enforcement in enhancing cooperation. But in the context of online crime, there is no physical identity one can place trust in or seek enforcement against. Instead, nicknames become of fundamental importance. They become the central identity signal, without which one cannot operate. As Carter, an American law enforcement agent with significant undercover experience, put it: your nickname is "basically all that you have" (US-LE-2).

Cybercriminal nicknames appear to differ considerably from how aliases are used by conventional criminals and others. There is only a small literature on criminal nicknames, but David Maurer and Allan Futrell argue that such monikers have been around since the development of professional crime in fifteenth-century Europe.[1] Diego Gambetta examines the phenomenon of aliases in the Mafia by looking at a sample of nicknames from Sicilian families.[2] Federico Varese extends this approach to consider the Russian Mafia.[3] In sociological terms, these last two works likely go the furthest in delineating a typology for making sense of criminal aliases.[4] Table 5 summarizes their approach and is reproduced from Varese's *The Russian Mafia* (itself adapted from previous work by Gambetta).

Table 5

TYPES OF ALIASES

	Source	Conferring mechanism	Motive	Content	Typical bearers
Nicknames	others	informal	expressive	mocking/ appreciative	Sicilian Mafiosi
Code names	self/others	informal	instrumental	neutral	spies
Noms de guerre	self/others	informal	instrumental	neutral/ appreciative	partisans
Noms de plume	self	informal	expressive	appreciative	writers
"Second" names	self	formal	instrumental	appreciative	priests

Source: Varese 2001, p. 195

Both Varese and Gambetta agree, as this table notes, that nicknames are generally chosen by people other than their bearers, and may involve a degree of fun. All other aliases can be self-applied. Code names, often used by intelligence operatives and others, have the instrumental purpose to hide identities and are not devised to carry any particular meaning. *Noms de guerre,* taken on by guerrillas and partisans, also have an element of secrecy and are designed to protect the identity of their bearers and those individuals' families. But unlike code names, a *nom de guerre* could become quite famous and could also have some meaning to the bearer. A *nom de plume* is chosen by a writer. Some writers might simply like the added flair of a pseudonym, while others may have reasons for cloaking their identities, perhaps because they are writing politically sensitive material in dangerous settings. The chosen name may have special meaning for the writer or it may operate like a code name, hiding the author's identity. Finally, Varese adds a new category to those originally considered by Gambetta: renaming. This is common among orthodox churches and secret societies when members join. The name may be chosen by the bearer, but it is formally bestowed by the institution. Perhaps the most famous renaming process is the one that occurs with the installation of a new pope.[5]

In many instances, criminal aliases appear to fit within the nickname category. Among gang or mafia members, names are often coined by others and include an element of mischief. With that said, they can also have a functional value, such as helping to distinguish between parties with similar legal names or to shield real identities from law enforcement.[6] But this does not appear to be a nickname's primary reason for being. There are other criminal groups that either don't use nicknames or use them in different ways. For instance, Varese's main finding was that *vory v zakone* (thieves-in-law), the effective bosses of the Russian Mafia, approach aliases more as renaming. *Vory* adopt their new names as part of a ceremony by which they become full members of the criminal fraternity.[7] This appears to be a more ceremonial, symbolic, and ritualistic process than a strategy for protecting members against law enforcement or other threats.

Cybercriminal nicknames differ again from most other criminal aliases. They are not even nicknames in the formal sense outlined above, because they are adopted by the bearers rather than applied by others. Nonetheless, I refer to them as nicknames because that is what they are commonly called within the cybercrime industry, along with the terms *niks* and *handles*. The chief function of a cybercriminal nickname is to protect the identity of the user, so these aliases have more in common with code names, noms de guerre, and noms de plume. But such handles differ from these categories in that they extend beyond simply covering true identities. The nickname functions as an identity signal for the user's very online existence. As we shall see below, in some sense, it becomes a bona fide second identity, sometimes with a persona different from the user's offline self. A writer might adopt a nom de plume to publish works, but writers rarely communicate and collaborate extensively with others under their aliases. They are not typically creating functional second identities. But for the cybercriminal, such an identity is essential for carrying out business online. If any categorization fits how cybercriminal nicknames operate within the industry, it is perhaps the concept of a *brand*, as will be discussed below.

This chapter examines how nicknames are used by cybercriminals to build identities online, and what challenges they face therein. Building an identity can be a complex and unstable process, given that nicknames can be altered far more easily than physical identities. A number of points will be addressed. The first section investigates the manner in which nicknames act as online brands for cybercriminals. The second section examines how cybercriminals choose these specific brand names and whether they are inherently meaningful. The third section builds on that discussion by determining whether nicknames can be successfully interpreted to provide insights about the users behind them. The last section investigates the central tension in the use of nicknames: that anonymity is both a benefit and a cost. Cybercriminals cannot operate without identity signals, yet they must still attempt to protect themselves with as many name variations as they can afford. They cannot completely abandon their identities, as this would waste the reputations they have developed; yet their reputations are the very things that can incriminate them or put them in danger with other criminals. This final section explores how cybercriminals attempt to manage this challenge with their nickname strategies.

Nicknames as Brands

Nicknames effectively act as brands for many cybercriminals. Each handle is the foundation of a cybercriminal's reputation; without it he has no presence in the online market. If, for instance, a cybercriminal builds a reputation as a trusted vendor of a certain type of illicit goods, he must maintain the same nickname to benefit from that reputation. If the cybercriminal starts using a different nik to sell his wares, all the goodwill he has accrued is lost and a new reputation must be built from scratch, with the associated costs of loss of business. It is like "being reborn," and best avoided unless one's previous account has been "messed up" (WE-(F)CC-3). This idea of a brand was confirmed by a number of former cybercriminals, hackers, and others I interviewed (WE-(F)H-1, NA-(F)CC-2, US-LE-10). Sean believed "nicknames not only act as a sense of reputation and identity, but depending on your reputation also acts as a medal of what your rank is within the hacking community" (WE-(F)CC-1). Eastern European former cybercriminal Andrey saw matters in this way, writing:

> for many nickname is a "brand," so when you choose it, it means a lot. It is even more so, if one elects to promote his services or sell proceeds of his activity. In such case his fame, reputation and standing relation is all dependent on his nickname (EE-(F)CC-2).

Ivan also believed that nicknames acted as brands and that the "only thing that should be known to cybercriminals about a person with whom they are doing business with is his or her nickname." As a result, a nickname is one of the few ways to identify a person online, with one of the only exceptions being when a cybercriminal is closely associated with a product or service, such as the author of a key piece of malware (EE-(F)CC-3).

But given that one's true identity is not directly associated with any nickname, this branding operates in potentially unstable ways. First, an individual can choose to operate under more than one nickname, and build more than one brand. This might be the case especially with vendors whose business is to sell products as best they can. Maintaining several brands offers a way of diversifying risk in case one nickname were to be tarnished, a strategy discussed in the final section of this chapter. But multiple brands can also be useful in day-to-day business practice. For instance, a cybercriminal might provide distinct types of service under different nicknames. In the Carder.su forum there was a user who advertised two lines of business under the separate names Bank Manager and Document Manager.[8]

Another reason to maintain multiple brands might be less honorable: it makes it possible to offer the same products at different prices, a practice known in legitimate business as *price discrimination*. Scott knew of one leading card data vendor, for example, who sold his wares through his own site. Scott later found out this same person had started a new "reseller" site under a different nickname—"but really it was in fact the same exact person on the backside of it, it was just a way that he could raise his prices to all the newcomers etc." (NA-(F)CC-2). It appears the vendor closed his first site to new members (unless they were specially invited) and charged higher prices on the second site. Presumably he hoped to keep his existing clientele happy while also expanding to serve a segment of less discerning, and perhaps less experienced, buyers who did not have the preexisting relationships to purchase data at lower prices. He could do this without raising much suspicion because having resellers is quite common for vendors of "dumps" (NA-(F)CC-2).[9] Usually, higher prices are expected, given the additional profit margin sought by the resellers. This vendor evidently appropriated that explanation as a tactic to gain additional profits for himself. For slightly different ends, former cybercriminal Leonid employed multiple nicknames as part of his business strategy:

> I had 3–4 pseudonyms for: 1—main, as an owner of carder forum, 2nd—for mt private messengers only for my private circle, 3rd—for sell dumps, 4th—for sell plastic, 5—for sell documents . . . it was my biz strategy—to sell dumps and recommend to buy plastic or docs from another man who was me too . . . (EE-(F)CC-4).

Eastern European former cybercriminal Ivan took a more pessimistic view of those who used more than one nickname:

Usually, people who have multiple nicknames and using them at the same time, are rippers (or "rats")—that is, they trying to make a deal like selling a product or service and then disappear without providing it; so then they can just pick up different nickname and continue their activity (EE-(F)CC-3).

A second source of branding instability involves essentially the inverse situation. Not only are there individual cybercriminals with multiple handles, there are also cases in which multiple users employ the same nickname. In some cases, people might make use of one core brand and have related nicknames to indicate support staff. For example, a nickname of XXXX might give rise to the additional nickname of XXXX Support, designating an employee of the main player. Such employee nicknames were more important in the past, before automated shop fronts dominated the business, because support staff were sometimes required to take orders manually when the boss was offline (NA-(F)CC-2). In other cases, more than one person might make use of exactly the same nickname. Trusted friends might share a login because one cannot be bothered to attain entry into a forum or, if it is a closed-access forum, has difficulty getting vouched in. A single nickname might even serve as the brand for an entire team working behind it (NA-(F)CC-2, US-LE-10). All these instances suggest the difficulties in ascertaining true identities when dealing with online actors.

Finally, linked to these issues, there are cases of confusion over genuine identities, along with opportunities for nicknames to be hijacked, and for other manipulations to take place in this virtual environment. Some mix-ups happen because certain nicknames are common, such as John Dillinger, Frank Abagnale, or other well-known criminals from the past (NA-(F)CC-2). Nicknames are also influenced by pop culture. Following the release of *The Matrix,* "Neo" became very popular among users, along with other names from the movie (NA-(F)CC-1). As will be discussed in the next section, many actively try to choose names that are uncommon to avoid this type of confusion. This allows them to establish their own brands.

But sometimes the opposite approach is taken. For instance, elite hacker and forum administrator Max Butler chose the name Iceman to administer CardersMarket precisely because it was not original. There were already other Icemen floating around the digital underground. Butler's logic was that if he ever attracted heat from law enforcement, these other users might complicate efforts to identify him.[10] In line with this approach, some also choose common words that will lead to countless hits on Google and therefore be harder to trace (EE-(F)CC-3, NLD(E)-CSP-1). Others have taken a more nefarious approach, trying deliberately to impersonate other users to appropriate the benefits of their reputation. This is sometimes the case when the cybercriminal in question has retired or been arrested and is no longer in a position to contest the brand (NA-(F)CC-2, EE-(F)CC-2). It should be noted that such a strategy is typically aimed at making a short-term gain, because if the ruse became apparent, the user would no longer be trusted. It is also not too difficult for old partners to verify that a user is the same as one from the past, by closely examining his wares, requesting to be contacted through chat accounts or emails that they know belonged to that user previously, or asking specific questions to which only the original user would know the answer (NA-(F)CC-2). These issues will be discussed further in the next chapter.

Of course, criminals are not the only ones who appropriate nicknames to impersonate others. This has also been a tactic of law enforcement. In one early case, a (now former) US law enforcement agent, Landon, was involved in the arrest of a major cybercriminal. But only a short time later, his network of informants began to report that the perpetrator's nickname had become active online again. When Landon investigated, his sense was that the nickname's use exhibited law enforcement traits, so he surmised that another agency was involved. He was able to track down those agents and make clear that they were potentially jeopardizing the case, as the defense could claim that the nickname had always been operated by law enforcement rather than the arrested suspect (US-(F)LE-8). In other cases, niks can be purchased for use by others (including law enforcement). Effectively, the purchaser has bought the reputation and access tied to that name. Law enforcement is most dangerous, however, when it is able to turn a cybercriminal into an informant. In that case, no impersonation has to take place. The individual already owns the brand and knows how to operate it.

Choosing Nicknames

With cybercriminal nicknames acting as brands, the question arises of how best to name one's brand. Choosing handles is more of an art than a science. While there do not appear to be any strict rules, certain general principles are apparent. The most fundamental of these is not to incorporate any part of one's real name or other identifying features. This is very much tied to protection from arrest or other harm (US-(F)LE-3). As Noah put it: "I don't want these guys to know who I am and they don't want me to know them. If you get arrested you can tell on them" (NA-(F)CC-1). Don also summed up the benefit of separating one's offline and online identities. He wrote that he did not have concern about law enforcement actions against him "because I was not 'me,' but rather a construct, puppeted from afar, invisible and anonymous" (NA-(F)CC-4).

It might seem obvious not to use variations of one's real name, but in the earlier days of cybercrime, when concerns about law enforcement were lower, users often made this mistake. Andrey used part of his real name when he began in the business, but later realized this was "stupid" and changed it (EE-(F)CC-2). In the days of Counterfeit Library, Lance actively counseled other users not to use niks linked to their real identities, such as middle names (NA-(F)CC-3). More recently, it has been less common to see people using nicknames hinting at their true identities, but there are still cases. For instance, the real name of the leading Ukrainian carding vendor Maksik is Maksim Yastremskiy.[11] In Brazil, where cybercrime is not perceived as a priority relative to concerns like widespread homicide, some offenders still operate somewhat openly on Facebook and in gaming channels, among other platforms. Many also make use of their real names, or variations and contractions of them, without major concern (BRA-CSP-2, SA-(F)CC-1).[12] The use of variations on real names was also observed in some other regions, such as Southeast Asia (SEA-(F)CC-2).

Beyond this key guideline of crafting a nickname different from one's real name, the specific choice appears to be a very personal one. As mentioned above, popular culture plays an important role in some choices, with movies being a regularly noted form of inspiration (EE-(F)CC-3; NA-(F)CC-1). David Thomas, a veteran of the carding underground, had a passion for movies and used the online nickname El Mariachi, which was inspired by the Robert Rodriguez film.[13] Mythological gods and figures are another common source (WE-(F)CC-2, EE-(F)CC-2, UKR-CSP-1). Robert Schifreen, the British former hacker whose early hobby exploits partly led to the introduction of the United Kingdom's 1990 Computer Misuse Act, took this in a comic direction by naming himself Triludan the Warrior, after the antihistamine medication he used.[14] On the whole, many appear to choose names based on whatever "sounds cool at the moment" (NA-(F)CC-1). Ivan chose one of his nicknames just because it sounded "funny" when his friend came up with it, even though it didn't relate to him directly (EE-(F)CC-3).

But, ultimately, the nickname effectively becomes the heart of an online persona. It should be something the cybercriminal in question likes and feels that he is well represented by:

> As to the significance of nickname, for each person it is his own. For me, as for many others, it is like short description of your alter ego, whatever you want it to be, behind the screen, because very often, your nickname is what people on the other side know first of you, it's your first impression on them (EE-(F)CC-2).

In Andrey's case, his key driver was to produce something "short" and "crisp," which he felt best reflected his persona (EE-(F)CC-2). While he had some technical ability, he did not view himself primarily as a hacker and thus did not choose a nickname that would indicate that. Ivan also chose another of his names because he thought it reflected an aspect of his character (EE-(F)CC-3). But in some instances, the reverse happens and cybercriminals appear to take on the personality traits of their nickname in their online behavior. Poulsen notes how Max Butler altered the way he acted in virtual settings according to the roles he was playing and the identities he had taken on. For instance, as the administrator Iceman, Max would be cool, ruthless, and aggressive—in contrast to his real personality, which was more affable and subdued.[15] This resonates with the broader idea that people are able to create a new persona for themselves online, which parallels clichés of Internet dating, among other online interactions.

The element of randomness in some nickname choices can be taken to the extreme. Dave originally had no attachment at all to the nickname he chose:

> I picked a random name out of the dictionary and I always stuck with that name. The best advice I had from someone was when I was probably about 15 on the Internet was he told me: have one name and use it and get a reputation. Okay, alright, so I got this alias and there are still people that I used to work with when I was cracking software when I was really young and I still talk to them. I am still . . . with that alias, and they know me and they have the same alias, they now have three like kids, and they're still doing it. But I guess can't stop. I just picked a name out of a dictionary, completely randomly. No attachment. But later I found out that the word was actually quite cool and I kind of liked it a lot, *it's a cool word* (SEA(E)-(F)CC-1).

Sometimes the randomness is built into the sign-up process itself. A person creating a nickname might encounter a character limit for a login ID, or simply realize that a shorter name is easier to type. In some cases, sites are set up to suggest nicknames. When South American former cybercriminal Thiago joined IRC, he typed in his real name and it gave him a suggested nickname contraction based on that, which he subsequently kept (SA-(F) CC-1). Western European former cybercriminal Jonas, who was a teenager when he originally chose his nickname, noted that choices are often spontaneous: "I wasn't planning this for a week." He used a random nickname generator and signed up with the handle it produced (WE-(F)CC-3).

Other names are much more functional, and far from randomly chosen. The above-noted nickname of Document Manager is one example of a name specifically linked to a business service on offer. Another would be Track2, referring to a component of the magstripe on bank cards, which was a handle that Roman Seleznev used to sell dumps.[16] In some cases, the functionality is less specific. For instance, while Max Butler chose Iceman to be the enforcer and leader of a criminal market, he used Generous and Digits for his personal vending of card data, implying positive dealings and attractive profits.[17]

Interpreting Nicknames

The previous sections indicated that the key importance of a nickname is twofold: to shield the true identity of its user and to build a recognized online brand. A successful brand can be built on even a random choice of handle. But in many cases, cybercriminals have some kind of reason, however vague or subconscious, for choosing their specific nicknames. Linked to this, some of those I interviewed believe that nicknames can be interpreted to find clues about a user's true identity. As Andrey wrote:

> More sophisticated nickname is, more sophisticated its author. It is clear that individual have to give some thought to his nick (and if he did not, you can tell it right away), and so, sometimes it is like a crypto with his thoughts he gave it, which are to decrypt—more layers, more sophisticated person or his activities is. Choosing a nickname, is somehow, like naming children. What you can tell from the name? If you use similar approach to nicknames, you will understand more (EE-(F)CC-2).

The collected data suggest that nicknames might indeed be interpreted to reveal aspects of age and experience, technical ability, and national, linguistic, or regional backgrounds. First, a number of interview subjects indicated that the age and relative experience of users can sometimes be determined from their nicknames (WE-(F)CC-1, NA-(F)CC-2, EE-(F) CC-2). The key markers are long and excessively complex handles. As Sean put it:

> You can modify it like either reverse it or you could add different characters to it or you could put things in star key, decorating it essentially changing it. Usually what happens is, the more elaborate the nickname the more nooby the person is. Your nickname starts to shrink down and simplify over the years. So mine started off as a ridiculously long one with decorations off the front and a star and now it is just four characters. The sign is when someone has a smaller nickname not bothering with upper case lower case, it shows they are more grown up, which is very strange. It is not an exact science, but it usually shows what mindset that person currently has (WE-(F)CC-1).

It appears that, over time, more experienced parties opt for the confident understatement and ease of use of much shorter and simpler handles. Noah, who also began hacking as a teenager, found after two years that his original nickname "was just too long. So I abbreviated it just like you would Jon, being called Jon" (NA-(F)CC-1). While this seems a useful rule of thumb, not all agree. Ivan argued that there were respected cybercriminals, and not just "script-kiddies," who had numbers and other decorations in their names (EE-(F)CC-3).

Second, some aspects of technical ability might be deduced from a nickname. Former cybercriminal Leonid believed that, while the handles of some carders were not particularly interesting, those chosen by people with hacking backgrounds tended to be more complex (EE-(F)CC-4). In a similar vein, Andrey wrote:

> For "carders" (this is a slang name for cybercriminals who specialize in credit card fraud), who primarily have more computer-related specialty (and skills), selection of nickname is deeply rooted in cyberpunk culture, not unlike hackers. Black-hat hackers, who turned to commit credit card fraud, elected to do so because of lucrativity

and simplicity of this business, comparable to other "areas" of for-profit black-hat hacking, but in context of this discussion on nicknames, it is worth notice, that sometimes (but not always) is relatively simple to identify "carders" with such a hacking background. On other hand, those who do not really have "underground computer culture" background, you can also spot by lack of "sophistication" to their "nick" . . . (EE-(F)CC-2).

The key idea here is that a nickname would reflect some technical knowledge that may not be known by the average user, who does not have the interest or experience in the relevant area. For instance, Andrey analyzed the nickname Segvec as a "non-standard array type descriptor in one of C++ libraries (I may be wrong, but it's along with, along with ::vector, ::segment and ::stdmap etc. descriptors)" (EE-(F)CC-2). Former cybercriminal Mohammed also provided an example of a well-known nickname that was a coding reference that would only be obvious to those with a knowledge of the subject (MENA-(F)CC-1).

Finally, nicknames might also provide useful clues as to the national, regional, or linguistic backgrounds of certain individuals. English-language names and references to western pop culture *might* suggest the user has such a background. Meanwhile, it is not uncommon for cybercriminals to spell out Russian words using the Latin alphabet, as in *Graf* or *Deputat*. Graf is an aristocratic title (akin to an earl or count), while Deputat means deputy (a position of political authority). Both imply power and a form of protection (NA-(F)CC-2). But, of course, a little knowledge of Russian or the use of Google Translate would not prevent the choice of such names by non-Russian speakers. Other names require a deeper familiarity with the Russian language or Eastern European culture. As Andrey explained, the name nCuX (another handle of Roman Seleznev) could be dismissed as somewhat random by English speakers. But someone comfortable with the Cyrillic alphabet would recognize its reference to псих, which means psycho (EE-(F)CC-2). This suggests a greater probability of a Russian speaker behind the nickname (though it should be noted that some of Seleznev's other names, like Track2, are in English). Another of Andrey's examples went further to show how a cultural reference can be suggestive of the user's background. He wrote:

"Borman" is likely to be character in popular soviet movie (as well as subject of many jokes), portrayed after Nazi Bormann, therefore, I can conclude that bearer of that nickname is either neo-Nazi or of Soviet origins, second thing likely, since westerners doesn't often bother themselves with such a study of history, and it is not likely that somebody in the Britain or US studied about Bormann outside college (EE-(F)CC-2).

Andrey acknowledged that his method of interpretation was not always accurate, but believed that, even subconsciously, elements of a nickname can give a feel for the user and whether you might like them or not (EE-(F) CC-2).

While the indications of age seem tied to exuberance and overstatement on the part of inexperienced users, the suggestions of technical, national, or linguistic backgrounds are connected to something deeper— some degree of investment by the bearer of a nik. In order to choose such names in the first place, one must have real experience or knowledge of certain topics. Choosing the name Segvec, for example, suggests a knowledge of a particular programming language. The names nCuX or Borman require at least some linguistic or cultural knowledge relating to a specific region. This means the person in question has likely either grown up in that region or actively sought knowledge of it. The nicknames that would better indicate someone is from a particular background would be those that require extensive knowledge of that culture. The more specific the reference, the more difficult it is for the nickname to be appropriated by someone of a different background. While beyond the scope of the present study, this aspect of cybercriminal nicknames might be well suited to analysis through a signaling theory framework.[18]

Balancing Anonymity with Identity

While these points about branding, handle choice, and interpretation are important, there is perhaps a more fundamental issue at the heart of this subject of nicknames. As noted above, the primary requirement of an effective handle is that it aids anonymity and cannot easily be used to identify the cybercriminal in question. It is the feature that, in effect, allows cybercriminals to advertise their criminality openly online. But one irony of the online underground economy is that anonymity is as much a cost as a benefit. On the Internet, one begins with no identity whatsoever. Cybercriminals must construct identities and attempt to reduce their anonymity in order to build brands and attract criminal partners. But they can do this only up to a point that they remain disguised to law enforcement and do not become vulnerable to other criminals who may wish to do them harm. They must attempt to pierce the veil of anonymity that the Internet affords them, but not discard it entirely.

This is the central tension of cybercriminal nicknames. On one hand there is an incentive to maintain the same nik or a variation of it over time. On the other, there is a competing incentive for cybercriminals to change online names regularly in order to distance themselves either from past crimes, should they ever attract the attention of the law, or from misdeeds against other cybercriminals. A calculation must be made as to what approach to take. Carter, an experienced undercover law enforcement agent, summed up the cybercriminal conundrum:

> It's kind of a paradox, like a catch 22, in that you want people to know your nickname because you have that business reputation, and they can come to you, but at the same time you don't want to keep a nickname too long to let law enforcement track you too much. So there's that fine line in that if you practice good operational security and you change your nickname frequently so people would never really know who you are, but at the same time if people don't really know who you are, how do people know who they're doing business with? (US-LE-2).

Rather than one equilibrium forming, there appear to be a number of approaches cybercriminals take to address this tension. These likely depend on their personal circumstances and preferences. Some use particular handles for different aspects of their business, or regularly change nicknames over time, in order to spread or reduce risk. At the other extreme, some choose to stick with one name, or as few as possible, because they treasure the reputation they have built more than they fear the risk this brings. Finally, many users appear to engage in a midway approach falling between these two extremes.

Regarding the first group, there are those who maintain a number of different handles or change them regularly in order to protect themselves (NLD(E)-CSP-1). While not the most extreme case, Max Butler operated several handles for particular purposes (US-LE-2), including Ghost23, Generous, Iceman, Digits, and Aphex. His story offers an interesting example of nickname strategies, an account of which is found in Kevin Poulsen's *Kingpin*.[19] The first two names he used respectively in the piracy scene and early in his career as a forum vendor of hacked credit card details. As noted above, Iceman was chosen as Butler's administrator nickname, as it was sufficiently common to perhaps subvert law enforcement investigations. But Butler also operated another nickname on CardersMarket, Digits, which he used to vend his own dumps. The thinking behind the two different handles was another strategic decision: if the heat ever came, Iceman could claim to be running an informational website, which Butler did not believe was illegal. Only Digits would go down; Iceman and CardersMarket would remain. Butler was essentially diversifying his risk. In reality, when the heat did come for Iceman, he simply retired this handle. After starting a cyber turf war with DarkMarket, attracting media attention, and (ironically, in hindsight) making unproven accusations that Master Splyntr was actually a "Fed," Butler decided that Iceman's reputation had become too damaged to continue. Instead, Butler as Aphex became the new leader of CardersMarket.

This example demonstrates how nicknames can be employed to address the tension involved in maintaining a brand while reducing the risks associated with it. Particular nicknames might be used to operate distinct brands and spread risk across them. The strategy here is to quarantine some online activities from others, such as selling bank card data from administering a forum (which also perhaps reduces the *appearance* of conflicts of interest). In other instances, users might employ distinct nicknames for the different groups and forums with which they are associated (EE-(F)CC-4). Noah had observed this approach and believed it was a good way to manage risk. He suggested that if hackers employ multiple nicknames they may keep them separate: "so this group of people knows me by this name, this group knows me by this name, the idea being that if this group ever got taken down they wouldn't be able to trace your activity to this other group because they all know you as something completely different" (NA-(F)CC-1). In a similar vein, some cybercriminals use different profile names for different activities, such as in public versus private forums, for personal contacts, for messaging accounts, and for financial accounts (EE-(F)CC-3, SEA-(F)CC-2, WE-(F)CC-3).

Nicknames may also be dropped if they become tarnished, and new ones adopted. In Butler's case, his handle was changed in response to specific developments. Southeast Asian former cybercriminal Tan suggested that such changes were used to throw off not only law enforcement interest, but possibly also forum administrators' attentions following a scam (SEA-(F)CC-2). Noah suggested that, under less dramatic circumstances, handles might be abandoned simply because one decided to move on and no longer be associated with particular activities (NA-(F)CC-1). But some cybercriminals also regularly change their names as a matter of operational security (EE-(F)CC-3). Carter, the undercover agent, observed this directly: "I know certain Russian malware writers that change their nickname about every three months. I look back at the last 5 years and they probably have 20 different nicknames we've been able to connect to one another" (US-LE-2). Andrey had seen the same practice, but noted that it was a relatively new development. In the past, it was common for a user to take great pains to develop a nickname and well-rounded "alter ego," but he said that trend was now "slipping away." The "younger generation" is much more likely to change niks often in the face of security concerns, and care less about the niks they choose (EE-(F)CC-2).

This leads to the second point concerning those cybercriminals who do choose to maintain one name for lengthy periods of time. Despite altering his own nickname at various points, Tan wrote that maintaining one handle was a common approach:

> I believe cybercriminals choose nicknames and stick to that nickname for a while, because they want to keep doing business with one nickname rather than using many different ones, as you know it took time to build trust, credit or reputation for a nickname. Nickname is chosen and represent them like an identity and also their signature (SEA-(F)CC-2).

For Eastern European former cybercriminal Ivan, the chance of being unmasked seemed remote and therefore he felt little need to alter his nickname regularly (EE-(F)CC-3). When Dave, as noted above, chose a nickname randomly out of a dictionary and then kept it over time, the clear reason was that the value of maintaining a brand outweighed any concerns of risk. This was despite the "real catch" that "if you google it, there's all sorts of stuff associated to it. So it sticks." Dave explained his reasoning for not changing names in order to protect himself:

> But then you'd have to start from scratch. It's like changing a real name. If you were no longer Jonathan and you are now known as Bob . . . ha-ha. You've got to start from scratch, it's not worth it. I mean I've got a reputation, I've got friends, people trust me, I've got a good working relationship with many people, and I like that. So no, I wouldn't change it (SEA(E)-(F)CC-1).

Now that he has moved into the legitimate security industry, there might be a threat of people finding out his past. But even this hasn't been a great concern for Dave: "To be honest, people have, clients have and they like it. They think that's awesome. You'll do an even better job because they know you are really fucking going for it" (SEA(E)-(F)CC-1). Thiago took a similar line. It was "so important" to him to maintain the same nickname (itself a contraction or variation of his real name) for his entire criminal career and following it (SA-(F)CC-1).

Part of Dave's approach could be explained by the fact that he began his on-and-off cybercriminal adventures when law enforcement was not as active in this space. The risks were simply lower, even only as far back as last decade. In Thiago's case, he did not see local law enforcement as a major threat but nonetheless took other steps to stay under their radar (SA-(F)CC-1). Yet, while it is now less common, hanging on to nicknames still continues. In fact, there appear to be particular roles within the cybercrime industry that encourage the use of one name for as long as possible. Carter noted that Russian malware writers change names regularly, but it may be that their place in the economy allows this. Such actors often work in smaller groups, or even alone, and the most cautious ones deal only with people they know relatively well. As such, it is much easier for them to keep their key contacts aware of any nickname changes. The high value of their services in the market allows them to keep a low profile. There are other types of cybercriminals, however, who benefit from using the same nik over time. These actors perform functions that require them to interact with many other users, including some with whom they have not dealt before. Foremost among these are vendors. Scott argued that someone who changed his name regularly as a matter of routine procedure was often "someone more behind the scenes," who might, for instance, provide dumps to vendors who would then resell them in smaller amounts. But it was rare for someone with a "'brand name' that they relied for vending" doing this. Scott wrote his summation like this:

> I would say this is more a problem for the people that depend on the "brand name" much more, such as vendors etc. It would be allot easier for someone on the hacking / cashing / buying side of the business to change niks if he had already established contacts etc. This is one reason most of the hackers stealing most of the data sell in bulk to the vendors that have the brand. They don't want to expose themselves to so much heat that the vendors already do (because

they can't really change nicks etc.) so they sell in bulk to the vendors (with the already established brand names) and let them piece them out (NA-(F)CC-2).

In a sense, the high-level suppliers are offloading unwanted risk along with the goods they sell. The vendors buy the risk because they otherwise can't access the product. This point underscores the argument that cybercriminals are not a homogeneous group. There are many specialized roles within the industry and it is not reasonable to expect they all operate in the same way.

Third, it is noteworthy that few cybercriminals actually fall at the remote extremes of either changing nicknames very regularly and not leaving trails, or clinging to single handles for their entire careers. Most lie somewhere in between, employing at least one of two key strategies. The first involves leaving a clear trail between their new and old nicknames (US-LE-2). Some might openly introduce themselves on a board or channel, for example, using a current handle but making reference to other niks:

> Your nicknames kind of follow you so what usually happens if you introduce yourself as someone, you'll join a channel with a usual nickname and then they might say aka Nick1 Nick2 Nick3 blah blah blah blah blah. So you kind of take a trail of these nicknames with you and you do use them to show people your reputation within the hacking community. And it can also work vice versa, if someone says I am affiliated with this this this person or I was known as this this and this, and that person says never heard of them then you know that that they are probably not really, well they are either from a different hacking group that you don't want to be part of or they're just a noob and you know to stay away from them (WE-(F)CC-1).

Others might be more secretive and choose to alert only trusted partners to their new or different identities. But in many cases, some link has to be made or their original reputation will be lost entirely (NA-(F)CC-1). While he had seen some cybercriminals change their nicknames very regularly, Carter also suggested that such links still needed to be made (US-LE-2).

There must be ways to signal credibly that one is the same person who was behind previous handles, but care must also be taken that the trail is not so obvious to everyone that the nickname change is rendered pointless. Scott wrote about how this works:

> If you were to change nicknames and still wanted a select few people to know it was the same person, there are a few ways someone can tell it's you or not. A lot of people will first check to see if the person is on the same ICQ / Jabber / email account (or has the ability to login to the old one still) and then will ask a verification question like I talked about before. Some people choose that drop the name and start all the way over, maybe sometimes later on confirming that it is the same only to a few people they trust really well. If you are a big ripper then they would most likely not reveal that because word travels etc. (NA-(F)CC-2).

Law enforcement agents and security professionals also believed that evidence of past dealings was an important means of confirming identity once a nickname had been changed (US-LE-2, NLD(E)-CSP-1).

This raises a related issue of importance: that online identities can be confirmed through technical markers. In this case, Scott mentions the ability to log into known accounts. Andrey attempted to use *supercookie* to determine if a machine was the same one. In basic terms, a supercookie is, like a cookie, a small piece of data deposited in a user's browser so that the user can be recognized as a repeat visitor by the site in the future. What makes a supercookie "super" is that it can't be removed, as a regular cookie can, simply by clearing one's browser. In his communications, Andrey described it as the "digital fingerprint of a client's machine derived from such a subtle settings as screen resolution, installed software, language configuration, regional settings or even very specific font sizes or flash, JavaScript, java vm settings, which are very specific for each machine. Thus, there several algorithms, which could tell you possibility that it is the same machine, whether client reset its configuration or not" (EE-(F)CC-2). In reality, there may be many breadcrumbs that could be used to identify a cybercriminal. As Jonas noted, many young users don't set out to become cybercriminals when they enter the hacking scene (WE-(F)CC-3). They are not always acting with operational security in mind. As one experienced private intelligence professional explained, it is "very difficult" to prevent active profiles having some enduring links to a past name, whether in the form of an old email address, messaging account, phone number, or technical marker (NLD(E)-CSP-1).

The second hedging strategy involves keeping the same core nickname but varying aspects of it over time. One alters the handle multiple times but maintains a similar strain throughout, so that there is a connection among the variations. Mentioned above was Sean's nickname, which started out very long and decorated then shrank down to just four letters. Its essence remained the same. Casper approached matters in a similar way. He took a core part of his handle and then changed the consonants at the front of it to create a series of different words (WE-(F)CC-2). Both Sean and Casper were young hackers, who may have made some naming choices based on fun rather than pure strategy. In Casper's case, his dealings with for-profit activities were also somewhat limited. Among older offenders, who are more fully engaged in cybercrime as a profession, this approach—of using permutations of a core name—appears more rarely (NA-(F)CC-4). Managing multiple, distinct names seems to be the much more common strategy.

Conclusion

While nicknames may be an interesting curiosity in the world of conventional crime, within the industry of cybercrime they are of utmost importance. One cannot exist online without an identity. Niks solve this problem to a degree but also lead to complications and paradoxes. This chapter suggests that anonymity presents an ironic challenge. Online criminals cannot operate without established identities, yet they must still attempt to protect themselves with as many name variations as they can afford. The reputations that allow them to do business on the Internet are the very things that can incriminate them. Anonymity can hide individuals from law enforcement, but it also makes it harder for them to determine which other users might be undercover agents. It can protect cybercriminals from the violence of other criminals, but it offers little recourse to enforce agreements with untrustworthy partners, lacking the traditional underworld option of "paying a visit." In short, anonymity on the Internet is not purely (or even primarily) a boon to cybercriminals. It brings with it great costs and leads users into a series of games to address the challenge of identifying those they wish to deal with, and those they should avoid.

This chapter has outlined the various ways in which cybercriminals attempt to overcome these obstacles. It covered how nicknames act as online brands; how specific nicknames are chosen; the means by which nicknames can be interpreted to provide hints on true identities; and the ways in which cybercriminals balance their needs to establish brands with their needs to maintain low profiles and distance themselves from past actions. Ultimately, cybercriminals manage these challenges as best they can. They must be able to establish functional reputations through their handles. While they act cautiously in this regard and sometimes forgo the value of the reputations they have built, without the ability of nicknames to establish brands online, cybercriminal cooperation would be next to impossible. The entire illicit industry online would collapse.

5

How Cybercriminals
Cooperate Online

FOR A CYBERCRIMINAL, the ability to establish and manage an identity (or multiple identities) in an online environment is of vital importance to cooperating with other cybercriminals. Without an identity, there is no vessel in which to place trust and there is no entity with which to forge agreements—or enforce them. While online identities remain somewhat flimsy and unstable relative to physical ones, the ability to maintain some form of brand is a prerequisite for collaboration. Once cybercriminals have brands to work with, the next step is determining how they will actually cooperate. Great distrust still remains, because all potential online partners are either anonymous criminals or, worse, undercover agents. Earlier chapters have argued that cybercrime is now an industry, and that industries require high levels of cooperation. This chapter examines what mechanisms have been developed online that allow sufficient cooperation to take place in such a low-trust environment.

This chapter draws heavily on theory outlined in the Introduction. The first section investigates the importance of trustworthiness for cybercriminals online. The second discusses the other key element that might conceivably lead to increased cooperation: enforcement. The third assesses how the lucrative rewards of cybercrime might encourage collaboration because the risks involved are outweighed. The final section allows for some variation and considers instances where cooperation is less successful among cybercriminals, and what these failures can teach us about the likely mechanisms that lead to more effective collaboration.

Trustworthiness

As noted in the Introduction to this book, it is trustworthiness rather than trust that is a core element in enhancing cooperation. Trust is essentially the risk one is willing to take on in a transaction, but higher levels of trustworthiness in partners will reduce that risk and make cooperation more likely. Following Piotr Sztompka's approach to trust, this section breaks down the discussion of trustworthiness into three key components: appearance, performance, and reputation.[1]

APPEARANCE

The first component, appearance, overlaps with certain issues of identity discussed in the previous chapter. Here, to avoid too much replication, the focus is specifically on how appearance is used by cybercriminals to determine trustworthiness, moving beyond nicknames alone. Sean, the hacker and former cybercriminal, explained matters this way:

> At the time, we didn't really see age as being a matter. For example, when someone came on we judged them purely based on their ability, their hacking mindset. Your ability to solve problems, your technical how technically minded you are, but mostly how quickly you learn. There are a lot of things that give you that hacker's mindset. We didn't really judge people based on age, gender anything like that. Females might get a bit more attention. But we didn't judge based on that. A lot of the time, I didn't even know how old any of these people were. I didn't know about what race or anything like that. We just judged people purely on how good their hacker's mindset was. And a lot of the time, you just know. It's hard to explain how you know. I can't think of how to explain it. You just get a feeling for how someone is after talking to them on the chat rooms, seeing how they respond, what sort of things they talk about, what sort of things they take an interest in. Very much like talking to someone, like we are talking now. I mean there are no facial expressions or anything like that go into it, but you can still judge someone fairly well just from text I think, sometimes easier . . . (WE-(F)CC-1).

Understanding "appearance" in the context of online interactions presents difficulties because in conventional settings, appearance is mainly physical—and fairly consistent. While some facets of physical appearance, such as clothing or hair style, may be easily changed, other features can't be altered as readily, such as size, shape, and skin color. By contrast, many aspects of appearance online can be manipulated. It is much more a construction of a persona, and is addressed here in such terms. With regard to trustworthiness, potential "tells" that cybercriminals can use to determine a partner's "true" appearance are of particular interest. These represent the limits of virtual persona creation. They include writing style, language or nationality, memberships and affiliations, and time span online.[2]

Regarding style, Scott supported Sean's view that cybercriminals could ascertain a great deal from the manner in which a user wrote and presented himself. Providing greater specificity, he wrote:

> Usually, you would kind of watch how this person would act in general on forums / chat rooms. Pay attention to how and what he talks about. If he talks allot about un-necessary stuff out loud and asks allot of stupid questions, or claims to have done things that just don't add up, red flag usually. Most of the people that are serious about business are generally quiet as can be in public (forums / cha-trooms) and straight to business over PM's etc. (unless you already know them, then you might have occasional chit chat etc.) (NA-(F) CC-2).

He also looked out for unusual behavior, or inconsistencies in typing patterns, which could suggest that a handle had been co-opted by undercover agents or a criminal imposter (NA-(F)CC-2). Still, it would not be impossible for someone to fake a particular style. Max Butler, for example, deliberately altered his writing to make it harder for anyone to connect his virtual identity to white papers and posts he had authored under his legal name.[3]

For cybercriminals, a key question relating to style is how it might serve as a reliable indicator of whether a user is an undercover agent. One former agent with such experience, Landon, suggested that acting against type could sometimes throw off a suspicious cybercriminal. One time when he was accused of being a "Fed" by another user, Landon responded by "cussing him out." The colorful language he typed out went far beyond what would be expected from law enforcement, and apparently convinced this person that Landon was okay to deal with (US-(F)LE-8). Another undercover agent,

Carter, also said his approach was to do "what cops wouldn't do." He took his time and often did a lot of "bullshitting," trying not to move too quickly to transactional matters because "cops always want to talk about business" (US-LE-2). Similar considerations apply to private sector intelligence operatives, as I heard from Daniel. When dealing with users in forums, he would pretend to be the "godfather of cybercrime"—extremely well-connected and too busy with his own affairs to engage much with someone new (NLD(E)-CSP-1).

After style, a second central aspect of online appearance is language or nationality. In some cases, a particular language can act as a deterrent to working with possible partners. For instance, in the wake of major arrests and takedowns of prominent markeplaces in the 2000s, Russian-speaking cybercriminals have become more cautious of English-speaking actors, with some operating solely in Russian. This may be in the interests of trying to shut out undercover agents from the West, or at minimum creating an extra obstacle for them (see Chapter 2). This point was emphasized by many interview subjects (US-LE-2, NLD(E)-CSP-1, NA-(F)CC-2). Nikita, a former Ukrainian law enforcement agent, argued that even if English-speaking researchers and agents could gain access to certain Russian-speaking forums, they would be shunned by most members (UKR-(F)LE-2). Of course, it is unrealistic to think that western law enforcement agencies and companies have not employed fluent Russian speakers to infiltrate this space (US-LE-2).

Russian-speaking cybercriminals are not the only ones who discriminate based on language. While Sean would work with almost anyone who was appropriately skilled, he listed one important proviso:

> When I said that we didn't bias anyone on race or anything like that. One thing that we did bias them on was their ability to speak English language properly, speak *the* English language properly rather. And usually that meant that if someone was foreign they wouldn't really be accepted into a group because they weren't able to speak English properly. So your groups would usually be separated based on the language barriers. I can't recall of any other previous group where you had intermixing language barriers. Because it is all online, you judge people on how they are typing what they are typing and one of those things if they are not very good at typing in that particular native language, it confuses things a little (WE-(F)CC-1).

Conversely, in certain sets, speaking the "correct" language can encourage cooperation. Scott wrote that, when looking for a good "supplier" (of card details), imperfect English could be a positive trait:

> I seemed to have noticed over the years also that if it is someone that is a supplier of something, if he seems to speak broken English, another good sign since allot of the suppliers come from eastern Europe / Russia (although this obviously can be faked but usually not too consistently, you can tell if it's real) (NA-(F)CC-2).

Scott provided some detail on the specific tells he might look for in determining nationality:

> Obviously, there is no way to always know if someone is faking where they are from for sure, but you begin to develop a "feel" for it. This falls back on the typing patterns a little. I noticed over time that allot of the eastern Europeans (and non-Americans in general) use the word "bro" allot or use words like "university" instead of college, put USD at the end of $ amounts, use the word "market" or "bazaar" when talking about a shopping center, says monies instead of money (makes words plural with "s" that are not supposed to be etc. Also, you can tell if they don't understand US slang words allot (or not well) (NA-(F)CC-2).

Interestingly, I heard from security researchers who go undercover on forums that one of the common tactics they employ is to affect broken English, attempting to impersonate non-native speakers. It is a tactic to gain greater criminal credibility (NLD(E)-CSP-1, UKR-(F)LE-2). This is akin to cybercriminals' pretending to be Eastern Europeans, trying to appropriate the latter's good reputation in the industry (NA-(F)CC-2).

The third notable component of online appearance is a cybercriminal's affiliations—that is, where the individual operates online and with what groups. In the offline world, conventional criminals may take note of who frequents the right places at the right times as one means of discriminating between bona fide criminals and "civilians." For example, when FBI agent Joseph Pistone went undercover in the Bonanno crime family in the late 1970s, he initially established a criminal appearance by hanging out at "wise guy" bars in New York.[4] My data suggest that cybercriminals similarly have their regular haunts, in their case online (UK-(F)LE-2). These places are often hidden and even more difficult to happen upon accidentally than the ones Pistone visited. Anyone found in one should have connections and the degree of knowledge needed to be there. In some instances, payment is required to join particular forums or to attain privileged status within them. These upfront dues provide more assurance that a user is serious about doing business and is not a poorly paid researcher or student (RUS-CSP-5, RUS-CSP-6). Even large fees, perhaps in the thousands, are not hard for successful cybercriminals to cover (US-LE-2). Ivan wrote about what fee payment signals (forum name is removed to preserve participant anonymity):

> For example, on [redacted] you could pay $100 to admin of the forum to have some kind of more respectable profile—so everybody will see that you actually spent $100 just to have it. That is why if you are trying to sell some cards for couple of hundred dollars, it is unlikely that you will rip the customer off (EE-(F)CC-3).

These points closely relate to the final aspect of appearance: time span online. This is a good indicator of whether someone might be a noob, or perhaps a ripper (a scammer of other criminals), or even a law enforcement agent. If they have maintained an enduring online presence, they may be more trustworthy (WE-(F)CC-1, US-LE-2). Some forums even require proof of an established, multiyear *existence* online, to keep out anyone new to the scene (UKR-CSP-1). Another common practice has forum profiles displaying user start dates, to make transparent the length of time they have been active. Nicknames provide a more esoteric way to discern whether someone is a newcomer. As discussed in Chapter 4, young, immature noobs are more likely to have more "decorated" handles that are long and complicated (WE-(F)CC-1, NA-(F)CC-2). More experienced actors tend toward simpler, shorter nicknames.

A sustained online presence is also an element of one's reputation, which will be discussed below. The more time someone has spent in the scene attached to a particular handle, the greater his investment in establishing that identity. This represents a sizeable cost. Because people realize that a person who has made a large time investment is probably less willing to jeopardize it, that investment can be perceived as a signal of trustworthiness. Sean emphasized the length of time required to build and, just as important, maintain an online persona. Having switched to full-time work in the legitimate IT sector, he believed he would no longer have the time to remain relevant online. It's "really a lifestyle thing," he explained, which requires hours and hours of time to show dedication (WE-(F)CC-1). Southeast Asian former cybercriminal Tan suggested that an important part of doing business was being available online as much as possible, in the event that customers wanted to be in touch. If something went wrong with a product and it was not promptly corrected, a buyer might provide a poor review or, worse, report the vendor as a ripper (SEA-(F)CC-2).

PERFORMANCE

The data I collected indicate that performance is also central to cybercriminals' assessments of trustworthiness. Potential partners might make generalized displays of their skills through broad advertisements. For example, prowess demonstrations are commonly found within forums (UK-LE-1). One such means of displaying ability is by providing a tutorial on a technical or criminal skill in the relevant sub-forum of a particular site. The impact of a prowess demonstration can be seen in the communications it generates, which range from deferential praise to offers of business. Tan suggested a related method of publishing e-books that might bolster an author's reputation among certain communities of online readers (SEA-(F)CC-2). (Throughout this section, it will become apparent that performance incrementally feeds into reputation.)

Performance can also be more specifically displayed in the context of a particular criminal endeavor. For instance, a cybercriminal might initially be entrusted with only a small amount of money, as a test of performance (NIG-(F)LE-1). This is a practice used with money mules.[5] As will be discussed further in the next subsection, mules must generally prove themselves by delivering minor amounts, after which they are entrusted with incrementally larger sums (UK-(F)LE-2). For online vendors, test buys and samples can be used to display product quality (UKR-(F)LE-2, RUS-CSP-5, RUS-CSP-6). Ivan originally provided samples of his malware when he was vending, and later provided "comprehensive documentation" to let potential buyers know what to expect from the product. After purchase, if a customer was not happy with the product, "he could sell his license to a new buyer. The only thing that buyer needed to do is to pay me a small fee" (EE-(F)CC-3). Western European former cybercriminal Jonas said he distributed an early version of his malware free of charge to well-respected figures online, in the hope that they would post positive reviews and that strong sales would follow (WE-(F)CC-3). Tan also noted that, because it can take some time to build up a good reputation, it makes sense in a product's early days to offer a "bonus" or "discounts" to initial customers. Once they have had a taste, the satisfied customers will return for more. To maintain these customers, Tan believed it was important to issue replacements if products don't function as promised, such as "dead" credit card data. From the opposite perspective, to avoid "bad buyers," he would insist on payment in advance (SEA-(F)CC-2).

Online marketplaces have incorporated performance-vetting mechanisms into their structures. They do this mainly by having forum officers, or others they endorse, test products and services on behalf of the community (UKR-(F)LE-2, RUS-CSP-5, RUS-CSP-6). This reduces the individual user's need to verify the quality of goods in every instance. Typically, when a product or service passes inspection, its seller receives the mark of a "verified" or "reviewed" vendor. Sometimes a report is published alongside the title being bestowed. While this process may be voluntary, it is clear how such approval helps sales. To attract more business, some also advertise the verified status they have earned on other forums.[6] And in some cases, such as on the forum Lampeduza, being reviewed is a required step before vending at all. Forum membership fees were discussed above in relation to appearance, but they can also be viewed as a type of performance test—demonstrating the ability to pay. Some marketplaces require these for entry instead of (or in addition to) vouches by existing members (RUS-CSP5, RUS-CSP-6, US-LE-2, SEA-(F)CC-2, UKR-(F)LE-2). While some fees are very large, others might only be $100 or so—enough, presumably, to deter the young and penniless noobs. While law enforcement agencies could certainly overcome this barrier with a simple payment, some security companies would fail to pass the test, as they have internal rules that forbid any payment of cybercriminals during an investigation (IRE-CSP-2, NLD(E)-CSP-1).

Some checks used by cybercriminals are less focused on assessing products, and more directly attuned to assessing potential partners (MENA-(F)CC-1). Scott explained his methodology for sizing up new collaborators, moving past appearance to measures that sound more like performance tests:

> As far as online goes, a good place to start when dealing with someone new that doesn't have much of a reputation is my talking to him and trying to see if he, in general, knows allot about the scene and terminology used in it as well. You can proceed this by asking questions that only someone that is actually a real worker would be likely to know off hand. For example, you could start up a conversation about common problems you have with certain brand ATMs, printers, software etc. and see if the guy can elaborate on it, or you could go the opposite way and make something up about it and see if he tries to agree with you on it (which is an obvious red flag). If he were to correct you, you could be like "oh yea, I was thinking of something else" or whatever. If, overall, he seems to be familiar with

what he claims to do off hand (not over email, I'm talking about in real time chat, ICQ / IRC / Jabber / whatever) then it's a good sign (of course not for sure though) (NA-(F)CC-2).

Scott emphasized that it is vital to make this evaluation in real time. If the person cannot provide immediate and credible responses, then the level of suspicion increases. But it is not certain that someone who can't provide timely answers is a ripper. It may only be that the person is a reseller who must check details with the original seller. Being a reseller is not a problem in itself, but it was Scott's preference to deal with original sellers whenever possible (NA-(F)CC-2).

Scott thought similar tests were appropriate for determining whether a nik had been hijacked by either a ripper or an undercover agent:

> If someone drops off out of nowhere and you haven't heard from them in a long time and they come back talking kind of strange with some weird excuse, it's always good to ask a verification question from the past that only they would know, just to make sure you are talking to the same person (although you can usually tell because of their typing patterns etc. after a while). Gotta try to make sure you are not talking to LE directly (although they could be working with them) or someone that hijacked their account, trying to rip you off (NA-(F)CC-2).

Examples of "a verification question" might include asking about the first project they had collaborated on, a shared password that was jointly used in a past project, or the nickname of the person who first introduced them (NA-(F)CC-2).

This leads to the more general concern about how cybercriminals can successfully detect undercover agents. Performance is important in this regard, particularly in providing evidence of criminality. Don, formerly an elite cybercriminal, believed there was only one true method that could unmask agents:

> The only consistent manner of uncovering American law enforcement is to get them to do something that they and their turned individuals cannot do. Usually in the USA this means getting them to hack a site, or abuse some piece of information that you know is an innocent third-party. I have often seen undercovers pretend to

provide dumps in or other resources but those were actually bogus accounts set up as part of an agreement with the bank, so the account was really not owned by a person, and therefor didn't break laws—they were giving away their own credit cards, basically (NA-(F)CC-4).

Eastern European agent Kirill agreed: "It's like in the movies when you are given a gun and you are said 'kill this person and I will trust you.' In this case, it's not that, but slightly similar" (UKR-LE-2). He suggested that cybercriminals are given small tasks to see if there are "bad consequences." Inquiries might then be made with (bent) law enforcement contacts to verify whether this information has been given to the authorities. Sometimes a specific task might be a "decoy" to test a newcomer and see if law enforcement acts on it (NIG-(F)LE-1). In line with this, in some groups, simply observing is not possible. Everyone is given some kind of job to bring them inside the conspiracy (UKR-LE-2, RUS-CSP5, RUS-CSP-6). This connects with the concept of *display crimes*. In underworld settings, these are crimes that are intended to prove one's criminality, and the most serious of such tests is to commit a murder.[7] The stakes are lower in cybercrime, but tests can function in the same way.

REPUTATION

Across many interviews, it became clear that reputation plays a large role in online interactions among cybercriminals (SEA(E)-(F)CC-1, US-LE-2, US(E)-CSP-1, UKR-LE-2, SEA-(F)CC-2, NA-(F)CC-2). As a mechanism for assessing trustworthiness, it is more significant than those discussed above. Indeed, as noted, both appearance and performance can play heavily into reputation. One former hacker, now an experienced cybersecurity professional, noted that the "whole world revolves around reputation, everything revolves around reputation" (UK-CSP-1). Western European former cybercriminal Jonas recalled that his malware customers were very aggressive in the early days. Once he had accrued a good reputation online, however, he was better trusted and could take more time in responding to requests (WE-(F)CC-3). Former spammer Dave, who focused on the more technical layer of cybercrime and stayed away from major forums, outlined the significance of reputation:

> most of these guys, it's small circles of friends. Little groups all like associates. That's why I said at the beginning like reputation. So if

your reputation gets tarnished and you get pushed out of your little bubble, word spreads pretty fast among the other little bubbles close to your bubble. Like you tell your friends, your friends tell your other friends oh that guy he fucking ripped me off, he's no good. So then you're working with, instead of the higher caliber people who are dealing with large sums of money then they would probably have to work with like Nigerians or, I don't know, someone who doesn't have that much cash. It wouldn't be worth it (SEA(E)-(F)CC-1).

Dave went on to add that he had mostly positive dealings in the underworld, with many players acting to keep their reputations intact. Now working as a cybersecurity professional, his more recent experiences have surprised him: "I've been ripped off more times by corporates and commercials. Like companies I'm working for legitimately, with a fucking contract, than I have by people you would consider the scum of the earth" (SEA(E)-(F)CC-1).

As discussed in the previous chapter, an online reputation is tied to a nickname rather than a physical identity. Handles effectively operate as brands for cybercriminals trying to participate in the market. Bearing in mind the instability of reputation in the world of cybercrime, three key elements became apparent through the collected data: the importance of repeated interaction; the regular use of referrals and background checks; and the role of forums in institutionalizing the reputation mechanism and scaling its usability to thousands of members.

Repeated interaction is key to building reputation in various social interactions, so it is unsurprising that the same would be true in cybercrime.[8] It is not hard to comprehend how cybercriminals might become increasingly comfortable doing business together the more regularly they interact. This is especially the case if the interactions take place over a span of years (UKR-LE-2, SEA-(F)CC-2). South American former cybercriminal Thiago had engaged with some online partners for well over a decade in a slow and organic trust-building process (SA-(F)CC-1). As noted in the Introduction, the value of numerous repeated interactions could be that, incrementally, partners are able to test each other's willingness and ability to make good on their sides of the bargain. Throughout the course of dealing, greater compliance might be achieved through partners being able to punish each other for defections. Meanwhile, the mere repetition of interaction in itself may cultivate greater cooperation over the development of the relationship. As Schelling argues, parties may see there is greater value in establishing a "tradition of trust," rather than cheating in a particular instance and jeopardizing future gains.[9]

Phillip, a former UK law enforcement agent, elaborated on how those employing money mules might benefit from repeated interactions:

> What would happen is that they would put an advert up on one of the sites and say, "I need a money mule to transfer money between the UK and Russia." So people would volunteer. So what the crooks would do is say, "Here's a hundred pounds." They'll go to wherever, get the hundred pounds or I'll transfer a hundred pounds into your account. "I need you to go to the Western Union office in Lewisham High Street in London and transfer it to this account in Russia. And, when you do that I will send ten pounds into your account." So they go and do it. So they passed trust test number one. So the crook, he doesn't really mind, because if the guy runs off with the hundred quid, he's run off with the hundred quid, but when you're dealing in millions does that really matter? So, the next time it'll be five hundred pounds, "do it and there's fifty quid in it for you." Next time, it's a thousand pounds, "do it and there's a hundred pounds in it for you." And so on and so on until it builds up. And then they get to really trust money mules. "You know he's had ten thousand pounds from me before and he transferred it and he's really reliable" (UK-(F)LE-2).

Eastern European former cybercriminal Ivan was even more explicit about the value of repeated interactions and, particularly, a Schelling-like tradition of trust. He wrote about his dealings with freelance programmers and others:

> After first couple of deals are done, that is where the trust is beginning to grow. So, if you have done successful deals with a person in the past, then it is unlikely that he will disappear after another one— it is just not in his best interest; it will not going to make any sense, because he will make more money by continuing doing business with you, than by ripping you off. So, growth of trust is based on analysis of a person's egoistic motives (EE-(F)CC-3).

UK law enforcement agent Colin saw reputation and its impact on future gains as crucial: "The trust element is probably more driven by the profit that's in it" (UK-LE-3).

There is already some support for the idea that repeated interactions can help build positive reputations for cybercriminals. For instance, Marti

Motoyama and colleagues look at personal messages responding to trading (advertisement) threads on forums, and find that a significant percentage came from prior acquaintances.[10] This could mean that, although other factors might be involved, forum users were more at ease working with past partners than finding new ones.[11]

North American former cybercriminal Scott preferred working with partners he had past experience with, so sometimes this meant not dealing with people on forums at all:

> A lot of times you find that a lot of good people wouldn't even be on forums at all (at least not with the same nick or not advertising lol) because they would rather just work with who they knew and avoid the added heat / attention from being on the forums. Once I found someone that could do a certain thing or provide a certain service well or whatever, I would just keep using him until he no longer could, ripped me off, or quit / disappeared or whatever (NA-(F)CC-2).

If the first key driver of a cybercriminal's online reputation is repeated interaction, then the second driver is referrals and background checks. This connects to the question of how a cybercriminal's network expands over time, and how others not directly known to him gain information about his reputation. After all, before repeated interaction is possible, potential collaborators must decide if the risks are sufficiently low to begin cooperating. One possible answer is that information about the cybercriminal passes through social networks, via gossip or otherwise, thereby allowing others to learn information about him. Even more valuable to a potential collaborator, as Mark Granovetter tells us, "is information from a trusted informant that he has dealt with that individual and found him so."[12] Referrals play an important role in the cybercrime sphere. As Scott explained:

> If you are not using a forum, then word-of-mouth is another thing people use. If you are looking for someone to provide a service you need and you have some other people you are already working with on other things, it's always good to ask them first if they know a good cashout guy, or dumps vendor, id vendor or whatever it may be. Usually, that is your best option (or it was for me) and used forums as a sort of last resort because of the ripper potential and its always better to work with a person that someone you already trust, trusts (ha) (NA-(F)CC-2).

Scott considered this approach equally important when trying to avoid working with undercover law enforcement (NA-(F)CC-2).

It is also possible for a cybercriminal to list potential references when introducing himself, inviting potential partners to contact them if they are interested in working with him. Eastern European former cybercriminal Andrey wrote that the major players always know where to find different specialists to perform the necessary roles in a scheme: "Big cybercrime is almost never game of one player of one team" (EE-(F)CC-2). Cybersecurity professional Daniel also saw deep value in referrals: "If you need to get to a person in the underground, don't go to them direct you go through people they know and trust" (NLD(E)-CSP-1).

Rather than depending solely on references, cybercriminals are also able to engage in background checks. They can gather the electronic footprints a user leaves behind, and compare these to the details they can extract directly from that user (WE-(F)CC-1, NA-(F)CC-2, UKR-CSP-1). Such footprints could include past affiliations with different groups and forums, or posts from the individual containing relevant information. Of course, as was shown by undercover FBI agent Keith Mularski, who managed to ascend to the top administrator rank on DarkMarket, it is possible to forge certain aspects of this trail. In that case, Mularski, operating under the handle Master Splyntr, became widely known as an elite Polish spammer after appearing on a list of the top ten spammers in the world. The publisher of the list, the anti-spam organization Spamhaus, had collaborated with the FBI to fabricate this impressive reputation.[13]

Some cybercriminals may go further in checking their would-be collaborators' backgrounds. One method of doing so involves hacking into the person's email or system to find out more details. Scott described engaging in this practice:

> Also, if you are able to conduct a little recon on your partners, it never hurts ;-). I have gotten into partners emails before to make sure I knew what they were up to, also tried to find any link to a real world name etc. anywhere else on the Internet with that same nickname etc. (some people slip up and use the same nickname they used when playing counterstrike or something for example and leave posts with their real name or something on other places on the Internet). The more you know, the better (NA-(F)CC-2).

The final point to note with regard to reputation is that forums—as with appearance and performance—have institutionalized this mechanism so it can be applied to sizeable clusters of strangers. The bigger the group, the higher the costs of doing background checks on, and seeking referrals for, every member. Large forums can have memberships in the thousands, which means it is probable that any two users may not be acquainted or know a user in common who could introduce them. In fact, as noted in Chapter 3, a person's very presence on the forum might indicate a lack of contacts in the first place. In order to cut the risk, virtual marketplaces have needed to develop means for scaling up the reputation mechanism. Some forums have crystalized reputation into numerical indices, by having members or forum officers rate the conduct of users. Other members can then use these scores to gauge whether it is advisable to do business with a specific individual.[14] Jonas chose his main business partner in part because he had many reputation points (WE-(F)CC-3). In line with this, Motoyama and coauthors find higher reputation scores to be correlated with larger numbers of private messages from other users, which are often suggestive of willingness to trade.[15] Some forums, like Ghostmarket, also award formal ranks such as "trusted member" to users who prove their "criminal credentials to the administrator and moderators."[16] Such designations may be a way for forums to confirm a user's good reputation for the reference of others.

While these systems might have some value, my empirical data suggest that qualitative reviews and feedback options are equally important in practice. These functions allow buyers to provide accounts of their experiences interacting with different sellers (RUS-CSP-5, RUS-CSP-6).[17] Scott explained the importance of this in selecting prospective partners:

> If you are advertising your service on a forum etc., then you have your own thread where people leave feedback for your service and products etc. Kind of like eBay, you do business with the guy, you leave feedback in his thread saying if he was helpful and legit or not or if you had any problems etc. If you see someone on there that has been dealing with several other people you know for a while and the people you already know and trust are leaving good feedback, then probably ok to deal with him (NA-(F)CC-2).

The reliance on reviews as a reputational measure was confirmed from the law enforcement perspective, as well, with a sense that they were even more important than various points systems (UKR-(F)LE-2). An extension of the review function is the "name and shame" section found on some forums.[18] These are areas where cybercriminals can provide evidence of bad behavior, warn about rippers, and identify other malefactors to steer clear of.

Being publicly shamed in this way damages reputations and can even lead to parties being ostracized, thereby discouraging other would-be scammers.

The vouching process required to enter some closed forums institutionalizes the way cybercriminals regularly seek and provide referrals before engaging with someone. These higher-level sites usually demand that at least two standing members vouch for the prospective entrant (UKR-CSP-1, NIG-(F)LE-1, RUS-CSP-5, RUS-CSP-6). Security researcher Rikard claimed that some are even more restrictive, requiring upwards of four existing members to provide recommendations, each of whom must have known the prospective member at least three years (UDL-CSP-1). This reduces the need to seek referrals for each new partner. Essentially, all potential partners are pre-vetted, which signals that the forum overall is a safe place to do business. To ensure that recommendations are genuine, there is often a rule by which the vouching members are held responsible for any misbehavior by a new member they have introduced to the community. They have to repay anyone who has been scammed, for example, or face being banned along with the ripper (UDL-CSP-1, NA-(F)CC-2).

Knowing someone's reputation is vital for cybercriminals to calculate the risk level of doing business with that person. But to properly understand how cybercriminals make use of reputation, one should recognize their approach as not entirely novel. Legal online auction sites like eBay, which bear some structural similarity to illicit trading forums, employ analogous reputation systems.[19] And there are also offline, historical parallels from entirely different contexts.[20]

The Champagne fairs in medieval France, which brought together merchants from across Europe, were one historical setting in which traders also faced major concerns related to enforcement and trust. The challenge was that sellers from diverse locations convened briefly and then decamped, making subsequent contract enforcement a challenge. The way the fairs dealt with this obstacle was with a system of private judges who maintained records of merchant behavior. Before entering a deal, a trader could consult with these judges and learn information about the reputation of a possible partner.[21] Today's reputational mechanisms in cybercriminal forums—including numerical indices, public reviews, and naming and shaming sections—are analogous to these private judges. They dramatically lower the costs that parties would otherwise have to incur to investigate each other individually, by making public the relevant information on past transactions. They are a strong advertisement for the importance of institutions in expanding exchange and supporting the development of the broader industry.

Enforcement

So far this chapter has focused on trustworthiness, but another key element required to support cooperation and the formation of a cybercrime industry is enforcement. This mechanism can function even when there is little trust between parties. Southeast Asian former cybercriminal Tan put it this way: "To me, the cybercriminals are working as the same mentality as the real world criminals, it's about trust, integrity, and so if ones wants to play the game, ones have to follow the rules or ones will get punishment" (SEA-(F) CC-2). There are three main forms of enforcement: self-enforcement, collective enforcement by a group, and enforcement by a third party who may act on behalf of an individual or group. As previously mentioned, monitoring and sanctions can play a key role in this regard. Establishing a credible commitment can also enhance cooperation through more esoteric means like cutting off options or exchanging information hostages.

Cybercriminals have only limited enforcement options available online, when they operate outside structures like forums. Unlike traditional criminals, they cannot employ outright violence. But they can, in very elementary terms, punish noncompliant collaborators by declining to cooperate with them again. More punitive options are possible, some of which seem to mirror violence in a virtual way, but these are mere shadows of the real thing. For example, Benoît Dupont describes one form of enforcement involving carrying out DDoS attacks against other hackers.[22] This method can be employed by a collective against a wayward member, or by individuals against others; even competing forums have engaged in these attacks against one another.[23] Their use is a relatively common cybercriminal tactic (NA-(F) CC-2).

Other means of virtual punishment have also evolved. *Doxing* involves tracking down personal details and then publishing them online to humiliate the target (US-(F)LE-8). It also effectively strips victims of their anonymity, the most precious possession of a cybercriminal. Scott wrote about an episode he observed:

> there are also sometimes repercussions for "ripping" etc. Take, for example, one cashout guy I used to know whose nick was [redacted].[24] His downfall came from under-estimating his supplier and deciding not to pay him $40k. Not soon after the rip was confirmed, he was kicked out of the IRC channel (where he was an operator at the time), banned from it, and the topic was changed to "Whoever

wants to fuck [redacted] click here." The link was to a page (on a hacked banking site lol) that had his picture, name, brother's name, address, phone, swift account #s, bank acct numbers etc. Two to three weeks later he was busted (NA-(F)CC-2).

This supplier's revenge illustrates the gravity of doxing. It not only leads to humiliation and a feeling of violation but also makes the victim vulnerable to further abusive or pecuniary attacks by others. Most damagingly, with their identifying information revealed, targets may quickly find themselves subject to arrest by the police. While almost any user can engage in doxing, there are people with a particular talent for this activity who offer their professional services for hire (NA-(F)CC-2). DDoS services can also be hired, but they often have more "legitimate" purposes than solely targeting other cybercriminals, such as extorting businesses whose trade relies on online sales.

Swatting is another associated method of punishment. This involves tricking the police into sending armed officers to the victim's location, under the misapprehension that a violent encounter has taken place on the premises. One famous example of swatting involved leading security blogger Brian Krebs, whose reporting is based on deep access to cybercriminal forums. It is not uncommon for Krebs to aggravate cybercriminals with his work, sometimes leading to threats. In this case, the blogger was surprised to find heavily armed police outside his home one evening, who immediately apprehended him. The event became the subject of a widely read and publicized post entitled "The World Has No Room for Cowards."[25]

These forms of punishment demonstrate how information can be used to cause damage. Gathering information also plays an important role in monitoring, perhaps with later punishment and coercion in mind. Scott outlined how seriously he took this task:

> I used to make a little notepad on each person I was suspicious of (or trusting allot of stuff with) and keep track of any little clues that I could get. Allot of times, people slip up and say or do things they don't mean to or don't think about. You have to pay attention to the details. Anything you can get that you can use to try to find more out with, save it in a file to create a profile on them kinda. Any email addresses they use, nicks that they use, ip addresses and even metadata from pictures they send could be helpful. Anytime they send money with WU or MG etc., keep any names that they use. There are

allot of people that will actually use real names (or close variations of) to do this or names of other people they know. You keep any addresses that you might have got from them (from mailing physical items). You could also do teamwork kinda with anyone else that might be involved. For example, if they were buying IDs or plastics from someone else you know well and work with, ask them if they have the addresses or pictures even that were used in their order. If you already know the seller better than them and let him know they ripped you, they might give it up (or sell it to you lol). You could always go with the virus approach if you thought you could pull it off and were really suspicious, but you better be pretty sure with what you are doing if you don't want to lose them (because if they figure it out they will not take it well). If you have a custom version of a key logger that is crypted just for that use that wont be detected most likely then try it out. Also, one thing that helps is addresses on receipts that are sent as pictures for verification possibly and if they happen to have a hand or something in the picture you could possibly tell their skin color (NA-(F)CC-2).

Even in cases where there isn't any suspicion, the gradual exchange of personal information often takes place over time between long-term partners, slowly chipping away at their anonymity. Former cybercriminals interviewed for this project provided examples of speaking on the phone with some collaborators and sharing personal details about their families, offline lives, and so on (WE-(F)CC-1, NA-(F)CC-2, SA-(F)CC-1). Such behavior was not universal and was often reserved for those who had already established a degree of trustworthiness. But it goes against the core idea that anonymity should always be maintained as a norm. (In Chapter 6, we will explore the even more curious cases of cybercriminals choosing to meet in person.)

One possible explanation for this behavior can be tied to Schelling's idea of information hostages. To restate the central idea from the Introduction, rather than trading people, the process involves the exchange of compromising information and encourages cooperation because each side has the power to incriminate the other with that information. This serves as a credible commitment. Consistent with this theory is the idea that once cybercriminals feel comfortable with one another, they might start to exchange personal or other information to cement the relationship. Some behaviors along these lines have been observed in the context of forums.

Those who wanted to join DarkMarket were required to upload data from a hundred compromised credit cards. Two reviewers would then check the data and produce reports. As one investigator of this case explained, if "the cards did what they were supposed to . . . they would be recommended. If not they weren't allowed in."[26] This mirrors similar processes in the other spheres of cybercrime, such as online pedophile groups that require the provision of a certain quantity of original child sexual abuse material to join.[27]

In recent years, however, such practices do not appear widespread among forums, with examples appearing relatively rarely, at least in the profit-driven sphere (NLD(E)-CSP-1). While verified vendor status commonly requires goods to be vetted by forum designates, such approaches have not been popular tests for basic entry into forums. Closed forums seem to have valued other barriers to entry whereby existing members vouch for new members. This is perhaps an admission that tests like DarkMarket's can be defeated by law enforcement, with the assistance of banks (although they might still keep security companies or noobs at bay). Instead, the primary application of information hostages appears to be in offline relationships, as will be seen in Chapter 6.

Aside from information hostages, forums expand and formalize aspects of private enforcement to keep cybercriminals in line. This brings the enforcement mechanism to an institutional level and scales its impact to much larger numbers. The most commonly reported punishment is banning from a site by the forum's hierarchy.[28] Administrators make the rules of forums and they can enforce them by whatever means they deem necessary. My data confirm that exclusion is a common form of punishment and a relatively powerful tool (UKR-CSP-1, MENA-(F)CC-1). But the process has its complexities. Scott wrote that exclusion might not always be suggestive of poor behavior; it might rather reflect an administrator with biases, who abuses his power or engages in "hating." If one wished to deal with a banned user, it might be wise to investigate further before writing him off. Here is how he phrased the point: "If it seemed like it was minor bullshit and possibly biased by the administrator or whoever, then you could still proceed if you thought it was worth it but obviously, be careful and take it as a warning ;-)" (NA-(F)CC-2). Clearly, if someone has been banned from multiple forums, it is best to avoid them. In this way, the process of banning again draws us back to the question of reputation. As Scott wrote:

> Your best bet is to check into the feedback to see if other people (that you already trust / deal with) left feedback and talk to them and get

their opinion. Overall, if it seems like the nick is banned for good reasons on a respectable forum, then that nick is basically dead. They could start over with another nick if they wanted to and build back up, but it would take time and more positive feedbacks to get it back up. Sometimes people can figure out if it's the same person though just by typing patterns or whatever and everyone will be scared off (NA-(F)CC-2).

The key weakness with banning as a means of punishment is that offenders can attempt to rejoin the same forum or other forums under a different nickname. After all, it is only their usernames that have been excluded. This means that the true cost of the expulsion from the forum is the need to build a new reputation from scratch. Though substantial, such a cost is far less than the sanction of being purged from, for example, a mafia group—which might well be death.

Linked to banning is the arbitration mechanism present within many marketplaces. The process is akin to an online trial (EE-(F)CC-3, RUS-CSP-5, RUS-CSP-6). Nikita, the Ukrainian former agent, provided an outline of how this might work in the Russian-speaking underground. While the arbitrator can be a forum administrator, in the Russian scene it is common to find people akin to professional specialist arbitrators, such as one known individual who was regularly called in to judge disputes across a number of different forums (UKR-(F)LE-2). Nikita described the arbiter's job:

> It's his role to research all the evidence. The guys present evidence and the usual evidence is the chats. So they usually communicate through Jabber and mostly they post chat logs or screen shots. In some cases, if it involved malware for example, they might give access to that malware control panel, for example, to the arbiter for him to see to test it and then after these several posts by both sides providing their evidence, the arbiter makes his decision. The usual decision is to expel the party that was involved in wrongdoing (UKR-(F)LE-2).

It is also not uncommon for others to have a say on the matter: "It's kind of like regular court hearings, but online in the underground world. There are witnesses, evidence, the judge—the arbiter—who makes the decisions" (UKR-(F)LE-2). A similar process takes place on the English-language forums, but the arbitrators are often forum administrators rather than professionals hired to perform the service (NA-(F)CC-2).

Online marketplaces also employ another tool to enforce agreements directly: escrow. In some instances, escrow is provided by forum officers, while in others well-trusted members can provide this function (UKR-(F)LE-2, UKR-CSP-1, NA-(F)CC-2, SEA-(F)CC-2, NLD(E)-CSP-1). Brendan described this third-party guarantor as someone who has "got a lot of posts, who is very trusted and has more to lose screwing people over" (IRE-CSP-2). Usually this person simply holds the money until the promised goods have been received or verified, but in some cases the person also serves as the middleman in the exchange of both the goods and the payment. Guarantors can take a commission, often around three to five percent (UKR-CSP-1, SEA-(F)CC-2). DarkMarket is a good example of an English-language forum which housed escrow services.[29]

The presence of escrow in the cybercriminal underground has often been noted in the academic literature, but there has been little in-depth discussion of how it functions in practice. Scott provided further details of when someone might use escrow:

> Also, there are escrow services that are usually offered by some of the higher people in the forums (Admin, Mods, etc). If you are doing a big deal with someone (say you are purchasing an entire database of dumps for $30,000 for example) and you want to make sure this person doesn't just take your $30k and run off, you would contact one of the escrow providers and ask for help. This way you have a third party (admin) that takes the $30k in Bitcoins or whatever and holds it until you confirm to him that you received the dumps you purchased and then he will take his fee out (5 percent or whatever he charges) and sends the money to the seller (NA-(F)CC-2).

But questions also remain concerning how the guarantors themselves are judged to be trustworthy. This, again, brings us back to reputation. Those who provide escrow services must have spotless reputations. These figures are often "wise old men" who have long been a presence in the underground and have invested heavily in establishing brands for honesty (RUS-CSP-5, RUS-CSP-6). Brendan put it this way: "Their business is their reputation" (IRE-CSP-2). They can be high-ranking forum officers who are widely trusted, but it would not be sufficient to be the administrator of a small, new forum with little standing of its own (UKR-CSP-1, NA-(F)CC-2). While guarantors will never be uniformly reliable, numerous participants believed these figures often took many years to develop their reputations and that it would be highly unusual for them to jeopardize them by carrying out a scam. "Everyone trusts them" (UKR-(F)LE-2). Maksym, a Ukrainian security researcher with government experience, described guarantor cheating as so rare that for it to happen would be like a "nuclear explosion" (UKR-CSP-1). These people have the "ultimate reputation," and maintaining their hard-earned status is the core of how they earn money (NA-(F)CC-2).[30]

It is clear that forums enlarge the role that enforcement can play for cybercriminals. Outside of them, one must rely on oneself or the help of other (friendly) individuals. But this makes dealing with anonymous strangers, who are not closely tied to one's existing contacts, challenging. It limits the extent of exchange that can take place. In line with Douglass North's views, it appears that forums and related groupings have developed institutions to enhance enforcement.[31] They create some order in a chaotic world. But the degree of private enforcement provided by these sites suggests an even further step. In cases where the forum hierarchies establish a system of rules and punishments, guarantee transactions, and arbitrate disputes, they are essentially providing a form of governance. Mohammed likened them to a "state of legit hackers" (MENA-(F)CC-1). As such, they begin to act like some traditional organized crime groups that seek to control the offline underworld. For instance, the Italian-American Mafia guaranteed trade of bootlegged alcohol during Prohibition. It protected the supply of alcohol, the makeshift "curb exchanges" that served as marketplaces, and the transactions that were carried out at these exchanges.[32]

Forums likely fall just short of being accurately classified as mafias or other organized crime groups. They do appear to comply, at least partially, with the theory of protection, where mafias operate in low-trust environments and provide protection for otherwise unstable transactions.[33] Thus they move toward the definition of a mafia as an organized crime group that "attempts to control the supply of protection."[34] But there are two main reasons that, even as they perform mafia-like functions, such forums are unlikely to qualify as mafias themselves. First, attempting to control the supply of protection is very challenging online. While some competition and friction exist among these sites, there isn't a rigid sense of territoriality in the world of cyber. Low barriers of entry mean that other protectors can easily emerge from across the globe. Forums provide only a relatively weak form of governance because enforcement is not physical but virtual. Although the modes of enforcement online may significantly enhance cooperation and exchange, they are only a shadow of the most powerful offline sanction: death. While exclusion may be seen as an online version of death, it is really only a form of severe reputational damage. Old nicknames can be shed and new identities built. But death is final.[35]

The second challenge in conceptualizing a cybercriminal forum as a form of mafia is that these digital structures are not true criminal organizations at all. Don, who played a key role in running a large marketpalce, said that to describe a forum as one large organization where everyone works for a boss would be "batshit insane." Instead, he suggested, it was more like "running a coffee shop with a bunch of whiteboards where visitors could scrawl notes" (NA-(F)CC-4). Acts of criminality are committed by forum members, but not necessarily with the direction or involvement of its leaders. Forums are somewhat ephemeral marketplaces, and the individuals behind them—the key forum officers—appear to lack the tight structure and cohesion that might define a bona fide criminal organization such as an offline mafia. In basic terms:

> A mafia is not a marketplace. A mafia may attempt to govern various marketplaces, but its existence is distinct from the individual enterprises it is involved with. For instance, while the mafia oversaw the curb exchanges during Prohibition, this was not its sole occupation as it was involved in a number of other activities. Likewise, while the Sicilian mafia has controlled the Palermo fish market for some time, the fish market is not itself a mafia. The Sicilian mafia is the mafia.[36]

Governance in the cybercriminal world is largely tied to specific sites, rather than autonomous criminal organizations. Their policing role looks more like the private judges of the Champagne fairs who regulated trading in those marketplaces.[37] If merchants did not abide by their rulings following disputes, these judges could exclude the recalcitrant ones from future fairs. In very similar fashion, forum officers exclude rippers from their marketplaces, and by doing so, deter would-be scammers and provide general assurance that the sites are safe places to do business. In both contexts, it is clear that institutions are enhancing opportunities for exchange and leading to economic development. Both also demonstrate some level of governance, but at a lower level than what is seen in genuine organized crime groups, who attempt to govern not only specific marketplaces but entire illicit markets. Nonetheless, the role of institutions and governance in cybercrime has been fundamental, effectively transforming small-scale trade into an industry.

Risk for Reward?

The mechanisms discussed above are built around the central objective to reduce risks in transactions and thereby increase cooperation, but they will never completely succeed in wiping out defection. As noted in the Introduction, universal cooperation is an unattainable goal, even in mature societies with well-functioning institutions and strong governance. To trust is to accept a certain level of risk. But the other part of the equation is the possible reward for that trust. If the stakes are high enough, there will be those who are willing to take on greater risk. Cybercriminals may engage in more enterprises not just because risks drop, but also because rewards increase.

Some might question why cybercriminals dare to operate online at all. The simple reason is that, even accounting for the shortcomings of an industry of anonymity, they can continue to earn money. While calculations vary and certainly are not beyond critique, it should be remembered that the annual, global cost of cybercrime is regularly estimated in the hundreds of billions of dollars.[38] Many cybercriminals appear happy to accept the costs of doing business in return for the large benefits they can reap. Scott argued that the "bottom line is you are always taking a bit of a risk or gamble, but when you do finally get a good team together, you keep it as long as you can" (NA-(F)CC-2). Lance was more direct: "you got ripped off . . . ? Guess what, you're in the business of stealing money, you're going to get ripped off. Suck it up and carry on with your business" (NA-(F)CC-3). Ivan summed up this attitude in his account of choosing to work with a programmer who had a longstanding profile on a forum for software developers, but with whom he had never worked before:

> And he had an excellent reputation as a reliable software developer. Also, such people love what they do. It is not in their interest to grab the money and run. BTW, he asked only for 30 percent of full price ($8k). But I decided to transfer 100 percent anyway. Because I did not needed money by then, did not know what to do with such a small amount. So I figured that [redacted] could buy some toys for himself quicker which would make him happier. What would I have done if he did not pay back? I might drop a post on [redacted] that he failed a project and refused to return a prepay. That would ruin his reputation. But likely I would do nothing—just accept a loss. Post on a forum will not help me anyhow anyway—why should I bother then? (EE-(F)CC-3)

A similar pragmatism appears to be common regarding the threat of law enforcement. While those who have been arrested might now see the folly in this view, cybercriminals often feel that their anonymity protects them against arrest (NA-(F)CC-2, NA-(F)CC-4). To ensure this protection, they have to take the appropriate steps of maintaining good security and not engaging in activities that might give their identities away, such as using non-anonymized payment systems or mailing physical items (NA-(F)CC-2). But once these precautions are taken, dealing with undercover agents is part of the business. As long as there are profits to be made, collaboration may still be worthwhile. Don wrote:

> In most cases of "trust" relations in the underground the underlying truth is that trust as we are used to thinking of it does not matter, what is important are the deliverables and the results. In other words, if a spammer buys access to an RDP to mass mail, and the server is really owned and operated by FBI, that doesn't really matter to him or her so long as emails are actually delivered and there is a profit, Likewise, when I was selling credit card data (ugh), then it didn't matter if my customer was LE because their money was as good as anyone else's. It didn't bother me at all and in fact I would greatly prefer to have sold all of my stock en masse to a single LE, because that was everyone would be happy—I'd get the money, the owners of the cards and the banks would not "lose" (really it would be insurance and FDIC), and the LE would get their score. But, sadly, for some reason American LE don't buy cards to get them off the underground market, which is an awful waste (NA-(F)CC-4).

When asked why people engage in cybercrime despite the risks involved, former cybercriminal Jim had a very simple explanation: "$, Greed" (NA-(F)CC-5). Eastern European former cybercriminal Leonid wrote: "my secret is how to get an access to heart of every cybercriminal—u have to make him rich" (EE-(F)CC-4). Former agent Landon agreed, arguing that it's easy not to worry too much about losses when the money is not yours to begin with (US-(F)LE-8).

The data referenced above perhaps lean toward a picture of the online underground as a trustless world where the prospect of large profits is the primary driver of cybercriminal collaboration. Many appear to ignore, or choose to overlook, the risks in light of what can be gained. There is also an element of pure risk-taking behavior at certain points. Lance, for example, suggested that sometimes cybercriminals throw caution to the wind and just say "fuck it, let's do it" (NA-(F)CC-3). These are certainly important factors. The rewards play a large role in driving cooperation. But it is also vital not to overstate their importance. This element does not demolish the central significance of trustworthiness and enforcement, enhanced by institutions and governance, or even replace them as the primary factor in explaining cybercriminal cooperation.

As the earlier sections in this chapter attest, there is very strong support in the data for the roles that trustworthiness and enforcement play in enhancing cybercriminal cooperation. Almost all the former offenders in this study indicated, for example, that reputation played a key role in deciding whom to work with. Lance and Scott were among these, despite their quotes just above on the importance of large rewards in decision-making. Jim was another who noted that greed was of vital importance, but also observed, "I guess what most people do is try to find a few people they can work with and just stick with them" (NA-(F)CC-5). Only Don, quoted at length above, strongly viewed profits as the defining factor in cybercriminal cooperation and didn't really convey the idea of having much trust with partners at all (NA-(F)CC-4).

In most interviews, there appeared to be real caution about potential collaborators, but also the sense that cybercriminals could trust some people more than others—and there were certain people with whom each participant would not do business. A number also clearly differentiated between particular forums in terms of how safe they were as places to conduct business (NA-(F)CC-2, NA-(F)CC-3). Even on occasions when they might have acted recklessly, there was usually some calculation involved. It seemed to be a badge of honor for certain cybercriminals to have successfully avoided engaging with someone who later turned out to be an undercover agent or serial scammer (EE-(F)CC-2). There is, of course, tremendous distrust in the cybercriminal underground. This doesn't mean, however, that cybercriminals all retreat into a nihilistic view and don't bother drawing distinctions between partners worth doing business with and those to be avoided.

In short, there is little evidence that cybercriminals engage with partners indiscriminately. The rewards are why this criminal industry exists in the first place and without the payoffs there would be few cybercriminals. But within this distrustful world, trustworthiness, enforcement, institutions, and governance all play key roles in driving cooperation. In most cases, cybercriminals make use of these elements to reduce the risks involved. If the prospect of large rewards encourages more venturesome deal-making in certain cases, this supplements rather than replaces the above mechanisms.

Failures of Cooperation

It is a fundamental aspect of social science methodology that, if one wishes to study the presence of a phenomenon and the factors that lead to it, one also needs to examine cases where it is not present. Some element of variation must be included within the sample. In other words, it is important not to select on the dependent variable.[39] As this chapter examines how cybercriminal cooperation online has been achieved so that an industry could be established and maintained, it is also vital to address cases where cooperation among cybercriminals was less than successful. For instance, North American former cybercriminal Jim wrote about some past challenges in the underground economy:

> There were fake escrow accts, fraudulent reviews, payoffs for vendor status, and sometimes selective ripping, or just building up a reputation and then one day taking off with the money. I think I already told you that many of the sites set up were completely fraudulent, they were set up, run by, and all the vendors and reviewers were the same person. It was a dirty business (NA-(F)CC-5).

Scott and Lance recounted similar stories of administrators who "turn bad." In some instances, they might accept bribes to allow rippers to return to a forum. In other cases, they might bide their time as they build up good reputations until one major scam presents itself and they disappear (NA-(F)CC-2, NA-(F)CC-3).

Southeast Asian former cybercriminal Tan was one of the few former offender participants who admitted to scamming at some point during his career. Most of the others suggested that their reputations were too important to jeopardize. As to why Tan might take this risk, he said, "I used to scam others when I see there's a high percentage of chance that I can have a safe getaway" (SEA-(F)CC-2). Meanwhile, he protected himself from being scammed by establishing clear rules for partners and ensuring his procedures (for example, requiring upfront payment) were followed. This suggests that scams occur when risks of being caught are low and therefore reputational damage and punishment are not a great concern. Ripping will likely always take place, but the threat is greater when the appropriate mechanisms to prevent it are not adequately employed. For instance, Scott lost a dispute with a well-known cybercriminal who scammed him because he did not record logs of their dealings which could have been used in the subsequent arbitration (NA-(F)CC-2).

Perhaps the most effective way that variation can be brought into this study is to examine historical shifts in cybercrime and the levels of cooperation at each point. As outlined in Chapter 2, the early days of profit-driven cybercrime, before the turn of the millennium, were largely characterized by lone wolves and limited collaboration. This all changed with the birth of forums and the development of mechanisms to enhance cooperation. As Lance pointed out, one of the fundamental problems in the era of IRC platforms was that no "record" of conversations was available so that one could not get the "vibe for the seller or the buyer to see if they were able to do business, if they were able to trust them" (NA-(F)CC-3). This was a fundamental problem of identity and branding.

Forums overcame this challenge and made it easier for cybercriminals to review past posts and essentially assess the reputation of other users. This then also allowed some aspects of enforcement to be applied to these identities. The institutional and governance aspects of forums also aided cooperation in these communities, by formalizing the reputation, performance, and appearance mechanisms, as well as enhancing some aspects of enforcement like punishment, arbitration, and guaranteeing certain transactions. As a result, trade began to thrive and the underground rapidly expanded in both size and reach. Firms of various sizes began to form. A strong case can be made, therefore, that the broader functioning of these mechanisms lowered the risks and thereby genuinely improved cooperation. In the pre-forum world, where these mechanisms functioned much more weakly, the risks were higher and cooperation was limited.

This approach can also be taken one step further by including the state of affairs after the Golden Age of forums. As recounted in Chapter 2, after it came to light that ShadowCrew was being run by a US Secret Service informant and that undercover FBI agent Keith Mularski had ascended to the rank of administrator on DarkMarket, further distrust was injected into the underground. Following these law enforcement successes, cybercriminals became much more wary of whom they dealt with. While large forums still exist, experienced players have often retracted into smaller groupings of more trusted partners. They engage with the forums and strangers only out of necessity, such as in Scott's case when his old partners disappeared (NA-(F)CC-2). The implication is that cooperation levels dropped as risk increased: law enforcement agents capable of carrying out arrests might be lurking online.

Further than that, law enforcement appeared to damage faith in cybercriminal institutions. Forums, those places that successfully expanded the operation of key mechanisms to allow successful exchange among large groups, were no longer considered safe. Cybercriminals closed ranks and relied on trustworthiness even more, and especially on reputation, with a strong preference to work with long-term partners of good standing. Some degree of enforcement is still possible, but there are fewer options for it than forums provide. As cybercriminals retract into compact groups, smaller-scale collaboration can still suceed, but large-scale cooperation is stunted. This is a clear illustration of the value of trustworthiness and enforcement, along with institutions and governance in particular.

This discussion points to a broader issue: cooperation failures can be driven by intrinsic weaknesses within cybercrime and among cyber-criminals, such as mistrust over potential ripping, but such failures can also be provoked by external factors, such as law enforcement action. The latter failures are more the product of disruption and sabotage. In practice, the two phenomena merge together somewhat. For instance, the suspected presence of undercover agents might influence cybercriminal behavior, even when no such agents are actually present. Even without direct intervention, law enforcement agents, security researchers, and journalists become part of the fabric of this underworld. In other cases, cybercriminals may have no qualms about dealing with suspected agents, so long as their collaborators pay up (NA-(F)CC-4). The impact of policing is discussed in further detail in the final chapter.

Conclusion

To build a successful industry, cybercriminals must be able to operate in an online environment, despite the risk of dealing with anonymous, criminal partners. This chapter has outlined how, in a world filled with ample opportunities for defection, cybercriminals can overcome this challenge and succeed in collaborating on a large scale. It has addressed the value of trustworthiness, along with the importance of virtual enforcement. It has also outlined how big rewards might be a factor in encouraging cooperation when risks abound. As a point of comparison, it has also considered instances where cooperation has been relatively unsuccessful.

Some key points emerge from this discussion. First, in an online setting, reputation is the mechanism of central importance. While appearance and performance play some role, reputation was mentioned time after time by participants as the critical factor in deciding whether to partner with a specific cybercriminal. Reputation also compares strongly to enforcement. This is perhaps not surprising, given that virtual enforcement is relatively weak. It is also possible that, in an online environment, enforcement itself becomes a manifestation of the broader reputation mechanism. Punishment in the form of exclusion from a forum or other grouping means the loss of a nickname's reputation, leading to all the costs associated with building a new brand. Third-party enforcement by means of arbitration or escrow is a way to reduce the risk associated with transactions by dealing with a more trustworthy third party, who has invested significant time and effort in building a spotless reputation. As these reputable middlemen lower the risk, cooperation is enhanced.

The second point is the importance of institutions and governance in expanding the industry. Without rehashing an argument made above, the point to underscore is that forums appear to be important providers of cybercriminal governance. The institutional order they deliver greatly enhances cooperation and scales it from intimate groups to an industrial level. They also offer a hybrid of self-governance and private governance. In terms of self-governance, the main contribution of these online marketplaces is to extend the reputation mechanism, through indices and feedback systems, so that information can be transmitted beyond a small group of cybercriminals. Information about specific users is not limited to direct past interactions or personal referrals. Within a forum, a tradition of trust can be built as much between each user and the whole community as between pairs of cooperators, making compliance more attractive than cheating.[40] But, while users can collectively choose not to cooperate with a scammer once he has been outed, in practice, the enforcement aspects of forums look more like private governance than self-governance. Forum officers create rules and directly police scamming and other misbehavior. They can provide guarantees for certain transactions and arbitrate disputes. While this private governance never quite reaches the levels provided by offline mafia groups, who seek to govern a variety of different markets, it is significant.

These elements have allowed the flourishing of the cybercrime industry online. Yet no matter how sophisticated cybercriminal institutions become, some risk will remain. Again, this is the case in all human contexts—but in cybercrime, while risks have been reduced to a manageable level, the overall problem of distrust remains more intractable. Part of the reason for this is the very problem that makes reputation so important in an online environment in the first place: it is because virtual enforcement is so weak. Even the most aggressive forms of enforcement, like doxing or banning, pale in comparison to the worst offline sanctions of physical harm and, ultimately, death. The shield of anonymity on the Internet makes monitoring and enforcement far more difficult. These continued challenges may help explain the subject of the next chapter: the offline dimension.

6

The Offline Dimension

THE ROLE THAT OFFLINE interaction plays in cybercriminal enterprises is often overlooked. Most people picture cybercriminals as operating wholly in the anonymous spaces of the Internet, wreaking havoc that cannot be tracked. The offline dimension is also not widely discussed in the academic literature.[1] This adds to the sense that cybercrime is purely a virtual phenomenon, when in reality it is always anchored in a physical context somewhere in the world. Behind every attack, there is a flesh-and-blood person, or people, taking deliberate action. In certain cases, these actors are personally known to each other, or come to know each other over the course of their dealings. This offline element was evident in various cases shared in Chapters 2 and 3. Perhaps the best-known example is the Carder-Planet conferences, which brought cybercriminals from across the world together to discuss their affairs. This was an extension of the business and community aspects of the online forum. In other cases, offline interactions appear to be the starting point of cybercriminal cooperation which may scarcely go online at all.

This chapter highlights the importance of cybercrime's offline dimension. This facet is somewhat counterintuitive and perhaps puzzling at first, but is actually a logical extension of Chapter 5. Coming out of that discussion, it's clear that online cooperation among cybercriminals has been surprisingly successful, but that some risk remains. Actors continue to be cautious in dealing with anonymous strangers. Firms remain relatively small, often limited to just a handful of people, because trust will extend no further. This chapter focuses on how offline dealings help to overcome some of the remaining challenges to cybercriminal cooperation and thereby enable greater expansion of the industry. Cybercriminals can feel more comfortable dealing with partners they know in real life. Firms can operate at larger scale, with more employees, fixed office space, and company hierarchies. It is possible to focus so much on the benefits of anonymity in protecting cybercriminals that one ignores the costs it brings in terms of distrust. For some cybercriminals, anonymity is more a liability than an asset.

In short, this chapter argues that, for some actors, the puzzle of cybercriminal cooperation is solved with a very basic solution: choosing to collaborate, at least partly, offline instead of only online. Because offline interactions allow much more sophisticated organizational structures to develop, it supports a larger and better-functioning industry than would be possible with online interactions alone. Four sections follow. The first provides an overview of the offline dimension of cybercrime. The second examines why this form of collaboration occurs. The third investigates failures of cooperation in offline settings and what they teach us about the topic. The final section addresses how many cybercriminals create a balance between offline and online interactions. It will likely remain the case that cybercriminals will choose different risk profiles according to what suits their contexts and their activities.

Offline Interactions

Much of the focus on cybercrime centers on online interactions. This is largely in keeping with the idea of cybercrime as a bold new world. In reality, however, as discussed in the Introduction, the phenomenon is simply an extension of older criminal behaviors. Just as Peter Reuter found that the often mythologized realm of organized crime is far more localized and small-scale than people realize, cybercrime is also rooted in local settings.[2] While a large amount of online activity takes place, many cybercriminals appear to know at least some of their collaborators in person. Such offline structures have already been highlighted by a number of publicly known investigations. Max Bulter's primary partner, Chris Aragon, had full knowledge of the hacker's offline and online identities. These two men met through a criminal who was a mutual acquaintance in the real world, and carried out extensive amounts of fraud together, until Aragon was caught and ratted Butler out.[3] In a similar vein, leading cybercriminal Albert Gonzalez operated with a core group of associates offline as part of his activities.

Other publicly known cases suggest sophisticated organizations have formed that mimic the structure of legitimate technology firms. The Carberp case discussed in Chapters 2 and 3 involved a malware group that operated out of a physical office space.[4] Even larger was the Russian Business Network, with its physical base in St. Petersburg and connections to the broader Russian technology sector.[5] As security researcher Ashley explained, RBN had a place of business and operated in the same way as other hosting providers, except that it had protection and criminal customers (US-CSP-14). Another example is Rove Digital, which was based in Estonia. It began in the mid-2000s as a domain registrar and was a professional "company at the end of the day," with an office and originally a good reputation (IRE-CSP-2). It came to light only later that the company was involved in many forms of criminality, including playing a central role in deploying malware that changed domain name system (DNS) settings on infected computers (NLD-CSP-1).[6]

To understand the scale of what is possible for offline cybercriminal businesses, one need only look at the case of Liberty Reserve, in its day perhaps the most popular virtual currency service used by cybercriminals. As Jake Halpern later reported in *The Atlantic*:

> By 2010, Liberty Reserve was gaining tens of thousands of new accounts each month. The company soon looked the part of a successful tech start-up. It had more than 50 employees in departments including human resources, accounting, marketing, and legal, and provided around-the-clock customer service and technical support. Liberty Reserve's headquarters were in the same office park in San José, the capital [of Costa Rica], as branches of Hewlett-Packard, Procter & Gamble, and Western Union. The company housed its servers in the Netherlands and employed programmers in Ukraine. Its customers, of course, were everywhere.[7]

While Liberty Reserve likely had some legitimate users and could claim to be a hybrid organization, there is little doubt that it had a significant criminal customer base. A substantial number of the former cybercriminals interviewed for this study had used Liberty Reserve and supported the view that it held a dominant place in the industry.

The data collected for this book reinforce these indications of a strong offline dimension to many cybercriminal activities. Actors' non-virtual interactions can be seen as falling into three main categories: meetings between individuals; more formal gatherings, often for a specific purpose; and offline groupings of people operating together consistently over periods of time, and sometimes to the extent that they should be considered firms.

Within this study's sample of cybercriminals, it was relatively common to hear of interactions in the first category—that is, individuals choosing to meet offline as part of their ongoing business or perhaps even for social reasons. As previously noted, some developed relationships with online partners to the point that they exchanged personal information or talked on the phone (WE-(F)CC-1, NA-(F)CC-2, NA-(F)CC-3). Those taking the process to the further extreme of meeting in person were relatively rare but certainly not anomalous. Scott arranged at one point to catch up with a collaborator who happened to be passing through town, although the meeting did not materialize (NA-(F)CC-2). Thiago and two of his criminal colleagues became good enough friends after meeting on IRC that they graduated to Skype calls and eventually met socially for drinks (SA-(F)CC-1). Lance met at least one local collaborator, and even traveled to Eastern Europe to meet with some leading cybercriminals there. This was ostensibly a business meeting but he also wanted to "tool around." Ultimately, he added, there's "always fraud committed" (NA-(F)CC-3). He stressed that such meetings are rare: "More often than not, and when I say that I mean 90 percent of the time—maybe 99 percent of the time—you never talk to these people over the phone, you never go and visit them. We had a standing rule that that was one of the things you should not do: you should never agree to meet these people in person" (NA-(F)CC-3). Yet other cases tracked by the police also reveal a social dimension being added to business dealings, such as when a pair of Romanians involved in a phishing scam visited their UK-based Nigerian money mule manager, with perhaps a key reason for the trip being "a bit of a night out" (UK-LE-3).

Ahmed, a former cybercriminal based in Southeast Asia, met one of his collaborators, but in his case the purpose was purely business. Ahmed operated when he was a teenager and, among other activities, had hacked various websites for user data. He met another user online and over time they chatted a lot and "grew close." Eventually this contact asked if he had any wares to sell and mentioned that he knew "a guy" who could use them. Ahmed's contact turned out to be from the same country as him and they arranged to meet face to face to carry out their transaction, albeit in a café in a different town from Ahmed's (SEA-(F)CC-1). Another former Southeast Asian cybercriminal, Tan, wrote about his offline meetings in this way:

> At first, we deal small business online first then we start to trust each
> other more, but when we see that member is a trustworthy one or
> a truly professional cybercriminal on a particular forum or website,
> we might think to do business in the real world, because in that
> sense we can see each other face by face, build more trust and improve business relationship (SEA-(F)CC-2).

In many cases, Tan's meetings involved the exchange of large sums of money, wholesale data, or sensitive information such as vulnerabilities—but some were "just for fun." The locations were often private or in quiet cafés where unwanted attention could be avoided (SEA-(F)CC-2).

As for the second form of offline interactions, larger gatherings of cyber-criminals, such events are geared toward coordination and networking. The CarderPlanet conferences of the early 2000s had a format similar to business conventions, or mafia meetings, allowing members from across the region and world to meet, interact, and discuss key matters relating to the enterprise. But while those large meetings attracted a lot of attention, smaller versions also took place. Within the CarderPlanet network, Andrey made clear that other gatherings occurred in the early 2000s, beyond the major conferences (EE-(F)CC-2). He wrote about a meeting he attended elsewhere in Ukraine, with an elite group of Eastern European cybercrim-inals, as a combination of business and pleasure:

> Anyway, Ukraine is praised for its summer nights by Gogol and many other classics, and loved by folks looking for recreation and romance. It is no need to say that Ukrainian women one of most beautiful in world, Ukraine's politician—one of most stupid, and Ukraine's police—one of most corrupted. Nothing than such a combination is better for a "carder's" and that's what attracted us. We drove expensive cars ignoring any rules, drunk to coma, snorted coke and meth, and then danced to exhaustion, meet girls and had sex daily and nightly. It was good times, and there wasn't no one to stop us. If we didn't drank or got high, we met at some rented apartment with network of laptops and brainstormed some ideas, hacked for fun, or developed new methods or con-cepts (EE-(F)CC-2).

At this meeting, the group hacked a number of targets. Much of this was in the interest of gathering information on companies and individuals that might be used in financially motivated attacks, but some was just for fun. Some ideas aired at this meeting were fully realized by the group at later times (EE-(F)CC-2). Another Eastern European former cybercriminal, Leonid, confirmed that a rather collegial environment existed among this network, and face-to-face relationships and social meetups—complete with alcohol and prostitutes—were common. While these gatherings were not essential for work, meeting up in different countries allowed a bit of "fun" between collaborators who might otherwise be based in distinct locations (EE-(F)CC-4). There are no known meetings of cybercriminals on this scale in the West. This could mean that their gatherings have simply never come to light. But it is probably due to the enhanced enforcement and penalties facing those who might attend. If such events have occurred, they have probably been hosted in much more subtle ways than the Ukrainian meetings of the early 2000s.

The third category of offline interactions noted above consists of operational groupings of people carrying out cybercrimes together. Often these groupings take the form of firms. As noted in Chapter 3, there are certainly *online* firms of people working together to commit various cybercrimes, distinct from forums which act as marketplaces for firms and individuals. But firms may also appear *offline*, and in some sense this is beneficial for their operations. A number of participants noted groups that operated together in person, sometimes out of the same business space (US-LE-10, UK-LE-3, US-LE-3). In the case of Eastern European cybercrime, the CarderPlanet era might be defined by that forum, but in practical terms it was a set of firms under that network umbrella that actually carried out the various attacks (US-(F)LE-8). As mentioned, Andrey described these groups as being "somehow related but competing teams." He named the key teams based on the geographical origins of their founders or most of their members (while allowing that some members might have moved): Odessa, Sebastopol, Donetsk, Kiev, and Moscow. Each was made up of people who physically met and worked together. While they operated in distinct units, some key players in these groups knew each other and also attended meetings like those discussed above (EE-(F)CC-2). Former Russian law enforcement agent Vasily described small "programming factories" of five to ten people that write modules for major pieces of malware and look somewhat like offshore companies, as they are not always in the same location as the organizer (RUS-(F)LE-1).

Also noted in Chapter 3 is that offline firms similarly play a very important role in other parts of the world. For instance, in Romania, online fraud has emerged as somewhat of a local specialty and a major employer. Relatively large firms there are well coordinated and operate out of physical spaces, such as rented apartments, which they regularly change to avoid detection (ROM-(F)LE-1, ROM-(F)LE-2, ROM-P-1). These groups became famous in the early 2000s for their expertise in online auction fraud, with eBay being a major target in the beginning. In short, they advertised and sold items online that did not exist, with discounted luxury cars a particularly well-known hook in the early days. Over time, they diversified the scam and also targeted other trading platforms—along with, for example, websites offering online accommodation rentals—with the same basic tactic of advertising nonexistent products.

While the scam seems relatively simple, the organizational structure behind it is not. Many of these frauds are carried out by firms rather than individuals. The scammers have a clear hierarchy. A boss oversees the work, and underlings often handle the front-line interactions with victims and elicit their payments. Depending on the scam, there may also be some need for "tech support," which could involve assisting with producing fraudulent documents used to enable the scam (ROM-(F)LE-1, ROM-(F)LE-2, ROM-LE-1). There might also be a separate team of money mules, known in Romania as *arrows*, who transfer the money from, for example, the victim's country back to Romania. Each team of arrows is usually led by a trusted manager who recruits and oversees them. This manager often has a degree of autonomy, perhaps even working with (rather than *for*) the central leader in Romania. In some cases, the arrow manager recruits only other Romanians to move the money around, but in others, he may also employ citizens in the country of operation or foreigners that are residents there. Such arrow groups usually appear to be distinct from the firms that carry out the scams back in Romania (ROM-(F)LE-1, ROM-(F)LE-2, ROM-LE-1).[8] Another distinct grouping is made up of those corrupt law enforcement and government officials who provide protection to these groups, along with those financial sector officials who might assist in scams by subverting anti-fraud measures or providing information on internal processes (ROM-(F)LE-2). The intersection of corruption and cybercrime is discussed in greater detail in the next chapter. This group structure is outlined in Figure 5.

While there is certainly evidence for offline cybercriminal firms, one must not get carried away and assume that all offline groupings are firms. Sometimes it can be quite hard to distinguish firms from outsourcing relationships and informal collaborative groupings. The Nigerian scene bears some similarities to Romania in that there is a strong focus on online fraud with significant offline interaction among the offenders. But in the case of Nigeria, some of this fraud is carried out by individuals, and the groups that do exist are generally more loosely structured. Nigeria became famous for *419 scams,* the name of which derives from the section number within the Nigerian Criminal Code that addresses fraud. The genus of this scam is also known as advance fee fraud. These scams involve the promise of sharing a larger amount of money (or valuable item) with a victim, if only they will pay a smaller amount in advance to unlock the windfall. But the windfall does not exist. The scam has been tailored to

Figure 5   Romanian Cybercrime Group Structure (Fraud)

promise unexpected inheritances, packages coming through customs, and job opportunities, among other bounty (NIG-(F)LE-1, NIG-CSP-1, NIG-LE-6). Nigerians are also known for romance scams, but these differ slightly in that the hook is a potential romantic involvement rather than a large sum of money. As noted, the Nigerian form of advance fee fraud began in the 1980s and originally took the form of letters in the mail.[9] But when the Internet came to Nigeria in the 1990s, the famous cyber cafés sprang up and provided locations where scammers could take their enterprises online and reach many more people. Later, as Internet access went mobile and into homes, these cafés became less of a feature (NIG-(F)LE-1, NIG-ITP-1).[10]

Interview subjects regularly struggled to give a clear idea of how Nigerian cybercrime is organized, which supports the likelihood that it is loosely structured, without clearly identifiable hierarchies. There is certainly evidence of specific groups forming, but there is not much evidence of tight, clear vertical structures. Participants are often made up of friends or others who have known each other for some time, through school, university, or the local community (NIG-(F)LE-1, NIG-LE-6). But the groups appear to be rather informal, with membership shifting and new associates joining based on past relationships rather than being formally recruited. Sole operators also exist. It seems much more like a network of people working on similar endeavors who share information and provide help when needed (US-P-2, US-(F)LE-6). As a result, some of the focal points for meeting and networking appear to be connected to broader community institutions, such as church services (US-(F)LE-6, NLD-LE-1, NLD-LE-2).

While these offline groupings have a strong localized element, they are also based around the world. There are Nigerian fraudsters operating out of numerous jurisdictions, including the United States, Canada, the United Kingdom, the Netherlands, Australia, Malaysia, the Philippines, India, South

Africa, Ghana, and possibly new locations such as China (MY-LE-3, US-P-2, NLD-LE-1, NLD-LE-2, UK-LE-2, US-LE-9, US-LE-10 US-(F)LE-6, IND-(F)LE-1). But this is no octopus-like global conspiracy with a clear leadership committee, it is a more banal network. Individuals do not appear to be actively sent to other locations to perform a role, but more likely happen to travel there for studies or other purposes and then seek to exploit the opportunities presented to them in their new environments (NIG-CSP-1). In each location, they often form new localized groups, even as they continue to work with others back in Nigeria (or elsewhere). Social networks are important, with one participant describing a "bond that never ends" that connects many offenders together around the world (NIG-(F)LE-1). In some cases, proceeds are sent back to Nigeria, though it is unclear whether they go to a leader there, are shared with family, or are added to a nest egg (UK-LE-3, NLD-LE-1, NLD-LE-2).

While overseas, Nigerian scammers might engage in any of three common activities. They might be undertaking training in hacking or computing, for instance, in Malaysia or India. They might offer a service that assists scammers back in Nigeria, such as coordinating money mules in victim-heavy countries or purchasing goods with illicit proceeds that can then be sent back to Nigeria. (One recent scam has involved renting cars overseas with stolen cards and then shipping them to Africa as loot). Or they might operate their own fully-fledged scams from these overseas bases (NIG-CSP-1, NIG-(F)LE-1). Where Nigerians do the latter, it appears quite common for them to incorporate locals into their scams, often by finding girlfriends who assist their operations by helping to give the scams more credibility (MY-LE-3, NLD-LE-1, NLD-LE-2, US-(F)LE-6). These associates might ensure that a scam makes accurate references to, for example, the correct airport in a customs scam, or they might answer calls to the phone number listed in a scam in the local language or with a more authentic accent. In other cases, girlfriends might be "insiders" at target organizations, who can provide the scammers with access to data or a knowledge of company systems. It also seems that victims of romance scams can be incorporated into broader criminal operations, perhaps as money mules (US-LE-10).

There are examples beyond the Nigerian case where the line between a firm and other types of offline grouping is less than clear. In South America, Thiago ran a network of mules recruited from somewhat loose contacts in his community. He would tell them they had one chance, and if they betrayed him he wouldn't work with them again. His belief that they had much more to lose than he did likely reflected the poor economic situation in his neighborhood (SA-(F)CC-1). In the West, many of those who work on the money side of cybercrime also operate in relatively loose group structures. In some cases, they are regular employees on salary, but in others, they have arrangements more like freelance contractors. For instance, Scott operated cash-out crews, which involved his overseeing a number of offline contacts who would withdraw cash from ATMs with counterfeit cards he provided. There was quite regular turnover in his workforce, and he didn't consider these people to be employees in a formal sense (NA-(F)CC-2). In a similar case, as Sean made online purchases with stolen funds as part of his enterprise, he needed workers who could receive the deliveries ("drops"). Eventually, he would handle more of the deliveries himself, but in its original form Sean described his system as more of a freelance affiliate scheme than a firm:

> I then either deal with the drop people, I called them drop girls because they were mostly girls, I dealt with the drop girls myself. Or I would have other people dealing with the drop girls for me, or arranging those contacts, kind of like referring them and I would give them something for doing that. Kind of like a referral / affiliate but in a very non-business manner. The deliveries would then go to the drop girls. They would then receive it. I would pay them per parcel rather than per item. The parcels would then come direct to me. I would give the person the money for referring, I would give the person the money for receiving the goods. Those goods would then go to an undisclosed location and then I would then get money from delivering them to the person it was to be delivered to. And there was never any sort of traffic back and forth (WE-(F) CC-1).

The final point to note with regard to offline groupings is that they do not need to be entirely divorced from online interactions. Those that meet in person after first establishing contact online clearly demonstrate this. But even when offline groups emerge out of local relationships, actors may also choose to collaborate online, especially with individuals who cannot be readily sourced through offline contacts. The Nigerian scammers provide a good example of this. Traditionally they operated within offline groupings and that largely remains their structure. But over the years, they have increasingly engaged with online forums to gain access to actors with greater technical expertise, to hire services, to buy tools or equipment, and to purchase data (NIG-(F)LE-1, NIG-CSP-1). Such activity has allowed Nigerian attacks to appear more *sophisticated*. While some skill improvement has likely taken place, many Nigerian scammers are simply piggybacking on the higher skill levels found in Eastern Europe and elsewhere. Similar mixing of the online and offline can be seen in other jurisdictions around the world, including Romania, Eastern Europe, and the West. This point will be addressed in greater detail in the last section of this chapter.

As with many aspects of cybercrime, it is best not to expect a hard line separating spheres—in this case, offline and online. The purpose here is to highlight the often overlooked offline aspects of cybercrime that play an extremely important role in the ecosystem. Cybercrime is not solely an online phenomenon, as much of it remains rooted in the real world where its inhabitants live and go to sleep at night.

Why Offline?

There are various reasons why offline cooperation might appeal to cybercriminals. One could start with the simplest explanation, that it is convenient and efficient to work with those in your vicinity who are already known to you. It certainly saves the time and effort of finding new partners online when you have a perfectly good pool of talent on your doorstep. But at its heart, this explanation is about a desire for trustworthiness. It might be convenient and efficient to work with local contacts, but the convenience and efficiency are probably tied to the fact that these contacts are already trusted to a degree. After all, it is not very inconvenient for those with an interest in technology to log into an open forum and either advertise for partners or respond to those who have already advertised their services. The true convenience offline is the lesser need to vet one's collaborators because they are not anonymous strangers. The key element, therefore, becomes the importance of offline reputation in dealings.

One could then move to examining trustworthiness as an explanation. There is some support for this, as it seems clear that many offline groupings originate or are sustained through existing social networks. Scott explained that his cash-out workers were "recruited offline just by being friends, know someone that you can trust that wants to make some money and put them to work" (NA-(F)CC-2). Sean, who used drugs as a teenager, sought help from others in the local drug community to act as drop girls:

I had a lot of contacts from general drug taking and stuff like that and that's why I managed to get a lot of these people and of course, when you are taking drugs, the people have the same lack of respect for the law and that same lack of, you don't understand the consequences, or not caring about the consequences. That made it very easy to find new people for these drop addresses (WE-(F)CC-1).

In other contexts, cybercriminals place a premium on those with whom they have had previous contact or who come recommended by a trusted contact. For instance, Romanians operating inside the country, and even some outside the country, choose to work with those who are well known to them from their local community. In fact, cybercrime in Romania is associated with very specific geographical locations. Râmnicu Vâlcea has gained a reputation as "Hackerville"—though "Fraudville" would be a more accurate descriptor given the local specialty of online auction fraud rather than technical exploits.[11] Among other centers of fraud is Alexandria, which may predate Râmnicu Vâlcea as the cradle of cybercrime in the country. As law enforcement attention increased, some actors moved from these centers to Bucharest, where is it easier to blend in, or even overseas (ROM-(F)LE-2).

This local dimension, with geographical hubs, seems curious at first. If one thinks about it, however, it is not unlike the localization of innovation hubs such as Silicon Valley. While the Internet and other technologies make collaboration possible across vast distances, there is still a role, even within the technology industry, for offline, human relationships.[12] In some areas of cybercrime, small-town origins suggest close links and neighborly connections that might approximate kin relationships, serving as a solid base on which to build successful cooperation. This is evidently the case with Romanian cybercrime, which seems embedded in offline locales. In one instance, it appeared that a whole community was implicated in the same scheme, which had spread among them "like a disease" (ROM-P-1). In the Nigerian context, actors also appear to work with others they have come to know by living in the same area, if not attending the same school or university (NIG-(F)LE-1). A similar phenomenon can be seen in Eastern Europe (UKR-LE-2). Former agent Landon believed that cybercriminal activities in many of these countries could probably be traced back to a small "pocket" of individuals in each case who initiated the activity in the first place (US-(F)LE-8). Strong bonds matter.

Close ties may also apply to those cybercriminals who connect with collaborators online and then later decide to meet offline. When asked directly why someone might take the risk of meeting in person, Andrey's answer was somewhat cryptic:

> Well. Maybe because they stupid? Careless? Dealing with the people is normal. And some people want to go beyond the screen and keyboard. This is a flaw, a flaw of human nature. Or is it a flaw? (EE-(F)CC-2).

But his further elaboration on these issues offered some clearer sense of motivation: "Sooner or later people normally getting close, trusting, and naturally want to meet, because 'life stories' is the part of online business, and people tell how they are, bragging, sharing and finally want to meet each one other in real life" (EE-(F)CC-2). In short, they want to get a better sense of whom they are dealing with. Actors will usually meet only with those they have known for some time online and have some trust in already. In the cases where Lance physically met with his collaborators, he had done "so much" business with them that he "knew these kids had nothing to do with law enforcement" (NA-(F)CC-3).

Whether offline interactions take place with contacts originally made online or with acquaintances already established in the community, it appears that trustworthiness plays an important role. Those who work with members of their community, friends, and relatives are trying to draw value out of their existing social relations. They have a history of past interactions with those already known to them, and as we saw previously, repeated interactions increase trustworthiness. This might offer a stronger alternative to making contacts online, even if a chain of interactions could be successfully built. Those online contacts who choose to meet in person might also be seeking to better verify and vet their partners in person. The desire to meet with partners is likely due to the inherent instability of dealing with anonymous online partners. Learning someone's physical identity gives you a better sense of who they are. How trustworthy someone might seem online can be supplemented with offline elements of their reputation, appearance, and performance, to paint a clearer picture. And by revealing your own identity you can more firmly establish trust with other actors. Physical identification of collaborators reduces the risk that a partner might simply vanish.

But the importance of identity goes beyond reputation and essentially links this discussion to enforcement. The chief significance of a physical identity is that a person can be located if need be. If trust is breached, the person can be found and punished accordingly. Prior to that, his activity can be more closely monitored to avoid defection in the first place. In such cases, the sanction may be social rather than violent. One famous example of this is cooperation among diamond traders, and specifically the Orthodox Jewish traders who play a key role in the New York City wholesale diamond market. In this case, stones of great value are passed to potential buyers for private inspection as part of a sale, without insurance against the possible theft or replacement of the diamonds with counterfeits. James Coleman notes that the close ties held by many in this business essentially lead to a closed community: the traders belong to the same religion, live in the same parts of Brooklyn, attend the same synagogues, and regularly intermarry among families.[13] Coleman provides this explanation as to how this market can sustain itself without any formal insurance mechanism:

> Observation of the wholesale diamond market indicates that these close ties, through family, community, and religious affiliation, provide the insurance that is necessary to facilitate the transactions in the market. If any member of this community defected through substituting other stones or through stealing stones in his temporary possession, he would lose family, religious, and community ties. The strength of these ties makes possible transactions in which trustworthiness is taken for granted and trade can occur with ease. In the absence of these ties, elaborate and expensive bonding and insurance devices would be necessary—or else the transactions could not take place.[14]

While diamond trading is a legitimate business, cooperation among cyber-criminals may not look much different. This illustration of enforcement helps explain why offenders might choose to work with those known to them offline, and why those with closer ties are likely to be more successful collaborators. Campana and Varese have argued a similar point with regard to broader criminal settings and kinship specifically. They suggest that "if the member of the crime group still decides to defect on his associates, the latter would be able to find him and his relatives more easily if he shares kin ties with other members. In effect, both he and his immediate family are hostages of the larger criminal group."[15] The same line of thinking should apply more widely to close relationships beyond kinship, and it would seem logical that a spectrum of the intensity of ties would predict the effectiveness of insurance against defection.

As a result, working offline and letting others know one's true (physical) identity acts as a credible commitment. This can be viewed in terms of cutting off options: once one's involvement in cybercrime is known, one cannot easily retreat back into online anonymity. Nonetheless, Schelling's concept of information hostages probably offers the closest fit. At this point it is useful to recall Gambetta's statement in the Introduction on the topic of online pedophiles meeting offline. When "identification is at a premium and must be kept secret, just showing one's face is itself like giving a hostage," he writes, "namely the knowledge of one's key sign of identity."[16] This very much applies to the case of profit-driven cybercrime, as well. As noted above, it is relatively common for cybercriminals to begin exchanging information online, gradually exchange more, and perhaps later even speak on the phone or meet in person. Thiago exemplified this process. While he largely interacted online, he had five close collaborators whom he had known from a young age and who knew his real name. Out of that group, he had met two in person. For Thiago, along with the years they had known each other, the other salient point was how the collaborators behaved when they began to make money together. The opinion he expressed was that, once money is involved, that is when betrayal is most likely to happen. So the process was slow and somewhat organic: collaborators got to know each other, gradually shared more information, and once some trust was established, money could enter the equation. The core of this gradual development was a very tight relationship between the group. As Thiago put it, if a collaborator betrays you, "he goes to jail too" (SA-(F)CC-1). The hostage exchange is clear.

The more that collaborators know about each other, the closer they are tied together, and the simpler it is for arrangements to be enforced. By involving themselves in offline networks, cybercriminals make conventional enforcement tools possible: threats, destruction of property, harassment, beatings, torture, and death. Having such options reduces the risks involved in dealing with others. Some specific means of enforcement became evident in the data collected for this study, including violence, monitoring, and social sanctions. Each of these deserves some focused discussion.

In traditional forms of crime, violence often serves as a key enforcement instrument. At first glance, the online dimension of cybercrime would seem to constitute a new realm in which violence is no longer an option and other means of enforcement, or other mechanisms to enhance cooperation, need to be developed (as discussed in Chapter 5). But this narrative holds true only if cybercriminal activity is limited to cyberspace. In offline settings, the specter of violence reemerges. Probably the most famous known example of violence by a cybercriminal was the kidnapping and torture of a hacker known as Kier by the Turkish cybercriminal Chao.[17] There are claims that the hacker was beaten and threatened at gunpoint for informing on Chao's group. Chao then posted a picture of Kier online in his under-wear commemorating the occasion, most likely aimed at embarrassing Kier even further. Kier was holding a sign:

> I AM KIER
> MY REAL NAME IS:
> MERT ORTAÇ
> I AM PARTNER OF [illegible]
> I AM RAT. I AM PIG.
> I AM REPORTER.
> I AM FUCKED BY CHAo[18]

In a sense, this is like an extreme form of doxing, the practice mentioned in Chapter 5 involving the online publication of personal information. Doxing online would have been sufficient to reveal Kier's legal name, but by kidnapping him and displaying his true, physical identity, Chao subjected him to even greater shame, and sent an even stronger message. But such an attack could be carried out only because those involved were personally known to each other and lived in the same country. This illustrates what offline relationships allow in terms of increased enforcement. While Chao's alleged connections to organized crime and corrupt Turkish government officials are not confirmed, his posturing as a hard man at minimum illus-trates that cybercrime can also entail physical violence (US-LE-2). Even homicides are potentially possible.

Throughout interviews for this project, a number of instances of violence were recounted. Sean mentioned that violence was an option in dealing with his offline contacts. He recalled one occasion where he had to "give someone a little bit of a seeing to because they were fucking me around. But that was only very light, just going around there with someone else just saying what's up, where's my money kind of thing" (WE-(F)CC-1). Ilya knew of a case where an arrangement between a group of Russian hackers and a company that was using their services had gone awry. When the company refused to acquiesce to the cybercriminals' demands, the group returned with base-ball bats and began laying waste to the office. He described the individuals involved as the type who are smart but have a liking for violence—a dan-gerous combination (RUS-CSP-8). Igor described many of those involved in Eastern European cashing-out operations as "real criminals" who are dangerous (UKR-CSP-3). In the Nigerian context, former law enforcement agent Idris claimed he had heard of cybercriminals killing each other. In certain cases when one collaborator knows where another lives, he said that the "penalty for breach of trust is death" (NIG-(F)LE-1).

Despite these instances, it is important not to depict cybercrime as extremely violent. Even when physical attacks become possible as part of offline interactions, the threat is not always carried out. Violent episodes among cybercriminals appear to be less common than in some other forms of crime, such as within traditional organized crime activities. The next chapter will discuss organized crime's involvement in cybercrime, and the physical threats that can come with it. But some evidence suggests that cybercriminals actively seek not to involve themselves in violence. Scott never employed it in his dealings with cash-out crews. He simply stopped working with a person if he or she was cheating him too much (NA-(F)CC-2). Several current and former law enforcement officers across various jurisdictions, including Eastern Europe and Nigeria, said they had rarely, if ever, seen instances of violence among cybercriminal groups (ROM-LE-1, ROM-P-1, NIG-LE-6, US-LE-9, NLD-LE-1, NLD-LE-2). In many instances, they described the actors centrally involved as being "smart" guys, whether the crimes involved were highly technical or not. These types are more willing to use their brains than their brawn.

While violence, or the threat thereof, plays some role, there are other enforcement tools made available by the offline dimension. Chief among these is the greater opportunity for monitoring a partner's activity. The way that arrows are overseen by Romanian managers is a good illustration. These workers perform a vital task in a scam by physically withdrawing or transferring money (and are at greatest risk of arrest). Their managers do not simply trust that they will do as they are told and not run away with the funds. According to former Romanian law enforcement agent Razvan, a manager will wait nearby and watch that things are being done as they should (ROM-(F)LE-2). The supervision, while short of actual violence, carries a degree of threat that is likely to encourage greater compliance among the arrows. In the North American context, Scott also monitored his cash-out crews, but rather than shadow his operatives everywhere, he employed a different method:

> As far as trusting them not to steal from you, you just have to give
> them a test run and if things don't add up on the results when they
> are done and you feel like they are screwing you, you just cut them
> off and tell them things are not working anymore or whatever. It is
> expected though, in my experience, that almost always they all end

up eventually stealing a little more and more as time goes on, but usually I didn't have any way to prove it for sure or I just didn't care enough to try because it wasn't enough to make a difference in profits. I had done some recon here though and kept tabs on what they were doing without their knowledge just to see. For example I have done the same thing with THEIR emails / phones whatever and also I had actually slipped in some prepaid greendot cards [a form of prepaid Visa or Mastercard] in batches that I paid for and had online access too etc. to see if they tried to say it didn't work when I know it did etc. and if I did find them being un-honest (lol funny huh, un-honest criminals?) then I would slowly just phase them out. What else can you do? (NA-(F)CC-2).

As with his online dealings, Scott demonstrated a degree of acceptance that he would never achieve full cooperation from his workers. As noted above, he would not resort to violence, but would simply cease working with them. This is not a perfect system, but it is a functional one.

In other cases, the offline dimension provides an opportunity for monitoring specific transactions rather than overall group activities. As noted above, Ahmed connected with a collaborator online but later physically met with him in cafés for the purpose of transactions. He now looks back on those interactions as risky. He remembers being scared at various points as he was dealing with an older contact and being on edge whenever he saw police. When asked why he did not simply carry out the transactions online, he said he would have preferred that, but his main concerns at the time were to ensure the money was paid for the goods and not to leave an electronic trail. He thought it was best to physically exchange the CD with the relevant data on it, directly for cash (SEA-(F)CC-1).

Finally, social sanctions can also play an important role in cybercrime, alongside violence and monitoring. The discussion above on this topic illustrates the manner in which this works in close-knit communities, where offenders are well known to each other and live in the same neighborhoods. Those who defect are shunned not only by their collaborators, but by the broader community, as well. The tighter the community, the more damaging the sanction. This is a somewhat standard manifestation that doesn't require extensive illustration. Instead, I will provide a sketch of one of the more unusual social sanctions that emerged over the course of this study: voodoo. In certain parts of Africa, including Nigeria, there is a fairly widespread belief in voodoo, known locally as *juju*.[19] Aspects of juju have taken on importance for a range of traditional criminal groups, including human traffickers, who use rituals to sanction agreements with victims and thereby keep them under their control.[20] But juju has also become important for cybercriminals.[21] Some shows of belief are rather perfunctory, and mainly involve rites before shrines, where appeals to spirits are made to achieve success in scams. Typically, payment must be made to a spiritual leader and the ritual might relate to a specific email about to be sent (NIG-LE-1, NIG-LE-2, NIG-LE-3, NIG-LE-4). The invocation of juju is hoped to enhance the duping of victims.

But there is another aspect of juju that relates directly to cooperation. Just as human traffickers use it as a substitute for violence, so too do cybercriminals. In the case of cybercrime, the targets of this violence-substitute are not the criminal's victims but his collaborators. Idris explained that a cybercriminal swears an oath to be part of a group and not to betray it. While the oath is the "first layer, the second layer is the violence." But for juju adherents, the oaths themselves are perceived as physical threats, and possibly as deadly ones. According to Idris, these cybercriminals believe that if you swear an oath at a shrine and break it, then you will die (NIG-(F)LE-1). Gideon, who works in the Nigerian technology sector but is also involved with investigations, agreed that oaths were important among cybercriminals. He, too, mentioned a common belief that breaking an oath is deadly, and claimed that this can even lead to oath-breakers going into convulsions. Gideon argued that these religious elements are the "critical factor" that maintains cooperation in these groups and prevents individuals from informing on other group members. They would prefer beatings and the threat of jail to breaking their oaths (NIG-CSP-1). This certainly seems a novel addition to the famous scenario of the prisoner's dilemma.

Failures of Cooperation

While the offline dimension offers important advantages in terms of enforcement, there are obviously cases where cybercriminal cooperation still falters. Adopting a similar approach to Chapter 5, it is also valuable to study these failures in offline settings as a way to incorporate variation and gain a more nuanced understanding of why cooperation succeeds or fails. To begin, Sean's use of drop girls brought enough problems that he eventually shifted to a different system that was largely self-managed. Relying on local people from his drug-using community produced a failure directly tied to their drug use. What made them an available pool of criminal workers happy to break the law also made them a risk: "The problem was with that, there was a lot of distrust in that. And I can recount quite a few occasions where people had said oh an item had not turned up when it clearly did and they were just trying to pull a fast one" (WE-(F)CC-1). Scott had similar problems with his cash-out crews, believing most would deceive him at some point. He was willing to accept such defections as a cost of doing business (NA-(F)CC-2). In Sean's case, however, his workers' unreliability went beyond cheating him into problems with law enforcement:

> That model fell apart. I explained in explicit detail to these people how not to get arrested and how to make sure you get released within those 72 hours of being arrested. And that is to say absolutely no fucking comment all the way. Don't say a single word, they cannot prove anything. Unless, if they ask you, just say I was just signing something, someone asked me to sign something for them, I didn't know what it was, I was just doing them a favor, I didn't know anything, I didn't realize I was doing anything illegal. That is the story to stick to. Either that or no comment. And then you'll be fine. But these people didn't realize that. But of course when you get arrested, I kind of assumed they would have the same hardened approach that I would have, and of course they didn't. Leave them in a cell for 12 hours to think about what they are doing and a lot of people will crack after that amount of time. Whereas if it's me, I would just sit there, go to sleep, wake up and oh interview time already? So that was my biggest flaw in that (WE-(F)CC-1).

This experience led Sean to the sad realization that "People are dumb" (WE-(F)CC-1). In an Eastern European context, Ivan likewise suffered a "miserable failure" with his offline collaborators. This was despite his knowing them for quite some time. In his case, he believed the source of the problem was clear: "Incompetence and unreliability of people. Or, better to say, my inability to detect them" (EE-(F)CC-3). This ties into a broader narrative of Ivan's self-diagnosed weaknesses as an organizer. He was better suited to technical pursuits rather than judging the suitability of collaborators (EE-(F) CC-3).

These examples are best contrasted with the Nigerian and Romanian contexts, where cooperation appears to be relatively successful. The key difference in these contexts versus the failures discussed just above is that a premium is put on working with trusted contacts who have been known for some time. In both Romania and Nigeria, collaborators often come from the same towns or neighborhoods. Some have familial connections or have been educated together. This contrasts with the cases above, where workers are chosen less carefully. Sean wasn't drawing on a close-knit community with strong ties and extensive social capital. He was working with people whose situation as regular drug users made them inherently untrustworthy. As noted, he later changed his system to become almost entirely reliant on himself, the most trusted person in the equation. Scott appeared to take some care with the people he chose as partners, but the bonds did not rival those in communities elsewhere. He was not working with close family or friends. Meanwhile, Ivan's "miserable failure" emphasizes the importance of having not just a pool of known local contacts, but also the ability to vet them as partners. Even in local communities, there will be some bad apples.

The broad point to be drawn from these examples of failures of cooperation is that, the closer the relationship, the more likely it is that successful cooperation will take place. Dealing with weak offline ties is quite similar to dealing with strangers on the Internet. There may be limited information about individuals' true identities, where they live, and their social circles. This creates difficulties in terms of not only reputation but also enforcement. It becomes much more difficult to monitor collaborators adequately and take action if the need arises. Social sanctions are also less likely to be effective. Defections still take place in the Nigerian and Romanian contexts, but at least anecdotally, the model of dealing with more closely known and vetted individuals seems to be a more fruitful one (ROM-(F)LE-1, ROM-LE-1, NIG-(F)LE-1, NIG-LE-6). The cases of failed cooperation appear to support the idea that greater enforcement is what the offline dimension really adds to cybercriminal cooperation.

A Balance Between Online and Offline?

The above sections have argued that there are strong incentives for cybercriminals to operate, at least to some degree, offline. US law enforcement agent Ethan sums up the situation in terms of the higher levels of trust that can be garnered through offline interactions and the risks that can come from online ones:

> And I know for a fact that people will fly. They will travel to meet each other to talk in person. And many times—and I've had personal experience with this—people only want to communicate via mobile phone now. They only want to communicate via text message over phone. They don't want to get online because the perceived

risks of even getting online to communicate . . . bad actors understand that they're just increasing the risk overall by doing that. So I think for them anytime they communicate over out-of-band channels, and mobile phones are really out-of-band channels, but when you talk about the majority of bad actors and the way they communicate most of them use the Internet. So I've personally seen a lot more of what I call high-level players only communicating with people they know. They've met in person. They have a phone number for. But I couldn't give you a specific example of a sophisticated malware campaign with any longevity that was operated by multiple players that were really globally-dispersed, and they had never met each other (US-(F)LE-1).

This idea was echoed by Ilya, a Russian security researcher, who argued that some of the leading cybercriminals in Russia, as a matter of strategy, try to keep an offline-only presence. They recognize the inherent risks of leaving digital traces through online interactions (RUS-CSP-8), which can become the evidence to tie them later to crimes. Such digital evidence simply will not exist if they engage only with offline confreres.

Of course, not all see matters in this same way. For many discussed in this chapter, a combination of online and offline interactions is key. As in Ahmed's case, cybercriminals might operate largely online and then seek to meet in person at certain key moments. Tan and Thiago also showed a preference for online interactions, with occasional offline meetings with trusted partners (SEA-(F)CC-2, SA-(F)CC-1). In other cases, there might be a strong offline structure that allows the group to function effectively, as with Andrey's elite "teams" spread throughout Eastern Europe. But in such cases, online interactions allow these groups and individuals to expand their contacts and partner with individuals in other locations. The Nigerian model noted above provides an interesting example of this. Many Nigerian cybercriminals operate with those personally known to them. But in recent years they have increasingly been going online and doing business on forums. The key reason is to access products and expertise that they cannot obtain from within their local communities. Online, they can engage with Eastern Europeans and others to purchase card data or malware, or perhaps to learn some new skills themselves. Rather than being a counterpoint to the offline dimension, in this case the online dimension is complementary.

On the other end of the extreme are those that choose to operate solely online. Within his orbit, former cybercriminal Jim believed that most people avoided offline interactions and focused on online activities. As he put it, it's "not a very trusting business" (NA-(F)CC-5). Former Western European cybercriminal Jonas never met his main partner (or anyone else), nor did he even speak to him on the phone (WE-(F)CC-3). Mohammed similarly kept his activities and criminal connections online because he didn't want anyone to know his true identity. He compared it to being "bipolar," as he shifted between one mode in the "real world and other one in the digital world" (MENA-(F)CC-1). For those who see too great a risk in partnering offline, the anxiety may center on the threat of arrest or simply the fear of other criminals they might find themselves dealing with. Operating from one's home certainly brings a degree of safety. Along these lines, Lance argued that "the anonymity that is provided by being online, enables a lot of these people to commit crime whereas they would not have committed crime if they had to show their face to other people" (NA-(F)CC-3). Law enforcement agent Carter agreed: "People do things behind a computer they wouldn't do in real life" (US-LE-2). In these cases, the ability to remain anonymous allows the number of instances of cybercrime to expand.

The approaches that cybercriminals take are likely very much tied to the contexts within which they operate. In the West, outside of cash-out groups and some other less technical offenders, offline collaboration is relatively rare. For many, a key rule, albeit sometimes ignored, is not to meet in person because this is viewed as unsafe. Anonymity is what protects cybercriminals from arrest (NA-(F)CC-3). But in other parts of the world where law enforcement capacity is lower and corruption levels are higher, offline groupings appear much more likely to occur. In those instances, going online and interacting broadly with other cybercriminals is more risky because this may put an actor on the radar of western law enforcement agencies. But as policing efforts improve in these regions, cybercriminals must also act more cautiously.

Even in Eastern Europe, the cybercriminals of today would be extremely brave to hold conferences like those of the CarderPlanet era. As outlined throughout this chapter, smaller gatherings, groupings, and firms still exist. But with increased attention from both local and international law enforcement agencies, careful operators have retreated further underground (US-LE-10). Former cybercriminal Leonid believed that if meetings do still take place, they are mostly with long-time partners (EE-(F)CC-4). Security researcher Ashley suggested that "centralization works if you are not worried about law enforcement or industry." Otherwise, it poses a clear threat (US-CSP-14). The very large cybercrime "companies" that Nikita observed earlier in his career in Ukraine are now less common (UKR-(F)LE-2). Given some improvements in the legal system, more Russian-speaking cybercriminals are choosing to collaborate largely online—and, notably, have begun to voice more fears about being caught (UKR-CSP-3, UKR-CSP-1).

Conclusion

The offline dimension of cybercrime is central to the success of the industry. It appears to overcome some of the deficiencies of solely online interactions—namely, the distrust that remains despite steps taken to address this challenge. Along with evidence of this aspect of cybercrime, this chapter has provided a rationale for why this type of physical collaboration occurs. Virtual cooperation has limits: online firms are generally small and short-lived. In contrast, the offline dimension allows for far larger, more sophisticated, stable, and enduring structures. This appears curious at first, but there are logical explanations, most notably a level of enforcement, through the threat of violence or other sanctions, that is not possible in a virtual world. While it brings its own risks, this type of offline activity makes up for problems that come with operating as a faceless user. Anonymity protects identities, but also makes it much more difficult to maintain cohesion among larger groups. Online institutions and a degree of governance allowed cybercrime to grow from small-scale interactions to large marketplaces with thousands of members trading together. But the larger firms, some of which provide fundamental "infrastructure" to the broader industry, appear possible only when rooted in the physical world.

This chapter has also addressed failures of offline cooperation, and how most cybercriminals make use of both online and offline dealings. Ultimately, there is no perfect equilibrium with regard to how they approach the online versus offline conundrum. Some work exclusively online, others almost exclusively offline. Many operate on a spectrum in between, forging the types of partnerships that best suit their needs given their operational contexts and the goals they seek to achieve. In some situations, like cashing-out operations, offline collaboration is almost a necessity. In many others, it is a choice. Each approach brings its own risks, whether of being scammed, arrested, or otherwise.

The offline cybercriminal firms, and the exchange they engage in outside of the Internet, should not be that surprising. Just because cybercriminals have the option of engaging solely in online dealings does not make this a *fait accompli*. This so-called offline dimension is simply how other financially motivated criminal enterprises have always operated, whether in the drug trade or other organized crime ventures.[22] There are also parallels between these cybercriminal businesses and some legitimate companies operating in the technology sector. In the case of Liberty Reserve, apart from tailoring services to criminal customers, there was little separating the operations of this payment processing company from a number of other start-ups. Of course, much of this ties into local law enforcement capacity and pressure. Cybercriminal firms are much more likely to expand and take on the appearance of larger legitimate enterprises when they are not being harassed by law enforcement. If they operate in grey areas of the law, shield their true dealings, or bribe the right people, success may follow and the industry will flourish even further—as we will see in the next chapter.

7

Cybercrime, Organized Crime, and Governance

CRIMINAL MARKETS benefit from order in the same way that legitimate ones do. But while licit companies can rely on contracts and a legal system to enforce them, criminal firms and individuals cannot. Routinely, the state intervenes in the private sector to ensure that chaos does not reign, but no one engaging in illegal activity can fall under its protection. As distrust takes hold in these markets, demand for institutions and governance rises, and must be met through alternative means.[1] Surprisingly, many groups operating outside the state's formal control do find avenues for extra-legal governance. This is the case among street gangs, prison gangs, pirates, mafias, and more.[2] In Chapter 5, we saw that cybercriminals have succeeded in establishing online institutions that promote trade, regulate the market, and provide aspects of enforcement. The argument of this chapter is that there is also a system of governance that supports the offline dimension discussed in Chapter 6. This offline governance is essential to the successful functioning of the cybercrime industry.

There are three ways that offline cybercriminals could possibly be governed. First, some cybercrime firms could evolve to such a level that they seek to monopolize the business and effectively take control of all relevant actors in their territory. Second, governance could be provided by organized crime groups, who arbitrate disputes, mete out punishments, drive out competitors, and protect cybercriminals from arrest. In the criminal underworld, governance is commonly delivered by such organizations. As noted in the Introduction, some scholars even define the term *organized crime* as referring to groups that seek to govern a criminal market in such ways.[3] It is conceivable that these groups could apply the skills they have developed regulating other markets to the cybercrime industry. Third, governance could be provided by corrupt government agents. This would not amount to the state asserting control over a criminal market, but would rather involve individual state agents performing this function counter to their official role. Around the globe and throughout history, it is not uncommon for corrupt agents to carry out this function in return for illicit payments. For instance, prior to the rise of the mafia in New York City, it was primarily crooked police officers who protected prostitution and gambling.[4]

The organic development of a cybercriminal group capable of carrying out governance is theoretically possible, but my data offer little indication of this happening. Numerous participants viewed cybercrime groups as organizational structures quite distinct from traditional organized crime. As discussed in the previous chapter, there are some instances of violence on the part of cybercriminals, but they don't reach the scale and intent of attempts at broad control of the industry. Possibly the closest example to this is found in Brian Krebs's book *Spam Nation*. Krebs recounts the early history of the famed Russian Business Network and a rare instance of violent behavior between cybercrime competitors. As has been discussed at the heart of this history is Alexander Rubatsky, a talented programmer who became involved in various aspects of cybercrime, including payment processing for child sexual abuse material sites. His story has been mentioned in previous chapters. Rubatsky ran a team of hackers to assist his operations, but was also supported by a group of heavies who provided a form of protection.[5] Krebs describes how the group dealt with a rival businessman named Evgeny Petrovsky, who was developing his own credit card processing business focused on child sexual abuse material sites:

> Petrovsky was stopped in his car by a man posing as a local policeman, and when he stepped out of the car as directed, he was kidnapped by masked men. Once they reached their safe house in the outskirts of Minsk, the abductors contacted Petrovsky's associates and demanded a million U.S. dollars for his safe return. But no money would be forthcoming. When local authorities began to close in on their location, the assailants fled with Petrovsky to Moscow. By November 2012, Russian and Belarusian authorities had located the Loginov gang's hideout and arrested the kidnappers. They found Petrovsky alive and relatively unharmed.[6]

This rare account is suggestive of cybercriminal governance, but falls short of it. What is telling in this case is that the group does not appear to be a cybercrime group that has developed organized crime functions, but rather an alliance between a group of hackers and a group of heavies that was associated with the Belarusian gang known as "The Village."[7] While theoretically it is possible that a cybercrime firm might evolve into an organized crime group, empirically, it appears more likely that a traditional organized crime group would become involved in the business in some way—or else, that corrupt law enforcement agents might play this role. The remainder of this chapter focuses on the latter two governance avenues. It investigates the role that each plays in regulating the cybercrime industry and which group is more centrally involved.

Cybercrime and Organized Crime

There is a strong sense in blogging and media circles, as well as among some in the cybersecurity sector, that organized crime is "taking over" cybercrime. Among the hyperbolic statements that have been made on this subject is one expert quote from an article in 2004 that the "Mafia, which has been using the Internet as a communication vehicle for some time, is using it increasingly as a resource for carrying out mass identity theft and financial fraud."[8] Some ascribe a central role to the Russian Mafia in particular. "The Russian Mafia are the most prolific cybercriminals in the world," claimed another expert in a 2011 article.[9] But little empirical evidence tends to be provided on these points. Unfortunately, the hypothesis is not tested much more rigorously within the academic literature, which suffers from a pronounced scarcity of credible data.[10]

As Rob McCusker argues, there is a theoretical tension concerning traditional organized crime groups and how likely they are to get involved in cybercrime.[11] On one side of this tension, it seems logical that organized criminals would seek to take advantage of new money-making avenues. The other side of the tension is the notion that these individuals might be satiated by their existing activities and feel no need to engage in cybercrime. There may also be technical barriers preventing them from doing so. The possibility of a technical barrier is a noteworthy point. Despite their popular image as global criminal masterminds, many mobsters are "street guys" who specialize in projecting toughness and carrying out violence. Far from being worldly, they often maintain tight connections to their communities and neighborhoods. The undercover FBI agent Joseph Pistone, who infiltrated the Bonanno crime family in the 1970s, noted in his memoir that some mobsters didn't even know how to book their own airline tickets.[12] While technology is increasingly pervading all levels of society, and has almost certainly been adopted by organized criminals—especially of the younger generations—the fundamentally localized nature of much organized crime cannot be overlooked. This was one of Peter Reuter's key findings in his classic study, *Disorganized Crime.*[13]

Moving past loose claims and theorizing, there are answers that can be offered empirically to the question of whether organized crime groups are governing cybercrime. Many participants in this study believed their involvement was substantial. But when pressed, they appeared to make a theoretical rather than empirical argument. A common formulation was that organized crime always moves to where the money is and the money is now in cybercrime. Therefore, logically, these criminals would involve themselves. But when participants were asked whether they had directly seen a case of a traditional organized crime group's involvement in cybercrime, few answered affirmatively. Those who had seen such cases produced only a small number of observations. As a result, the data collected for this project suggest that organized crime does play a role in cybercrime, but that its involvement is far from a complete takeover. Security researcher Brendan ventured an explanation: "To be fair, getting into the cybercrime thing is a deeply technical subject, and these guys aren't deeply technical" (IRE-CSP-2).

On the basic question of whether organized crime groups are moving into cybercrime and supplying protection, there is some evidence, but it is not overwhelming. Like any other criminals, cybercriminals who are known to make large amounts of money can become targets of theft and extortion by others in the criminal community, and even by corrupt law enforcement agents (IRE-CSP-2, US-(F)LE-8, US(E)-CSP-1). They may also need protection from legitimate investigations into their activities (RUS-(F)LE-1). In enterprises involving collaboration with others locally, it may make sense to arrange for enforcement by a "trustworthy" local mobster. The need for protection was clear during Rubatsky's early days in Minsk, mentioned above. Later, RBN was suspected of having connections to organized crime and benefiting from protection by law enforcement and political figures in Russia, as well—a development that will be discussed more below.[14]

My data do not suggest widespread occurrences of organized criminals protecting cybercriminals. For example, in Romania, former law enforcement agents Virgil and Razvan knew of violent criminal groups who made contact with cybercriminals. There were also cases of cybercriminal groups stealing money from each other (ROM-(F)LE-1, ROM-(F)LE-2). But these behaviors were not the norm. Instead, many fraudsters seemed to be somewhat friendly with each other and felt little real need for protection. Participants often expressed the belief that offenders tend to be quiet, intelligent, nonviolent, and unconnected to organized crime groups (ROM-LE-1, ROM-P-1). In the Nigerian context, Idris also said it would be very unusual for cybercriminals to pay protection racketeers (NIG-(F)LE-1). Ukrainian former law enforcement agent Nikita suggested that connections between Eastern European cybercriminals and mafia groups were usually service-based rather than built on protection (UKR-(F)LE-2). Former cyber-criminal Andrey also did not believe there was an especially strong association between cybercrime and Eastern European organized crime. He wrote:

> All the relations between traditional mafia and gangs are eventual and personal, so there's no more connections than in any other industry or enterprise. Some individuals do, and if they do, they use it. Others don't. There are various individuals with different backgrounds, some came from "IT" world to carding, other from world of crime. Of course, regular criminals show interest in certain aspects of cybercrime, but they show interest in many other things. More advanced carders and hackers, however, usually show strong disgust to "traditional" criminals and usually join whatever cause there might be on temporary basis. In turn, "traditional" criminals often regard cybercriminals as "milk cows" and nerds (EE-(F)CC-2).

Another Eastern European former cybercriminal, Ivan, stated that he had never encountered a direct connection between cybercriminals and traditional organized crime groups (EE-(F)CC-3). In a South American context, Thiago said that he and his collaborators never engaged with organized criminals, and actively avoided them (SA-(F)CC-1).

There is much stronger empirical evidence that organized crime groups are involved in cybercrime in ways other than providing protection. Rather than seeking to govern cybercrime as an external party, organized criminals are much more likely to operate within the industry. This involvement some-times sees them acting as investors in certain enterprises, which requires little specialist knowledge. To be an investor, one need only make contact with a cybercriminal group and have a pool of capital available. My data did not suggest too many pure instances of investment, but there were some. Perhaps the best example was provided by UK former law enforcement agent Peter, who shared the story of a group involved in credit card fraud on what he described as an "industrial" scale. Because the case was sensitive I respect Peter's wishes to provide limited details, but essentially the scheme involved hiring a programmer to develop software to access card details from banks. There were significant upfront costs associated with this, and Peter believed the head of the enterprise sought the backing of a well-established British organized crime group to bankroll the operation. But a falling-out led to the cybercriminal's life being threatened by these gangsters and his going on the run (UK-(F)LE-4)

Beyond the two roles of offering protection and investment, organized crime groups can also potentially play a third role within cybercrime of service provider. This involves selling their skills in, for instance, money laundering and the physical enforcement of group arrangements. The money side of cybercrime is the part that commonly requires offline networks to collect and then transfer cash, purchase goods with stolen funds, or launder the gains. While in many cases this activity is carried out by groups not connected to traditional organized crime (NA-(F)CC-2), monitoring and enforcing this process is a plausible point for their involvement (IRE-CSP-2, US(E)-CSP-1, UK-LE-3, RUS-CSP-3, RUS-(F)LE-1). The collected data confirm this supposition, as organized crime groups appeared somewhat regularly in this role. Perhaps the most famous case of this was the Citibank hack of 1994 involving Vladimir Levin, who managed to infiltrate the bank's networks and arrange for illicit money transfers worth millions of dollars. According to Nathan, a US former law enforcement agent, the Tambov gang, a powerful Russian mafia group in St. Petersburg, was responsible for coordinating the delivery of the proceeds to Russia. A substantial network of people made up of individuals operating in the US, Israel, the Netherlands, and elsewhere had to be mobilized to receive and move the money. The gang used coercion and threats of violence to enforce compliance, particularly when arrests were made. In one case, it paid the legal fees of an arrested mule. In another, it attempted to murder one of its own members, whose wife was in American custody and had begun cooperating with the authorities. More than likely because of some form of government protection, the organized criminals at the top of the scheme in Russia were able to avoid jail time (US-(F)LE-5).

This type of activity continued to be relevant into the twenty-first century. Eastern European former cybercriminal Leonid knew of organized criminals involved in cybercrime. His account suggested that their key pathway was adapting their traditional skill set to be of value to the carding community (EE-(F)CC-4). This accorded with Jack's experience, who had investigated groups that smuggled card skimmers and "white plastic" between Eastern and Western Europe (US-LE-3). White plastic refers to blank cards that can be encoded with stolen data and then used in shops or at ATMs. The Turkish cybercriminal Chao was also heavily involved in the skimming business. As a key vendor of the required hardware on DarkMarket, he had a production line in China and many underlings. Though he may not have been a traditional mobster, he certainly styled himself as one (US-LE-2).

Other examples also show organized crime groups exploiting new opportunities concerning the monetary aspects of cybercrime. These cases commonly feature the leveraging of existing resources within the group for new purposes. Particularly instructive in this regard are certain Los Angeles street gangs where factions devoted to fraud are now part of the hierarchy (US-LE-1). Similar developments have been observed elsewhere in the United States, such as in New York.[15] This new activity is a direct offshoot of the gang's existing structure. As US law enforcement agent Lucas outlined, one gang member acts as the "fraud pimp" and manages low-level runners (US-LE-1). The pimp's role includes buying compromised credit and debit card details online and overseeing an operation that manufactures the counterfeit cards. This offers a point of connection with the online world of cybercrime, since the logical place to purchase these is on forums that are populated by cybercriminals from across the world. Here, gang members can learn aspects of cybercrime and purchase the goods and services they might require. Lucas recalled amusing conversations he had seen online between Eastern European cybercriminals and American gang members whose respective uses of unconventional language, and divergent approaches to the business, offered an interesting contrast (US-LE-1). Once the card data have been purchased and the physical cards have been manufactured, the fraud pimp then distributes the cards to lieutenants to arrange the cashing out. The split heavily favors the pimp, leaving the lieutenants to perform their role for surprisingly little. A cut also has to be paid to the gang's leadership (US-LE-1).

What is most interesting about these operations is the use of existing resources within the gang. The key actors in the cash-out crews are women who might otherwise have been sent out for "tricks" (US-LE-1). It is a shift from a prostitution model to a fraud model, using the same individuals. While a trick might be rewarded with $50 to $100, a cashing-out run might net close to $1,000. The products purchased by these cash-out crews appear to vary depending on the geographical base of the gang. Monthly passes for the Long Island Rail Road were popular for New York gangs, while Walmart goods were favored in Texas, and Apple products tended to be bought by gangs in California. Whatever is purchased can then be sold via conventional fencing methods or otherwise. Lucas stated that street gangs carry out this fraud alongside their traditional operations, such as drug dealing (US-LE-1).

A fourth way for organized criminals to play a role in cybercrime is to get directly involved and act as the guiding hand of certain operations. This usually involves recruiting people with technical skills, among others, to carry out the jobs (IRE-CSP-2, US-CSP-14, RUS-(F)LE-1). One instance of this saw Southeast Asian former cybercriminal Tan being approached by a group involved in a range of illicit activities—drugs, money laundering, nightclubs, political corruption, and real estate—that hoped he would take a monthly salary and other benefits to oversee its stolen credit card business. He refused the offer, saying he preferred to be his "own boss" (SEA-(F)CC-2). In Tan's case, a long-term arrangement was being sought. But some collaborations are centered on just one "job." One of the best examples was the failed Sumitomo Mitsui Bank heist in 2006, which attempted to steal £229 million. In that case, two men—one of them a hacker, the other his overseer—were admitted to the bank's premises in London by a security supervisor. Their goal, though they did not succeed, was to install keylogging software on the computers and then return to carry out fraudulent bank transfers.[16] The plot involved a global network of conspirators, but at the center of it, according to former law enforcement agent Phillip, was an organized crime group in London and another such group on the Continent. They were the ones, he believed, who recruited and coordinated the various actors and oversaw the operation. Phillip chose not to name the two groups, noting that they were "ominous people" (UK-(F)LE-2).

Of the four different ways discussed here for organized crime groups to get involved in cybercrime, the last two—acting as a service provider or taking charge as the guiding hand in a scheme—are essentially two sides of the same coin. In both instances, groups make use of their traditional skills on the money side and enforcing arrangements, and leave the technical elements of the job to others. The difference comes down to who initiated contact. Did the hackers and programmers reach out to the organized crime group so they could help with cashing out, or did the organized crime group recruit these more technical actors to carry out its own job? Sometimes it is hard to distinguish.

Finally, there may also be a fifth form of collaboration, which possibly falls outside the scope of cybercrime. In these cases, organized crime groups seek to recruit or partner with technical talent in order to enhance their existing operations, rather than engaging in cybercrime *per se*. For instance, Hong Kong's triads have traditionally run prostitution, but have found that new technologies can improve the marketing of this service. They have built online websites to showcase the different prostitutes available and allow johns to make online bookings (HK-(F)LE-2). Such websites are not unusual in the world of modern prostitution, but in this case they are run by serious organized criminals and operated in a way to keep them safe from law enforcement—for instance, by housing the servers in mainland China (HK-(F)LE-2).

The triads are also active in online gambling, as an extension of their existing, offline gambling operations. The casinos of Macao have been traditionally linked to triads and their money-laundering operations.[17] In Malaysia, the triads have found an intriguing way of providing gambling in a jurisdiction where it is illegal. Patrons enter a location where they can place bets on games such as roulette. But the casino itself is located in the Philippines, with only a video link to the room in Malaysia. This geographical dispersion, along with the placement of servers overseas, complicates law enforcement attempts to curb the practice (MY-CSP-1, MY-LE-3). In the world of true online gambling, where games are played on websites, there have also been suggestions of involvement by the Italian-American Mafia. This expands on their traditional control of illicit gambling in the United States. The sites in question have also been hosted offshore in jurisdictions like Costa Rica.[18]

This fifth category was the most commonly reported in this study by former cybercriminals and hackers. Ahmed, the former cybercriminal from Southeast Asia (later turned security professional), mentioned that he regularly turns down people seeking his services for illicit activities. In one instance, he was contacted by a drug dealer with connections to a major syndicate, who wanted to recruit him to gather intelligence, most likely by hacking the dealer's competitors (SEA-(F)CC-1). Irfan, a Malaysian security professional, claimed that a friend of his had provided IT services to drug traffickers in the Golden Triangle in Southeast Asia (MY-CSP-4). Apparently even drug barons need Internet, email, and adequate security. There are murmurs of Mexican drug cartels recruiting (or even kidnapping) programmers to carry out tasks for them. Background information I gathered suggested that such tasks might include hacking US agencies like Customs and Border Protection to gain intelligence and aid smuggling operations. But perhaps the most famous instance of a drug ring getting involved in hacking was the breach discovered in 2013 at the port of Antwerp. Drugs were hidden in containers that were moved through the port. It appears that a Netherlands-based group partnered with hackers to compromise the port systems so that it could locate and haul away these containers before their true owners claimed them.[19]

Sometimes it may be difficult to distinguish between this fifth category and the role that organized crime groups play in guiding certain cybercriminal schemes. Both involve the recruitment of technical actors. For example, Western European hacker, Casper, recounted a story of being approached by what he called "real criminals, very big criminals." These men jetted into town to meet Casper and, by his account, were friendly and respectful toward him. The criminal activity they hoped to woo him into included a major jewelry heist in Europe, in which his role would be to hack the target's alarm system. Casper politely declined (WE-(F)CC-2). The difference between this example and the Sumitomo heist is largely in the nature of what was to be stolen and how—physically removing items like jewelry, compared to carrying out electronic money transfers.

The distinction essentially returns to the functional definition of cybercrime settled on in the Introduction. If the use of the technology plays a central role, the crime might best be considered cybercrime. If cyber is merely tangential to a crime, it probably should not be considered cybercrime. Of course, many examples fall between these two ends of the spectrum. Some readers might view certain examples discussed in category four as correctly belonging in category five, and vice versa. Others might view an act like hacking to gain intelligence, for example, as tangential to the core crime of trafficking drugs, but also as an independent case of cybercrime in itself. As many of these questions become matters of degree, not easily classified, the central point remains that the strict categorization of what is and isn't cybercrime is not always helpful in making sense of what is happening out in the world. Organized crime groups clearly do not draw such strict delineations in their own activities.

To sum up, while organized crime groups are involved in cybercrime, they do not necessarily play a large role in governing it. Examples of such groups providing protection to cybercriminals are not particularly widespread, but they do exist and may help with some ordering of the business. It is much more likely that organized criminals are playing a role within the industry rather than seeking to control it. Sometimes they act as investors, in other cases they handle the money side of schemes, or act as guiding hands in managing specific cybercrime operations. Still, it is important not to overstate matters and represent such involvement as a large-scale takeover of the business, as some have. While younger mobsters might be making inroads, the leading, older mobsters may not really understand cyber in a way that would allow them to take control of it (US-CSP-14). While organized crime groups seem like a logical suspect for offline cyber-criminal governance, the evidence is not strong. Instead it is sensible to move onto the second suspect and examine the role that corrupt government agents might be playing in protecting the cybercrime industry.

Corruption and Protection

While there is only limited evidence that organized crime controls the cybercrime industry on a wide scale, it appears that corrupt state officials and agents play a more vital role in this regard.[20] They provide a key governance function that helps the cybercrime industry flourish in certain locations around the globe. In this section we will explore how corrupt state agents act as protectors of cybercriminals by neglecting to arrest the relevant offenders, tipping them off about upcoming operations against them, and even intervening after arrests have been made. The latter claim might seem extreme but it is not without precedent. When Dmitry Golubov, aka Script, was arrested in Ukraine in 2005, he was held in custody for just six months before being released by a judge on the recommendation of two local politicians.[21]

In my data, instances of protection by officials appear much more regularly than protection by organized crime groups. Many of those who had not observed organized crime involvement in cybercrime were well aware of the law enforcement corruption that helps facilitate the phenomenon. This is the case in Russian cybercrime, which often does not involve organized criminals but instead enjoys protection by crooked law enforcement (RUS-CSP-5, RUS-CSP-6). Ukrainian former law enforcement agent Nikita believed that corruption was a major reason that cybercrime flourished in the country. For him, Ukraine's core need was not about reforming the law, but enforcing it properly. In many instances, he believed the lack of enforcement was due to agents taking bribes (UKR-(F)LE-2).

While these instances suggest corruption among agents, the problem may go much higher. Brian Krebs's investigation of Russian spam "businesses" suggests that large operations may seek protection from the highest levels of law enforcement and government. Drawing on databases of leaked communications and interviews, Krebs reports that rival spammers Pavel

Vrublevsky and Igor Gusev were donating money to Russian sports associations as a way of funneling it to the highly influential political and law enforcement figures who administered them.[22] A surprising number of other cases involve cybercriminals whose relatives are law enforcement officials or important political figures. The leading carder Roman Seleznev, who was arrested in the Maldives and extradited to the United States in 2014, is the son of a member of parliament in Russia.[23] Flyman, who was placed in charge of the feared RBN, is the son of someone with significant political influence (US-CSP-14).[24] On the law enforcement side, Alexander Rubatsky's father was a high-ranking police officer in Belarus.[25] In *Fatal System Error,* Joseph Menn recounts an episode where UK agent Andy Crocker attempted to arrest a Russian cybercriminal based in Astrakhan. The suspect's father turned out to be the local police chief, leaving Crocker and his colleague holed up in a hotel room fearing for their safety.[26]

Participants in my study also pointed to corruption in other places around the globe. Post-communist Romania was said to have instances of protection similar to those found in the former Soviet states, such as payments to local law enforcement to prevent arrest (US-CSP-10). In Râmnicu Vâlcea, one of the geographical hubs of cyber fraud, there have been a number of arrests made of high-ranking law enforcement and political figures.[27] Such arrests may be a positive development, as part of broader Romanian efforts to stamp out corruption and improve cybercrime policing capacity (ROM-(F)LE-1, ROM-LE-1). In his Southeast Asian location, Tan wrote about how he had some governmental contacts through his family and would "hang around with some of the law enforcements to get protection relationships." This tactic also worked for a leading cybercriminal in the same country, who had strong relationships with senior police. Tan recounted stories of others escaping serious implications for their cybercriminal activities: "I have some friends who got arrested but got out in same day." One was an administrator of an underground forum who paid to be released. Another operated "a rogue Western Union, using it as a middle man to laundry money for other cyber-criminals, he got caught and got out in the same day, law enforcement just took his Western Union's license, he paid some money and just go home" (SEA-(F)CC-2).

Corruption is also a major feature in the Nigerian cybercrime scene. When President Muhammadu Buhari was elected in 2015 on a platform to stamp out corruption, it had long been a challenge facing the country. Nigeria is regularly rated as one of the most corrupt countries in the world.[28] One participant, based on his past interactions with Nigerian agents, pointed to the low salaries which he said made them "very shaky" (US-(F)LE-6).

Here, protection of cybercriminals appears to be somewhat "transactional." Rather than paying a regular protector, as one might in Eastern Europe, some Nigerian cybercriminals simply pay bribes upon apprehension to avoid an arrest or to be released subsequently (NIG-(F)LE-1). Yinka recalled a time in the earlier days of Nigerian cybercrime when he was in a cyber café where most of the other patrons were conducting illicit activities. When the police raided the location and promptly demanded bribes from anyone who wanted to be released, it became clear that this was not a genuine investigation but rather a coordinated extortion attempt (NIG-CSP-4).

Corrupt law enforcement agents in the West do not show up in my data, although it is unlikely that this phenomenon is nonexistent.[29] Interestingly, one of the few examples of western corruption that emerged related to criminal grey areas and the private-sector investigation of them. Todd, a security professional with experience in such investigations, said, "I've come across cases in click fraud where the criminal attempted to gain protection by bribing officials at the company being victimized or their agents." In one instance, he uncovered a large-scale operation and sought explanations from them as to how they were driving their traffic. In response, they offered to send a representative to the victim headquarters, which Todd read as code for a bribe (US-CSP-6). Shawn Hogan, who was later convicted of fraud, ran a successful but less-than-legitimate affiliate revenue scheme connected to eBay. He blogged about buying a car and other products for his contact at the company, which looks like a possible kickback to avoid potential investigations of his methods.[30]

This range of cases suggests that corruption interacts with cybercrime in different ways depending on the location in question. While it is well beyond the scope of this chapter to engage in a country-by-country analysis, the key point is that understanding these local variations is important. Nonetheless, it does make sense to give some focused attention to the system of corruption found in many former Soviet states, given the significant contribution that those countries make to cybercrime. Addressing their specific situation will help to clarify both how corruption supports the cybercrime industry in that region, and how this particular system of protection functions.

CORRUPTION AND PROTECTION IN THE FORMER USSR

To understand how the cybercrime industry, corruption, and protection interact, it is instructive to study how corruption functions within the former USSR. As various participants noted, in this region, there has long been an interplay among businessmen, gangsters, and the government (US-(F)

LE-5; US-LE-3). Within this environment, the typical cybercriminal lives a "normal life" and is a "regular" guy who doesn't particularly stand out from other technology professionals (UKR-LE-2). In such contexts, corruption is also much more of an ingrained aspect of the economy and political system than the pure moral failing some would consider it. While many locals resent it or wish matters were different, corruption is a part of daily life for much of the region's (and the world's) population.[31] Perhaps counterintuitive for some, Andrey wrote about his own view of the subject:

> If fact, if you regard what you call "Russian corruption" as the factor, I'd say it is much beneficial for emerging businesses. It is very fertile grounds for unorthodox methods. They asking me a lot, whether it is bad, my answer, though that "chaos is not a disorder, it is just another type of order we do not understand." So it is with Russia, it have its own ways, and they not always bad. You just have to learn how to operate in Russian environment, and soon you will learn that it is more pleasant that doing so in West. Although I don't advocate corruption, I regard it as inevitable, and, sometimes, lesser evil (EE-(F)CC-2).

Andrey's understanding of this Russian order accords theoretically with the concept of extra-legal governance.[32] While aspects of power and governance relate to formal political and legal institutions, there is a less formal system of conventions that also applies.[33] One might disagree with Andrey's analysis at particular points, but here I quote his unvarnished views at length, to illustrate a way of thinking probably alien to most western perspectives:

> Russia is very specific country, with very special order of things. It will be very hard to outline how the police works in Russia and it will take a lot to explain this. So, let's define, that in "western" understanding, methods of operations of Russian police are corrupt. But this "corruption" is very questionable depending on the angle how you regard it. See, I very familiar with methods of works of Russian police, and generally they follow the orders of superiors and respect hierarchy, for example it will be very hard to believe that lieutenant investigating cybercrime will take bribe and sabotage case without knowledge of his superior. From this, it is evident that whole line of policing, "corrupt" as you call it, is well defined from

high-above, they also follow the orders and rules, it is just so that those orders and rules are not in the book. So, it may be very good for you in Russia if you know "rules of the game," and follow it. And, knowing system, in both countries, I don't see how the American policing is less "corrupted" than Russian one, it is just that it is different kind of corruption. If in Russia it is bribe-taking and law-avoidance in favor of vague (let's call it) "game rules," in US it is bureaucracy, dictature, arrogance, embezzlement, and if we convert how much those "plagues" cost to system, I am sure that American ones will cost more to American taxpayers (EE-(F)CC-2).

Andrey's account suggests that corruption in Eastern Europe is not so much the work of rogue agents as it is institutionalized within the power structure. Many "illegal" actions fall under the influence of "legitimate" authorities. As a result, to make sense of many aspects of life in the former Soviet Union, it is vitally important to understand how the structures of authority function. Gilles Favarel-Garrigues provides a detailed history of policing of economic crimes in Russia, suggesting a degree of continuity between Soviet policing practices and those that followed.[34] This includes instances of corruption and a degree of "tolerance" for economic crimes during the Soviet period, even though this contradicted official ideology. His view is that the Soviet policeman exhibited a degree of autonomy and was best understood as a "street-level bureaucrat."[35] But to fully comprehend the post-Soviet system, one must also grasp the central concept of a protector (US-(F)LE-5). Federico Varese outlines how this idea functions in the Russian context:

> In Russian slang, the word for protection is *krysha* (lit. "roof"). It was used during the Soviet period to refer to front activities for Committee of State Security (KGB), Military Intelligence (GRU), and Ministry of Internal Affairs (MVD) agents both in the country and abroad. Cultural institutions, publishing houses, embassies, and ministries all supplied a cover to people engaged in intelligence gathering. Since the Soviet Union collapsed, *krysha* refers to protection against ordinary criminals and "unprofessional" racketeers, unruly business partners, and competitors. A *krysha* may ensure tax evasion and help in finding investment and credit opportunities. A Russian businessman, in his testimony to a US Senate committee, maintains that to operate a successful business in Moscow one must "pay the right government officials" and "purchase a *krysha* . . .

which has come to mean protection. The more important you are, the higher the roof must be." Reputable newspapers advise Russians to obtain a sound protection before starting any business. The search for a safe "roof" is considered by *Komsomol'skaya Pravda* as the "the most important element in the modern business world."[36]

Protection might be provided by organized criminals, Varese explains, but it might just as easily be provided by state officials who are legally allowed to moonlight as private protectors.[37] By law, their activity is not corrupt unless they are involved in protecting illicit enterprises. Private protection may also be provided by security firms or by firms developing their own internal security arms.[38] Former cybercriminal Leonid compared cyber-crime investigators who work both sides to werewolves (EE-(F)CC-4). US law enforcement agent Jack recalled a case he worked on in which a high-level Ukrainian police officer was arrested for organizing a cybercriminal group. Jack also suspected that one or more law enforcement agents had been involved in the foundation of CarderPlanet itself (US-LE-3).

The system of protection works within a broader context in which aspects of criminal or corrupt behavior have become somewhat normalized. Andrey believed that this model of governance originated even before the Soviets, but that the tradition was enhanced under communism. He shared his belief that one of the "few positive changes that communism inflicted on Soviet society is that feeling of social unity, relation, not so wrongly called 'camaraderie.' Though, origins of such unity and trust, I suppose, had nothing to do with communist theory, but rather with necessity to survive regime's oppression or to thrive and cheer at the times of hardships" (EE-(F)CC-2). In his view, those sent to prisons under the Soviet regime returned to society having adopted aspects of criminal culture. This counterculture then spread throughout society more generally, as it was useful to "thwart Soviet dictature and oppressions and survive in environment of suspicions, dictature and deprivations, some of those took roots too deeply among Soviet population" (EE-(F)CC-2). These traditions and growing cultural norms became an important aspect of life when the Soviet Union fell:

> Thus, post-Soviet society inherited this rich and controversial ruleset, and my generation were bought to it, as we learned about "camaraderie," help, mutual respect as well as distrust to authority from very young age; it is, naturally, was also very evident at the times when I grow up, that living and obeying by law will most likely not leads to prosperity or success, and it became even more

evident, as capitalist values and goods, attractive and of high quality, flowed through "iron curtain" to the Soviet markets. It was very hard to prosper for a doctor or engineer, as those had miserable (though well respected) lives, and little or no salary, while crooks and swindlers prospered. This social difference became even more evident after Soviet Union collapse, and it was time when artful fraud, praised by such authors like Ilf and Petrov in their "12 chairs" and "Golden Calf," really became a form of art, well respected and loathed if successful. It is no wonder that new generation didn't want to be a doctors, they wanted to be crooks, and some wanted to be crooked doctors or engineers. Cyber-criminals, in turn, is not much different, and learned very same rules of the game. However, they grew even more ruthless, since in real life criminal society and individuals, who you inevitably have to deal with if you choose life of fraud, will punish you for treason or disobedience, but cybercriminals were shield by the screen and keyboard from those, as well as they believed, from law and prosecution. For some, in late '90s cybercrime became form of ideal crime, undetected and unpunishable, while profitable and complex in its nature (EE-(F)CC-2).

Interestingly, Nathan pointed out that one of the Russian conspirators in the Citibank case was a neurosurgeon. As he observed, "there was more money in computer crime than brain surgery" (US-(F)LE-5). In his memoirs, the Belarusian carder Sergey Pavlovich (aka PoliceDog), provides a similar analysis:

Had my friends and I had begun life in a different country and at a different time, many of us could have been bank employees, businessmen or owners of companies. Some, of course, would still have become criminals. But we were born in the Soviet Union at the turn of an epoch and we became adults in the 1990s when old moral values had been rejected and new ones hadn't yet appeared. We became cyber-criminals not because we were naturals, but because of the times: our parents were working two or three jobs to make ends meet, and we, the kids, were left on our own. No-one told us stealing was a sin, and even if they did, no one bothered to explain why. But everyone around us was stealing, from civil servants to businessmen: and almost everyone got away with it. Why couldn't we do the same?[39]

In practical terms, high-level state agents become commanding figures. Their authority is partly drawn from their official status, but they also derive great power from the unofficial social standing these positions bring:

> Thus, "corruption," in Russian interpretation, is none other than giving "due" to authority, not unlike paying taxes, or showing respect (read Nicholas Gogol's) to those in position of authority, as they were able to "get there" and you did not. In post-Soviet mind, paying bribes is not unlike paying taxes, and assisting you friends and your family to advance on social ladder in first place, it is very natural and unquestionable. So, to further this thinking, you can also note that in such mindset, it is not uncommon for one social layer to protect another in exchange for certain favors and benefits, each of those social layers could provide, not unlike old communist "camaraderie" (EE-(F)CC-2).

The cybercrime industry operates firmly within this system. A roof is of vital importance and it is common for cybercriminals in former Soviet states to have a protector of one variety or another. This is part of doing business in the region. For cybercriminals, whose primary fear is arrest, corrupt state officials can present the best option to lessen such concerns. This is fundamental to the success of the cybercrime industry in the region, and the world, because it provides the space for cybercriminals to build this illicit technology sector. It allows them to operate relatively openly and, as a result, to build firms at the scale and level of sophistication described in the previous chapter. The former Soviet Union is the technical engine of the global cybercrime industry. This system of patronage, corruption, and protection is central to its proper functioning.

With that said, it would be wrong to assume that political protection is apparent in all cases in Eastern Europe. Former cybercriminal Ivan was somewhat surprised when questioned about the connection between cybercrime and corruption. "Corrupt law enforcement agents or official involved with cybercriminals? Never heard about it," he wrote. "The point of doing business online is to be anonymous" (EE-(F)CC-3). When I broadly outlined some previous findings as a means of verification, he went on:

> I am totally surprised to hear from you that some other cybercriminals actually paid law enforcement to protect them. Isn't it simpler not to be caught? I mean, a cybercriminal can use a prepaid phone to access Internet, use bunch of VPN servers, use

PGP etc. to complicate finding of his real identity and location (EE-(F) CC-3).

The argument Ivan presents here is an intuitive one. If a cybercriminal can sufficiently separate his online identity from his offline one, he should have little need for protection in a traditional sense. This is the same view expressed earlier by Don, who did not fear law enforcement because essentially he believed he was a ghost. From what Ivan described of his activities, he seemed to be far less known within his local networks than some other Eastern European cybercriminals I encountered, such as Andrey. According to Ivan, precisely seven people knew of his "occupation," most of whom he had known since school, and two of whom he had met through online circles and never met in person. Given that he started his career while living in regional centers, he also might not initially have had the same visibility as people who were part of "the scene" in business hubs or capital cities. While Ivan denied having a steady protector, even he provided evidence of how corruption can assist in cybercriminal endeavors. When an offline confrere who was involved in his cybercrime activities was arrested for unrelated sexual offenses, Ivan bribed law enforcement to have him released: "I paid about $12k to cops to let him go after just three months of 'serving time' in detention center (it was in Ukraine; corruption allowed such things)" (EE-(F)CC-3).

Conclusion

This chapter has argued that the protection of cybercriminals is central to the effective functioning of the industry. Just as in the online setting, a system of offline governance creates order that allows cybercriminals to operate more efficiently. In many criminal contexts, this role is performed by organized crime groups. The first section suggested that while there is some evidence of organized criminals protecting cybercriminals, this does not appear to be a widespread occurrence. Rather than seeking to govern cybercrime, these groups are more likely to be involved *within* the industry, playing a specific role. But even this function is not as widespread as many would believe. Instead, the second section argued that true cybercriminal governance is commonly delivered by corrupt state officials and agents. Acting outside of their lawful authority, the central service that these agents provide is to protect cybercriminals from arrest by tipping them off or subverting possible investigations. This is a vital service because it allows

cybercriminals to operate in the relative open. Without strong requirements for secrecy, they can collaborate with less fear, and the size of their
enterprises grows accordingly. This offline protection helps explain much
about the size of firms and the overall maturation of the industry discussed
in the last chapter. (Of course, another related element is law enforcement
capacity, which is addressed in the Conclusion. Even when corruption is
not a problem, a lack of policing resources, training, or interest might also
allow cybercriminals to operate freely).

Nonetheless, this manifestation of governance is curious in some ways.
First, organized crime groups play a fairly limited role, despite their often
seeking to control other criminal industries. It would not be a stretch for
them to apply their skills to this new context, yet they do not in many
instances. Second, the involvement of corrupt agents is often focused on
protection from arrest rather than arbitrating disputes between cybercriminals, or driving competitors out of business. These are forms of protection commonly required by criminals, alongside protection from arrest.
But cybercriminals do not appear to require these services on a broad scale.
This chapter did not attempt to address these issues in detail, but one could
surmise that a lack of strong offline competition between cybercriminals might be a key factor in why these other governance services are not
as popular. When there are countless victims located across the world, and
any "turf" is virtual, disputes between cybercriminals in offline settings are
rare. Such altercations are likely to emerge only when cybercriminals are operating in the same specific business, where they are geographically located
in the same place, and where there are limited targets or customers available.
Genuine competition may emerge in such cases. In these instances, protectors may find their other services in greater demand. Broadly speaking,
however, this does not appear to be the case across much of the cybercrime
industry.

8

Conclusion

THIS BOOK BEGAN with the story of Roman Seleznev, whose tale is somewhat emblematic of what cybercrime has become in recent years. Gone are the days when cybercrime consisted solely of hobby hacking and mischief. It is now a serious business. The big players look like illicit technology entrepreneurs, running their own firms with teams of programmers working for them. Other players sell products on marketplaces or perform various support functions. Enterprising types like Seleznev can bring in millions of dollars and live the high life. They can collaborate and trade with partners from around the globe—and they can threaten victims everywhere. It has been the central argument of this book that a bona fide cybercrime industry has developed. In short, cybercrime has gone professional.

But this industrialization is also puzzling. How can cybercriminals successfully cooperate on such a scale when their potential partners are anonymous criminals? Without the protection of state institutions, it is challenging enough to deal with traditional criminals. Adding the layer of anonymity makes the instability of the situation even more extreme. One might expect cybercriminals to act alone or in small groups. But, as this book argues, the opposite is occurring. There has been widespread collaboration, the formation of large marketplaces, and the development of significant firms among other operational groupings. This puzzle provided the second focus of the book, with its investigation into the mechanisms that have allowed this widespread cooperation and industrialization to take place. As much as this is a study of industry, it is also a study of anonymity—the obstacles it throws up and the ways it can be managed to achieve positive outcomes.

While this book is based on substantial fieldwork over a seven-year period, its findings can only be suggestive. This is due in part to the nature of qualitative data. But the bigger reason is that the world this study has sought to uncover is simply too big for one scholar to investigate in considerable detail. It sounds like a significant number to interview 238 subjects, but the population connected to cybercrime is vast. Not all perspectives can be represented here. My objective instead has been to draw a map that, by showing how the seemingly disparate elements relate to one another, can better explain how the cybercrime industry functions. Future studies will, I hope, zero in on specific issues identified here. They will uncover new data and apply different research methods. In so doing, they may suggest nuances that have been missed, or analyze data that contradict some of the findings here. At times, this felt like an endless project. And it is. But there comes a point when insights must be shared so that the broader community can benefit and new research projects can be launched.

One of the challenges of this project has been the retrospective nature of many interviews. Numerous qualitative studies have a retrospective dimension to them. This offers benefits, such as allowing the participation of subjects who might have been unable to contribute in their former roles or situations. It also allows the discussion of topics that might have been sensitive in the moment, but become less so over time. Of course, the passing of time can also fray memories. Meta-narratives can come into existence, informed by writings on various topics. Participants may partly reconstruct their recollections based on this material. This is particularly challenging when discussing long-past events. For instance, the historical components of this book often draw on an oral history of cybercrime, which may be influenced by what has been written on the topic already. This was one reason I tried to limit my publication output while fieldwork was ongoing, so as not to taint the data with participants restating elements of what they read in advance of meeting me. I also took pains to challenge any narratives that seemed too neat, and to triangulate findings with reference to additional sources. Complete accuracy, however, can never be assured. Within such limitations, this book contributes as much as it can.

Summary

The early chapters of this book examined the industrialization of cybercrime. The analysis began with an historical investigation of profit-driven cybercrime. Chapter 2 traced the evolution from the early days when hacking was largely a matter of intellectual curiosity, to the heavy focus on financially motivated activities that arrived later. This industrialization also occurred organizationally, with the development of large online marketplaces such as CarderPlanet and the subsequent operational group-ings that followed. Working as teams to carry out cybercriminal acts, they left behind the archetype of the lone-wolf hacker. Drawing on this his-tory, Chapter 3 analyzed cybercrime within a broad framework of indus-trial organization. It noted the presence of key elements that one would expect to find in other illicit and licit industries: specialization, profession-alization, markets, and firms.

The following chapters then moved to examine how this industrializa-tion could take place, given the challenges of anonymity. Chapter 4 ad-dressed the question of identity online and the way in which cybercriminal nicknames function as brands, making some level of cooperation possible in the first place. These brands, however, were shown to be somewhat un-stable, as nicknames can be quickly abandoned, albeit at the cost of losing accrued reputation. Cybercriminals face a key tension in this regard: the longer they maintain their nicknames, the more their reputations can de-velop, but maintaining a given nickname for a long time makes a cyber-criminal increasingly vulnerable to law enforcement investigations, and ties him to his past actions. There is no perfect solution to overcoming this tension; each cybercriminal must choose the strategy that best suits his needs. While one might accept the risk of holding onto a handle, another will switch handles regularly, trying to maintain a reputational trail of sorts with trusted partners.

Within the context of unstable identities and brands, Chapter 5 exam-ined what mechanisms cybercriminals employ to enhance cooperation. This discussion was built around trustworthiness and enforcement. In terms of trustworthiness, it was clear that reputation played a central role, but that appearance and performance were also important. Meanwhile, in an on-line setting, monitoring and enforcement are challenging. Some forms of punishment are available, like DDoS and doxing, but these are far less threat-ening than physical violence. Key institutions, mainly tied to forums, have developed to make avenues of enforcement (and assessing trustworthiness) more effective and scalable to much larger numbers. For instance, the estab-lishment of rules and the threat of exclusion, along with escrow services and arbitration, appear particularly important. Overall, such forums seem to inject a level of governance into the underground economy and help grease the wheels of exchange. Of course, another key factor in this discussion is the ample money that can be made through cybercrime, which may outweigh the residual risks of collaborating with anonymous criminal partners.

Chapter 6 addressed an aspect of cybercrime that is often overlooked: its offline dimension. In some ways, this provides a very simple solution to the puzzle of how cybercriminals cooperate with anonymous partners. This chapter suggested that some cybercriminals simply sidestep this challenge by dealing with partners in the physical world instead of, or in addition to, those online. They might sacrifice their anonymity, or never seek to hide their identities from partners in the first place. Some might view this type of behavior as puzzling in itself, but it rests on the realization that anonymity has both benefits and costs. It may provide more protection from law enforcement, but it also creates barriers to successful cooperation. This chapter suggested that by forgoing anonymity, cybercriminals enhance aspects of enforcement available to them. They can work with known partners locally and employ a range of sanctions, including the threat of violence. Without the concerns of dealing with virtual strangers, cooperation is improved. Firms can become more stable and grow much larger, thereby buttressing the cybercrime industry as a whole.

Chapter 7 continued the discussion of the offline dimension and argued that the protection of cybercriminals is essential to the overall success of the industry. While organized crime groups play a number of roles in cybercrime, they are not taking over and governing the business on a wide scale. Instead, corrupt agents of the state are the ones primarily governing cybercrime in the physical world. As competition and disputes among cybercriminals are not a major concern, the chief function of these agents is to protect them from arrest. This allows cybercriminals in some countries to operate in a relatively open way. As a result, the sorts of large firms and enterprises identified in Chapters 3 and 6, which begin to approximate licit technology companies, can flourish. Such corruption allows the cybercrime industry to reach the heights that it has.

It is hoped that these findings help to demystify cybercrime. There can be a tendency to view the phenomenon as some new plane of sorcery that is hidden and beyond comprehension. It can be seen as something so foreign that it must challenge what we already know about crime and the world more broadly. In all honesty, there does not appear to be that much that is new about cybercrime. The definitions of cybercrime we use should probably reflect this. Certainly, there is little to justify the development of new theoretical frameworks around this type of crime. Some details may differ, but the data I gathered brought no substantial challenge to the existing theory I employed, which has been widely applied to many other contexts. It may well be that other established frameworks from a range of disciplines are also applicable to cybercrime when matched to solid empirical evidence.

The findings presented in this book do indeed fit very well with the theoretical expectations outlined in the Introduction. Consistent with prior literature, trustworthiness is an important component of cooperation in the world of cybercrime, with reputation playing a particularly important role. The other key theoretical plank, enforcement, was also present. The importance of institutions was clearly evident, particularly with regard to the development of online marketplaces. In keeping with the work of Douglass North and others, the evolution of cybercriminal institutions had precisely the effect that one would predict: trade and collaboration were enhanced. Some level of governance was also apparent in this context, further improving cooperation and linking with theoretical expectations that some system of order will emerge even in unexpected settings. The offline dimension of cybercrime also supported, rather than challenged, existing theory. Giving up anonymity served as a credible commitment and opened up new (or rather, old) avenues of enforcement, including the threat of physical violence. Offline cybercrime is also supported by a system of governance, in keeping with many other forms of crime. But it is corrupt agents of the state, rather than organized criminals, that are most likely to protect the cybercrime industry.

The Impact of Policing

Moving past theory, there are numerous hypotheses that could follow from this study. Here, I choose to focus on just one central supposition. There are limits to the success of cybercriminal cooperation and the smooth running of the industry, particularly when cybercriminal institutions are disrupted. One of the key variables is law enforcement, in terms of its capacity, its transparency, and its willingness to tackle the problem. In short, when the state challenges cybercriminals in an effective way, the industry shrinks. I will explore the nuances of this hypothesis in the following paragraphs, as some might argue that certain initial studies on the effectiveness of cyber-policing have already contradicted this claim.

For instance, studies of the online drug trade have suggested that trading activity on cryptomarkets is not hampered over the long term by major police operations (arrests or site takedowns), or media coverage of this police action. Sales volume might even *increase* soon after these efforts, thanks to the unintended advertisement of such online marketplaces.[1] But while there are certain similarities, these studies cannot be directly applied to the case of profit-driven cybercrime. The motivations of online drug offenders are not identical to cybercriminals, nor is the nature of their product. The addictive or habitual aspects of drugs could produce a more stable form of demand than for cybercriminal products. And many might continue to use online drug markets, despite the risks, because offline drug markets bring their own major problems with regard to both law enforcement action and threats from certain dealers.

In the profit-driven cybercrime space itself, there has been some doubt about the efficacy of current law enforcement approaches.[2] Such doubts, however, are not supported by a large body of evidence. In their review of disruption and intervention strategies against stolen data markets, Alice Hutchings and Thomas Holt argue that much of the research in this area still needs to be done:

> At present, there is virtually no criminological inquiry with respect to evaluations of cybercrime intervention strategies or prevention programs generally. Such research is, however, pivotal to ensure a technique or strategy is effective, delivering value for money, and that there are no unforeseen or undesirable consequences. There is also need for evaluating perceptions of legitimacy and the fairness of the processes in which decisions are being made, how power is being exercised as well as oversight and supervision of powers.[3]

One cannot yet rule out the role of the state in addressing cybercrime, despite the enormous transnational challenges to policing that are habitually noted (and mentioned by too many interview subjects to list). This subject needs to be investigated in much greater detail. With testing, it is possible that the hypothesis may in fact not bear out. But there are also some elements of this study that suggest it might.

In an online setting, when cybercriminals are able to build institutions and operate within a system of governance, cooperation thrives and the industry expands. In basic terms, the cooperation is scaled up from low-level interactions to the industrial level. But when law enforcement makes arrests, knocks out institutions, and damages faith in the system of the governance, cybercriminals become cautious and retract into smaller groupings, where trustworthiness plays a more important role. This was clearly the case after CarderPlanet, ShadowCrew, and DarkMarket were compromised and shut down. This study has presented evidence from cybercriminals themselves, who became less trusting as a result of these interventions, and altered their behavior and hangouts. Many (though not all) of the former cybercriminals I interviewed spoke of a serious fear of being arrested when they were active. One quit the business largely because he was worried about the impact it would have on his parents if he were arrested. For those who had been arrested, the resulting trauma was clear. One participant kept me waiting for an hour, as he was paranoid the meeting we had set up might be a sting (despite his no longer being involved in crime). Another recounted how he keeps himself awake every night until after 6 a.m., as that was the time that his house was raided by law enforcement agents.

Various findings within this book suggest that law enforcement has some effect in cyberspace. But is it an effect that reduces the overall scale and impact of profit-driven cybercrime? That requires considerably more study. In particular, the effects of targeting institutions that enhance trust among criminals online should be investigated. While takedowns of key forums appear to have some effect, at least on the psyche of cybercriminals, it is unclear what long-term effect they have on the overall threat. Since the initial takedowns of sites like DarkMarket, it is possible that cybercrime has evolved to respond differently to such events, with cybercriminals simply factoring in such threats as a standard cost of doing business and acting accordingly. The deterrent element may have weakened over time for those committed to the craft.

For an interesting comparison, one can turn to Brazil, where such policing actions are not widely employed. Given that violent crimes and other threats in that country take precedence, cybercrime is not a major priority and relatively few cases are prosecuted. As a result, Brazilian cybercriminals still largely operate in the open, on platforms like Facebook, Skype, WhatsApp, Telegram, and gaming app channels (BRA-CSP-2, BRA-CSP-3, BRA-CSP-7). Presumably, if the enforcement situation changed and these actors were more aggressively pursued, they would quickly change their operations and move underground into more secure settings. The effect would be dramatic in the short term. But it is possible that the new reality would simply yield a new equilibrium, with some offenders changing their operations and hangouts, rather than all of them giving up entirely.

The question becomes whether law enforcement action simply displaces online crime to new locations.[4] For instance, after a takedown, cybercriminals might migrate to other existing forums or else initiate new ones. In some ways, law enforcement can be a victim of its own success. When it successfully disrupts cybercriminal institutions, it pushes various actors into smaller, more closed groups, making it more difficult to track, investigate, and arrest them. This might become a frustration, but it is not necessarily a failure. That depends on whether these operations reduce the overall impact of cybercrime, even if only through a deterrent effect.[5] This is very difficult to evaluate due to a dearth of data and the scale of the topic. One could also argue that, even if cybercrime grew in spite of police action, it is possible that it would have grown even more without that action. This would fit with a "cutting the weeds" analogy, even if critics prefer to see more of a "whack a mole" challenge. Finally, there is the controversial question of capacity. Are agencies simply in need of greater skills, resources, and manpower to take on the threat in a much more successful way?

The issue of capacity is a concern that affects agencies across the globe. This book makes clear that cybercrime thrives in certain geographical locations, and is far more offline and local than people often realize. As a result, it would not be surprising if effective approaches in policing the threat involve targeting those locations where cybercriminals operate with near impunity. As much as technical defenses and the education of potential victims might help, there is still a role for the state in fighting cybercrime. But it is the nations that are producing the most (and most successful) cybercriminals that need to act directly against them, as victim countries face enormous investigation challenges when crossing borders. Along with improving international cooperation, this often ties into broader issues of local capacity, anti-corruption measures, and overall good governance. In order to take on these challenges and fight cybercrime at its roots, these states likely need great help from the international community. Some programs are already in place to increase capacity and stamp out corruption, but it is an area that would benefit from perhaps greater investment and certainly much further study.[6]

Given the novelty of the cybercrime challenge, it is also important not to expect too much from the state in responding to the threat. Like all crime, it will always exist in some form (SWI(E)-CSP-1). Law enforcement can never wipe out cybercrime entirely; all it can do is limit its scale. The United States has invested the most of any country in building a large cyber-policing capability. It also prosecutes cases with gusto whether inside the country or internationally. Yet there should be no expectation of eradicating the problem. Instead, success may be better measured by the fact that, while many American cybercriminals still operate inside the country, these offenders must operate in secret, in small groupings, and in a guarded way. Organizational structures tend to grow when the activity is a grey area, or one that is more challenging to prosecute. (Consumer fraud, for example, often has a large number of victims taken for small sums of money.) In contrast to some Eastern European settings, it is difficult for cybercriminals in America to scale their cooperation upwards, because law enforcement restricts the space for institutions of criminal governance to form. With points on both sides of the debate, considerably more research is required to properly evaluate the impact of cybercrime policing and particular strategies within it. As yet, this hypothesis remains largely untested. But, as the next section makes clear, it is possible that some efforts to reduce cybercrime may be better placed elsewhere.

Policy Outcomes: A Problem of Underemployment

The final point of this discussion is policy. What can be done about an industry that is responsible for billions of losses and threatens victims across the world? Here, for a number of reasons, I choose not to focus on law enforcement strategies and tactics. First, this has not been a focus of my study, and other methodologies are probably better suited to making sense of the subject. Second, while certain former cybercriminals might have contributed to this project to right past wrongs or establish more trustworthy versions of themselves going forward, their intention was not to develop ways by which their old colleagues could be arrested or their operations infiltrated. In fact, in one case, this position was specifically stated. Third, as noted directly above, police action can only accomplish so much. Certain cybercriminals can be arrested and enterprises can be disrupted, but the scale of the threat remains immense. As one law enforcement agent put it to me, we "can't arrest our way out" of this situation (US-LE-3). Some attempt must be made to stem the flow of cybercriminals in the first instance.

The cybercrime industry is a tragedy. While some actors are simply career criminals who have found a new revenue source, across the world, numerous intelligent, capable, and driven individuals are also becoming involved in this enormous illicit enterprise. Many spend considerable time innovating and refining their businesses. They make large amounts of money doing so, and are the heart of the industry. But, ultimately, all this effort is destructive rather than constructive. If this talent pool could be diverted away from cybercrime and into legitimate industry, there would be two positive developments. Not only would levels of cybercrime drop dramatically, but many positive contributions could emerge from the endeavors of these capable individuals.

At the heart of the cybercrime industry are unemployment and underemployment. When highly capable individuals can't find legitimate job opportunities that challenge them and pay well, they turn elsewhere. When they find themselves in environments where criminal behavior is relatively acceptable and law enforcement attention is limited, they hesitate all the less. In the end, cybercrime is work, whether someone is simply looking for a steady job as a programmer or has the makings of an entrepreneur hoping to make millions. Without legitimate opportunities, they have created their own jobs. As noted earlier, Russian former law enforcement agent Vasily believed that the leading cybercriminals in Russia were effectively just entrepreneurs. The economy in Russia was simply not set up for these types of emerging technologists. The market is instead dominated by a small number of large companies (RUS-(F)LE-1). It probably does not help that these firms are often intimately connected to the state and thereby protected from much competition. If we take the case of Andrey, his central challenge as an entrepreneur was a lack of access to capital. It is important to note that he ran a number of legitimate enterprises alongside his illicit activities. But he had far greater financial success with his cybercrime and therefore diverted much of his time away from his legitimate businesses (EE-(F)CC-2). Ivan also felt he had little choice but to go into cybercrime to make the level of income he wanted (EE-(F)CC-3). As we have seen throughout these pages, the quality and scale of the illicit work of people like Andrey and Ivan is impressive. Collectively, they have built an enormous profit-driven industry. It is a criminal Silicon Valley.

The great challenge of dramatically reducing cybercrime is to find ways to divert those who would become cybercriminals into legitimate employment. This could be achieved by widely recruiting technical talent out of regions where cybercrime is a particular problem. Another method might be to invest heavily in the local technology sectors directly in those hot spots. This type of investment would provide the capital that entrepreneurs have difficulty accessing, create more jobs, and possibly have a positive effect on the broader economy. Such proposals are likely to succeed best in those places where offenders are more technical and opportunities in the technology sector would be attractive. Focusing on the former Soviet Union might make sense, given the outsize role that coders and programmers in that region play in cybercrime. As one Russian malware expert saw it, the wide availability of talent for criminal activities is a central problem: "If there will be no technical specialists there will be no cybercrime" (RUS-CSP-3). In places like Romania or Nigeria, where offenders are smart but less directly connected to technical expertise, the challenge would be greater. In such cases, possible solutions would need to be more focused on the dynamics of the local economy and ways to improve overall employment prospects. The success of the technology sector in Romania, and employment avenues for Romanians in the EU and further abroad, suggest that increased technology jobs might divert the more technical offenders out of the cybercrime business. But those focused on lower-level fraud might still remain.

Of course, any attempt to divert cybercriminals out of the criminal Silicon Valley and into legitimate employment would face challenges. There are questions about whether those already steeped in the business could be reformed or if they would make untrustworthy employees. Considerably more research is needed on such issues. A number of the former cybercriminals interviewed as part of this study had either begun careers in legitimate industry or were wishing to do so. I certainly had faith, and hope, that a number would find success on their new paths. I was not alone in this hope. While half of my participants were hesitant to trust former cybercriminals placed in the private sector or government, the other half thought they deserved a second chance and had something to offer. Landon, a former US agent with considerable experience investigating Eastern European offenders, believed that, if given the opportunity to turn legitimate, many cybercriminals would: "The truth is, they would take it in a heartbeat," he said, and the only ones left behind would be "the morally corrupt hackers who want to do this anyways" (US-(F)LE-8). Former Ukrainian agent Misha believed that many cybercriminals harbored a desire to start a "white business." While it would be challenging to wean them off the "drug" of cybercrime, he believed that even a small number of actors leaving the underground could have a profound impact, given that relatively few people are driving this criminal industry (UKR-(F)LE-3).

In line with this, there should be programs addressing how talented former inmates might be recruited into suitable jobs. In the course of this study, it became apparent that numerous (unconvicted) former cybercriminals are employed throughout the technology sector. Sometimes their backgrounds are widely known, but in many cases they are not. It seems strange that this occurs, while those with criminal records who have "paid their debts" with significant prison terms are barred from some jobs that would allow them to contribute, follow their passion, and build a new life once they are released. Nonetheless, if past involvement in cybercrime turns out to be a risk factor, successful programs may have to target younger individuals and try to establish pathways toward the technology sector before cybercrime becomes attractive. This is something that is already being experimented with in the West and should be applied more widely.

There are many nuances to explore here. It is one thing to have programs in place, but another to ensure that they are connecting with their targets. In this study, a number of former offenders came from major cities, but others came from more regional hubs and thus even further away from paths that might lead them into legitimate industry. Even in western settings, where greater opportunities abound, some can feel isolated and blocked from pathways to legitimate success. Jonas, a former cybercriminal with considerable technical ability, described his commitment to programming, which he viewed as an "art." But he also talked about the strong isolation he felt in his community. He couldn't find investors for his work, and there wasn't even much of a local population of programmers he could share his interests with. This search for belonging and success led him to online forums, and eventually to cybercrime (WE-(F)CC-3).

There are both risks and rewards in carrying out such employment and investment programs internationally. A story that Andrey shared about his youth and the early days of the Internet in Eastern Europe illustrates this:

> Once they installed Internet at our school, my friends, some are winners of regional and country competitions themselves, used this access to beg from western companies, successfully, sending letters like "I am poor, but talented student, and here is example of my work, but in our broke country we have no chance to advance our projects, because we simply don't have no reliable equipment to work on," and so, and so. And it worked. People got laptops sent from Intel, ZIP drives from Microsoft, or money from Soros. We laughed at western "idiots" and even established "begging" competition, where everything counted from booklets to money and laptops. In fact, this begging gave good ideas to some of my friends to immigrate later, for example couple of them living in US and working for big companies, others live in Europe (EE-(F)CC-2).

What's interesting about this account is that it displays an attitude of condescension toward those who are trying to help: the technology sector, philanthropists, and the West in general. It sums up the ideological cross-purposes of the different players in this game. Yet as much as these companies and individuals might be dismissed as suckers, their charity appears to have paid off in the long term. As Andrey notes, some of these students are now gainfully employed in the technology sector. They are earning a living and contributing to broader society, rather than working as full-time, professional cybercriminals. The begging competition achieved its aims for all involved—but it is also important for both sides of a transaction to save face.

In terms of investing in local technology sectors, the main challenge is likely to be corruption. A core argument of this book has been that corruption facilitates cybercrime on a broad scale. As a result, one might be hesitant to inject large sums of money into an economic system where the funds might be quickly misappropriated. One could also take steps to reduce overall corruption, but this is an intractable problem and moving well beyond the scope of this book. In basic terms, such an investment, and any other strategy to encourage potential cybercriminals to join the licit industry, should be encouraged. But considerably more study needs to be conducted in these areas to determine how successful programs could be implemented.

To sum up this overall point on employment, and conclude this book, I end with a famous anecdote from the early days of profit-driven cyber-crime.[7] On November 10, 2000, twenty-year-old Alexey Ivanov was interviewing for a job in Seattle. Ivanov was a talented programmer from Chelyabinsk, in Russia, who had caught the attention of an American computer security start-up called Invita. The company was looking to expand its operations into Eastern Europe and thought Ivanov and his team of coders might be a perfect fit. Vasiliy Gorshkov accompanied Ivanov to the meeting, acting as his business manager of sorts. The meeting went well. Ivanov completed a hacking test that had been set up by the company and answered a series of questions. At one point, the CEO of Invita also asked Gorshkov about some recent computer intrusions in the United States. He was curious if the two had been involved. He wanted to know how good they were.

After the interview was completed, the two Russians were driven away from the office toward their accommodation. But then the car stopped. The doors opened and FBI agents arrested both Ivanov and Gorshkov. It turned out that the two did know something about the recent computer intrusions the CEO had mentioned. Ivanov—aka subbsta—had been one of the leaders of a group called the Expert Group of Protection against Hackers. Their *modus operandi* was extortion: to hack into American Internet companies and steal credit card details or other data. They would then contact the company demanding payment not to release the data and, in return, would fix the holes that had allowed them access in the first place. If the companies didn't comply, they would then threaten to damage their systems. After this group hit a series of companies, the FBI began to uncover Ivanov's involvement.

Invita was not a real company. The office and its staff were not real, either. They were all part of an elaborate sting to lure Ivanov into the country, after Russian authorities failed to take action. Unbeknownst to the two Russians, the office was filled with undercover FBI agents. The entire interview had been recorded with hidden cameras and microphones. Key-logging software had been installed on the computers so that everything Ivanov typed was preserved. It was in this way that an agent gained the password that afforded him access to a server in Russia and, controversially, to a trove of intelligence on the group's operations. From this, it was clear that their activities were coordinated, extensive, and extremely lucrative. This evidence was suggestive of the enormous cybercrime industry that would soon follow.

For those involved, even in the early days, it had always been about the desire to make a good living. Ivanov was a skilled coder. The sad irony is that he flew all the way to America because he wanted to work in the technology sector. He was willing to take the risk and shed his anonymity for it. He was not born to be a cybercriminal. He wanted a better life.

Appendix 1

List of Participants

AUSTRALIA (AUS)

No.	Alias	Description	Year	Type	Code
	Lachlan	Australian Cybersecurity Professional 1	2013	In Person / 47.40	AUS-CSP-1
	Liam	Former Australian Law Enforcement Agent 1	2013	In Person / 39.13	AUS-(F)LE-1
4	Max, Harrison	Australian Law Enforcement Agent 1, Australian Law Enforcement Agent 2	2013	In Person / Unrecorded Interview	AUS-LE-1; AUS-LE-2
6	Mia, Amelia	Australian Law Enforcement Agent 3, Australian Law Enforcement Agent 4	2013	In Person / Informal Discussion	AUS-LE-3; AUS-LE-4
	Isaac	Australian Cybersecurity Professional 2	2013	In Person / 48.09	AUS-CSP-2
	Mitchell	Australian Cybersecurity Professional 3	2013	Phone / 27.51	AUS-CSP-3

BRAZIL (BRA)

No.	Alias	Description	Year	Type	Code
1	Antonio	Former Brazilian Law Enforcement Agent 1	2014	In Person / 29.11	BRA-(F)LE-1
2	Rodrigo	Brazilian Cybersecurity Professional 1	2014	In Person / 44.47	BRA-CSP-1
3	José	Brazilian Cybersecurity Professional 2	2017	In Person / 58.16	BRA-CSP-2
4	Cris	Brazilian Cybersecurity Professional 3	2017	In Person / Unrecorded Interview	BRA-CSP-3
5	Vitor	Brazilian Law Enforcement Agent 1	2017	Phone / Unrecorded Interview	BRA-LE-1
6	Maurício	Brazilian Cybersecurity Professional 4	2017	In Person / 49.25	BRA-CSP-4
7	Rafael	Brazilian Cybsecurity Professional 5	2017	In Person / 40.23	BRA-CSP-5
8	Ricardo	Brazilian Cybersecurity Professional 6	2017	In Person / Unrecorded Interview	BRA-CSP-6
9	Wanderlei	Brazilian Cybersecurity Professional 7	2017	Phone / 47.28	BRA-CSP-7

CHINA (CHN)

No.	Alias	Description	Year	Type	Code
1	Neil	Expatriate Cybersecurity Professional based in China 1	2014	In Person / 41.49	CHN(E)-CSP
2	Charles	Former Expatriate Cybersecurity Professional based in China 1	2014	In Person / Informal Discussion	CHN(E)-(F) CSP-1
3	Zhou	Chinese Cybersecurity Professional 1	2014	In Person / 49.38	CHN-CSP-1
4	Tony	Chinese Cybersecurity Professional 2	2014	In Person / Informal Discussion	CHN-CSP-2
5,6	Albert, Eric	Expatriate Financial Sector Professional based in China 1, Expatriate Financial Sector Professional Based in China 2	2014	In Person / Informal Discussion	CHN(E)-FSP CHN(E)-FSP
7	Wang	Former Chinese Law Enforcement Agent 1	2014	In Person / 31.28	CHN-(F)LE-1

ᴳERMANY (GER)

ᴺo.	Alias	Description	Year	Type	Code
	Bastian	German Cybersecurity Professional 1	2013	In Person / 44.27	GER-CSP-1

ᴴONG KONG (HK)

ᴺo.	Alias	Description	Year	Type	Code
	Franklin	Expatriate Cybersecurity Professional Based in Hong Kong 1	2012	In Person / 44.14	HK(E)-CSP-1
	Oscar	Former Hong Kong Law Enforcement Agent 1	2012	In Person / Unrecorded Interview	HK-(F)LE-1
	Nathaniel	Hong Kong Cybersecurity Professional 1	2012	In Person / Informal Discussion	HK-CSP-1
₅	Irving, Win	Hong Kong Prosecutor 1, Hong Kong Prosecutor 2	2012	In Person / Informal Discussion	HK-P-1; HK-P-2
	Billy	Former Hong Kong Law Enforcement Agent 2	2012	In Person / Unrecorded Interview	HK-(F)LE-2
	Jackson	Hong Kong Cybersecurity Professional 2	2012	In Person / Informal Discussion	HK-CSP-2

ᴵNDIA (IND)

ᴺo.	Alias	Description	Year	Type	Code
	Rahul	Indian Cybersecurity Professional 1	2015	In Person / 25.15	IND-CSP-1
	Sachin	Indian Cybersecurity Professional 2	2015	In Person / 36.32	IND-CSP-2
	Raj	Former Indian Law Enforcement Agent 1	2015	In Person / 32.17	IND-(F)LE-1

ᴵRELAND (IRE)

ᴺo.	Alias	Description	Year	Type	Code
	Jennifer	Irish Cybersecurity Professional 1	2011	Phone / 16.10	IRE-CSP-1
	Brendan	Irish Cybersecurity Professional 2	2014, 2018	In Person / 28.16 and Written Communication	IRE-CSP-2

LATVIA (LAT)

No.	Alias	Description	Year	Type	Code
1	Ivo	Latvian Law Enforcement Agent 1	2015	In Person / 38.29	LAT-LE-1
2	Kristiana	Latvian Financial Sector Professional 1	2015	In Person / Informal Discussion	LAT-FSP-
3	Artis	Latvian Cybersecurity Professional 1	2015	In Person / 30.05	LAT-CSP-

MALAYSIA (MY)

No.	Alias	Description	Year	Type	Code
1,2	Richard, Issam	Malaysian Law Enforcement Agent 1, Malaysian Law Enforcement Agent 2	2012	In Person / 67.48	MY-LE-1; MY-LE-2
3	Amin	Malaysian Cybersecurity Professional 1	2013	In Person / Unrecorded Interview	MY-CSP-1
4,5	Elisabeth, Firdaus	Malaysian Cybersecurity Professional 2, Malaysian Cybersecurity Professional 3	2013	In Person / Informal Discussion	MY-CSP-2 MY-CSP-3
6	Irfan	Malaysian Cybersecurity Professional 4	2013	In Person / 64.23	MY-CSP-4
7	Haziq	Malaysian Law Enforcement Agent 3	2013	In Person / Unrecorded Interview	MY-LE-3
8	Kelvin	Malaysian Hacker 1	2015	In Person / 48.11	MY-H-1

NETHERLANDS (NLD)

No.	Alias	Description	Year	Type	Code
1,2	Dingeman, Christian	Dutch Law Enforcement Agent 1, Dutch Law Enforcement Agent 2	2014	In Person / 53.34	NLD-LE-1; NLD-LE-2
3	Daniel	Expatriate Cybersecurity Professional Based in the Netherlands 1	2014	In Person / 36.43	NLD(E)-CSP-
4	Rafael	Dutch Cybersecurity Professional 1	2014	In Person / 49.26	NLD-CSP-1

NIGERIA (NIG)

No.	Alias	Description	Year	Type	Code
	Gideon	Nigerian Cybersecurity Professional 1	2016	In Person / Unrecorded Interview	NIG-CSP-1
3,4,5	Samuel, Olawale, Micah, Godwin	Nigerian Law Enforcement Agent 1, Nigerian Law Enforcement Agent 2, Nigerian Law Enforcement Agent 3, Nigerian Law Enforcement Agent 4	2016	In Person / Unrecorded Interview	NIG-LE-1; NIG-LE-2; NIG-LE-3; NIG-LE-4
	Adewale	Nigerian Law Enforcement Agent 5	2016	In Person / Informal Discussion	NIG-LE-5
	Solomon	Nigerian IT Professional 1	2016	In Person / 80.33	NIG-ITP-1
	Idris	Former Nigerian Law Enforcement Agent 1	2016	In Person / Unrecorded Interview	NIG-(F)LE-1
10	Sunday, Kingsley	Nigerian Cybersecurity Professional 2, Nigerian Cybersecurity Professional 3	2016	In Person / 49.36	NIG-CSP-2; NIG-CSP-3
	Joseph	Expatriate Journalist based in Nigeria 1	2016	In Person / Informal Discussion	NIG(E)-J-1
	Ayo	Nigerian Law Enforcement Agent 6	2016	In Person / Unrecorded Interview	NIG-LE-6
	Lawrence	Nigerian Financial Sector Professional 1	2016	In Person / 50.10	NIG-FSP-1
	Chris	Nigerian Financial Sector Professional 2	2016	In Person / 51.54	NIG-FSP-2
	Yinka	Nigerian Cybersecurity Professional 4	2016	In Person / 41.53	NIG-CSP-4

ROMANIA (ROM)

No.	Alias	Description	Year	Type	Code
1	Virgil	Former Romanian Law Enforcement Agent 1	2014	In Person / Unrecorded Interview	ROM-(F)LE-
2	Alexandru	Romanian Law Enforcement Agent 1	2014	In Person / Unrecorded Interview	ROM-LE-1
3	Razvan	Former Romanian Law Enforcement Agent 2	2014	In Person / 43.38	ROM-(F)LE-
4	Maria	Romanian Prosecutor 1	2014	In Person / Unrecorded Interview	ROM-P-1
5	Iulia	Romanian Law Enforcement Agent 2	2014	In Person / Informal Discussion	ROM-LE-2
6	Adrian	Romanian Cybersecurity Professional 1	2015	In Person / Unrecorded Background Interview	ROM-CSP-1
7	Silviu	Romanian Law Enforcement Agent 3	2015	In Person / Unrecorded Background Interview	ROM-LE-3
8,9	Dorian, Ionut	Romanian Academic 1, Romanian Hacker 1	2015	In Person / Informal Discussion	ROM-A-1; ROM-H-1
10,11,12	Sophia, Madalin, Cristian	Romanian Journalist 1, Romanian Prosecutor 2, Former Romanian Law Enforcement Agent 3	2015	In Person / Unrecorded Background Interview	ROM-J-1; ROM-P-2; ROM-(F)LE-
13	Mihai	Romanian Cybersecurity Professional 2	2015	In Person / Informal Discussion	ROM-CSP-2
14,15	Marcel, Gheorghe	Romanian Cybersecurity Professional 3, Romanian Cybersecurity Professional 4	2015	In Person / Unrecorded Background Interview	ROM-CSP-3 ROM-CSP-4
16	Tiberius	Romanian Prosecutor 3	2015	In Person / Informal Discussion	ROM-P-3

RUSSIA (RUS)

No.	Alias	Description	Year	Type	Code
	Anton	Russian Cybersecurity Professional 1	2013	In Person / 33.49	RUS-CSP-1
	Arkady	Russian Cybersecurity Professional 2	2013	In Person / 41.02	RUS-CSP-2
,4	Vladislav, Vasily	Russian Cybersecurity Professional 3, Former Russian Law Enforcement Agent 1	2013	In Person / 92.37	RUS-CSP-3; RUS-(F)LE-1
	Bogdan	Russian Financial Sector Professional 1	2013	In Person / Informal Discussion	RUS-FSP-1
	Artyom	Russian IT Professional 1	2013	In Person / 19.29	RUS-ITP-1
	Mikhail	Russian Cybersecurity Professional 4	2013	In Person / 39.42	RUS-CSP-4
	Valery	Russian Financial Sector Professional 2	2013	In Person / Informal Discussion	RUS-FSP-2
,10	Vladimir, Aleks	Russian Cybersecurity Professional 5, Russian Cybersecurity Professional 6	2014	In Person / Unrecorded Interview	RUS-CSP-5; RUS-CSP-6
	Sasha	Russian Cybersecurity Professional 7	2015	In Person / 54.07	RUS-CSP-7
2	Ilya	Russian Cybersecurity Professional 8	2015	In Person / Unrecorded Interview	RUS-CSP-8
3	Alexei	Russian Cybersecurity Professional 9	2015	In Person / 50.47	RUS-CSP-9
4,15,16	Dmitry, Petro, Fyodor	Russian Financial Sector Professional 3, Russian Cybersecurity Professional 10, Russian Cybersecurity Professional 11	2015	In Person / Unrecorded Interview	RUS-FSP-3; RUS-CSP-10; RUS-CSP-11
7	Anatoly	Russian Cybersecurity Professional 12	2015	In Person / 35.42	RUS-CSP-12
8	Evgeny	Russian Cybersecurity Professional 13	2015	Phone / 21.55	RUS-CSP-13

SINGAPORE (SGP)

No.	Alias	Description	Year	Type	Code
1	Geoff	Expatriate Hacker Based in Singapore 1	2012	In Person / 51.38	SGP(E)-H-1
2	Alvin	Former Singaporean Prosecutor 1	2012	In Person / 31.46	SGP-(F)P-1
3	Raymond	Singaporean Cybersecurity Professional 1	2012	In Person / 28.39	SGP-CSP-1
4	Vincent	Former Singaporean Law Enforcement Agent 1	2012	In Person / Informal Discussion	SGP-(F)LE-
5	Adrian	Former Singaporean Law Enforcement Agent 2	2013	Phone / 20.32	SGP-(F)LE-
6	Andrew	Singaporean Cybersecurity Professional 2	2015	In Person / 41.02	SGP-CSP-2

SOUTH KOREA (KOR)

No.	Alias	Description	Year	Type	Code
1,2	Seojun, Siu	South Korean Law Enforcement Agent 1, South Korean Law Enforcement Agent 2	2016	In Person / 83.49	KOR-LE-1 KOR-LE-2
3	Hyeonu	South Korean Cybersecurity Professional 1	2016	In Person / 47.12	KOR-CSP-
4	Junseo	South Korean Cybersecurity Professional 2	2016	In Person / Unrecorded Interview	KOR-CSP-
5	Jihun	South Korean Cybersecurity Professional 3	2016	In Person / Unrecorded Interview	KOR-CSP-

SWITZERLAND (SWI)

No.	Alias	Description	Year	Type	Code
	Denis	Swiss Cybersecurity Professional 1	2013	In Person / 41.58	SWI-CSP-1
	Victor	Expatriate Cybersecurity Professional based in Switzerland 1	2013	In Person / 44.24	SWI(E)-CSP-1

THAILAND (THA)

No.	Alias	Description	Year	Type	Code
	Jerome	Expatriate Cybersecurity Professional based in Thailand 1	2014	In Person / 39.47	THA(E)-CSP-1
	Kittinan	Thai Cybersecurity Professional 1	2014	In Person / Informal Discussion	THA-CSP-1
4	Sirawit, Adisak	Thai Law Enforcement Agent 1, Thai Law Enforcement Agent 2	2014	In Person / 34.02	THA-LE-1; THA-LE-2

UKRAINE (UKR)

No.	Alias	Description	Year	Type	Code
1	Artem	Former Ukrainian Law Enforcement Agent 1	2015	Written Communication	UKR-(F)LE-
2	Dima	Ukrainian IT Professional 1	2015	In Person / Informal Discussion	UKR-ITP-1
3	Sergey	Ukrainian Law Enforcement Agent 1	2015	In Person / 29.41	UKR-LE-1
4	Keith	Expatriate Cybersecurity Professional based in Ukraine 1	2015	In Person / 68.16	UKR(E)-CSF
5	Maksym	Ukrainian Cybersecurity Professional 1	2015	In Person / Unrecorded Interview	UKR-CSP-1
6	Oleg	Ukrainian Cybersecurity Professional 2	2015	In Person / Unrecorded Interview	UKR-CSP-2
7	Nikita	Former Ukrainian Law Enforcement Agent 2	2015	In Person / 56.22	UKR-(F)LE-2
8	Kirill	Ukrainian Law Enforcement Agent 2	2015	In Person / 20.33	UKR-LE-2
9	Misha	Former Ukrainian Law Enforcement Agent 3	2015	In Person / Unrecorded Interview	UKR-(F)LE-3
10	Igor	Ukrainian Cybersecurity Professional 3	2015	In Person / Unrecorded Interview	UKR-CSP-3

NITED KINGDOM (UK)

o.	Alias	Description	Year	Type	Code
	Nithan	British Cybersecurity Professional 1	2011	In Person / 48.27	UK-CSP-1
	Alex	Former UK Law Enforcement Agent 1	2011	In Person / 44.50	UK-(F)LE-1
	Phillip	Former UK Law Enforcement Agent 2	2011	In Person / 63.03	UK-(F)LE-2
	Tom	UK Law Enforcement Agent 1	2011	Phone / 54.15	UK-LE-1
	Amber	Expatriate IT professional based in the UK 1	2011	In Person / Informal Discussion	UK(E)-ITP-1
	Edward	UK Prosecutor 1	2011	In Person / Informal Discussion	UK-P-1
	Jake	British Cybersecurity Professional 2	2013	Phone / 26.56	UK-CSP-2
9,10	Frank, Luke, Daisy	British Cybersecurity Professional 3, Expatriate Cybersecurity Professional based in the UK 1, Expatriate Cybersecurity Professional based in the UK 2	2013	In Person / Informal Discussion	UK-CSP-3; UK(E)-CSP-1; UK(E)-CSP-2
	Nigel	British Financial Sector Professional 1	2014	In Person / 43.50	UK-FSP-1
₂	Elenor	Former UK Law Enforcement Agent 3	2014	In Person / 30.45	UK-(F)LE-3
₃	Peter	Former UK Law Enforcement Agent 4	2014	In Person / 50.53	UK-(F)LE-4
₄	Craig	British Cybersecurity Professional 4	2014	In Person / 73.31	UK-CSP-4
₅	Owen	Former UK Law Enforcement Agent 5	2015	In Person / 84.22	UK-(F)LE-5
₆	Jason	Former UK Law Enforcement Agent 6	2015	In Person / Informal Discussion	UK-(F)LE-6
₇	Trevor	UK Law Enforcement Agent 2	2015	In Person / 29.57	UK-LE-2
₈	Paul	British Cybersecurity Professional 5	2015	In Person / 40.11	UK-CSP-5
₉	Colin	UK Law Enforcement Agent 3	2015	In Person / 54.19	UK-LE-3
o	Connor	British Cybersecurity Professional 6	2015	In Person / 35.56	UK-CSP-6
1	Angus	British Financial Sector Professional 2	2015	In Person / Informal Discussion	UK-FSP-2
2	Jay	UK Prosecutor 2	2015	In Person / Informal Discussion	UK-P-2
3	Cameron	British Financial Sector Professional 3	2015	Phone / Informal Discussion	UK-FSP-3
4	Spencer	British Cybersecurity Professional 7	2016	Phone / 51.54	UK-CSP-7

UNITED STATES (US)

No.	Alias	Description	Year	Type	Code
1	Olivia	American Cybersecurity Professional 1	2012	In Person / 34.39	US-CSP-1
2	Ethan	Former US Law Enforcement Agent 1	2012	Phone / 35.26	US-(F)LE-1
3	William	Former US Law Enforcement Agent 2	2012	In Person / 36.08	US-(F)LE-2
4	Ryan	American Cybersecurity Professional 2	2012	In Person / 54.59	US-CSP-2
5	Michael	Former US Law Enforcement Agent 3	2012	In Person / 37.33	US-(F)LE-3
6	Matthew	Former US Law Enforcement Agent 4	2012	In Person / 41.07	US-(F)LE-4
7	Jacob	American Cybersecurity Professional 3	2012	In Person / 62.29	US-CSP-3
8	Aiden	Former US Prosecutor 1	2012	In Person / 26.53	US-(F)P-1;
9	Nathan	Former US Law Enforcement Agent 5	2012	In Person / 40.42	US-(F)LE-5
10	Caleb	Former US Prosecutor 2	2012	In Person / 20.15	US-(F)P-2;
11	Samantha	Former US Prosecutor 3	2012	In Person / 9.48	US-(F)P-3;
12	Adam	Former US Law Enforcement Agent 6	2012	In Person / 26.58	US-(F)LE-6
13	Jordan	American Cybersecurity Professional 4	2012	In Person / 60.29	US-CSP-4
14	Benjamin	American Cybersecurity Professional 5	2012	In Person / 54.40	US-CSP-5
15	Todd	American Cybersecurity Professional 6	2012– 2017	In Person / 58.28 and Written Communication	US-CSP-6
16	Gavin	American Cybersecurity Professional 7	2012	In Person / 34.57	US-CSP-7
17	Logan	American Cybersecurity Professional 8	2012	In Person / 45.58	US-CSP-8

	Alias	Description	Year	Type	Code
	Anne	US Prosecutor 1	2012	In Person / Informal Discussion	US-P-1
	Lucas	US Law Enforcement Agent 1	2012	In Person / Unrecorded Interview	US-LE-1
	Eugene	American Cybersecurity Professional 9	2012	In Person / 24.05	US-CSP-9
	Alexander	Former US Law Enforcement Agent 7	2012	In Person / 55.5	US-(F)LE-7
	John	Expatriate Cybersecurity Professional based in America 1	2012	Phone / 16.37	US(E)-CSP-1
	Dylan	American Cybersecurity Professional 10	2013	Phone / 32.59	US-CSP-10
	Jed	US Prosecutor 2	2013	Phone / 40.17	US-P-2;
	Carter	US Law Enforcement Agent 2	2013	Phone / 53.34	US-LE-2
,27	Christopher, Wyatt	American Cybersecurity Professional 11, American Cybersecurity Professional 12	2013	Phone / 46.41	US-CSP-11; US-CSP-12
	Joshua	American Cybersecurity Professional 13	2013	Phone / 28.57	US-CSP-13
	Abbie	Former US Prosecutor 4	2013	In Person / 53.41	US-(F)P-4;
	Ashley	American Cybersecurity Professional 14	2013	In Person / 57.24	US-CSP-14
	Andy	American Journalist 1	2013	In Person / Informal Discussion	US-J-1
	Jack	US Law Enforcement Agent 3	2013	In Person / 50.28	US-LE-3
,34	Rick, Simon	US Law Enforcement Agent 4, US Law Enforcement Agent 5	2013	In Person / Informal Discussion	US-LE-4; US-LE-5
	Landon	Former US Law Enforcement Agent 8	2014	In Person / 93.30	US-(F)LE-8
	Elijah	Former US Prosecutor 5	2014	In Person / 37.20	US-(F)P-5;
,38	Danielle, Leo	US Law Enforcement Agent 6, US Law Enforcement Agent 7	2014	In Person / 38.29	US-LE-6; US-LE-7

No.	Alias	Description	Year	Type	Code
39	Ryder	US Law Enforcement Agent 8	2015	Phone / Unrecorded Interview	US-LE-8
40	Clark	US Law Enforcement Agent 9	2016	Phone / 31.07	US-LE-9
41	Terry	US Law Enforcement Agent 10	2017	Phone / Unrecorded Interview	US-LE-10

VIETNAM (VN)

No.	Alias	Description	Year	Type	Code
1	Ahn	Vietnamese Hacker 1	2017	In Person / 58.13	VN-H-1
2	Minh	Vietnamese Cybersecurity Professional 1	2017	In Person / 24.25	VN-CSP
3,4	Phuc, Thanh	Vietnamese Cybersecurity Profession 2, Vietnamese Cybersecurity Professional 3	2017	In Person / Unrecorded Interview	VN-CSP VN-CSP
5	Linh	Vietnamese Law Enforcement Agent 1	2017	In Person / Unrecorded Interview	VN-LE-1
6,7,8	Hoang, Dinh, Nam	Vietnamese Cybersecurity Professional 4, Vietnamese Cybersecurity Professional 5, Vietnamese Cybersecurity Professional 6	2017	In Person / Unrecorded Interview	VN-CSP VN-CSP VN-CSP
9	Ngan	Vietnamese Cybersecurity Professional 7	2017	In Person / Unrecorded Interview	VN-CSP
10,11	Quang, Thien	Vietnamese Law Enforcement Agent 2, Vietnamese Law Enforcement Agent 3	2017	In Person / Unrecorded Interview	VN-LE-2 VN-LE-3
12,13	Truong, Van	Vietnamese Cybersecurity Professional 8, Vietnamese Cybersecurity Professional 9	2017	In Person / Unrecorded Interview	VN-CSP VN-CSP

REDACTED OR UNDISCLOSED (INT / UDL / RDT)

No.	Alias	Description	Year	Type	Code
1	Neville	International Organization Officer 1	2013	Phone / 20.51	INT-OO-1
2	Florian	International Organization Officer 2	2013	In Person / 34.23	INT-OO-2
3	Timothy	International Organization Officer 3	2013	In Person / 16.33	INT-OO-3
4	Rikard	Cybersecurity Professional (Undisclosed Location / Nationality) 1	2013	Written Communication	UDL-CSP-1
5	Patrice	International Organization Officer 4	2015	In Person / Unrecorded Interview	INT-OO-4
6	Slavoj	International Organization Officer 5	2015	In Person / 59.20	INT-OO-5
7	Vincent	International Organization Officer 6	2015	In Person / 34.40	INT-OO-6
8,9	Casey, Claude	Redacted 1, Redacted 2	2016	Phone / Background Interview	RDT-RDT-1; RDT-RDT-2
10,11	Sebastian, Tomas	Redacted 3, Redacted 4	2016	In Person / Unrecorded Background Interview	RDT-RDT-3; RDT-RDT-4
12	George	Redacted 5	2016	Phone / Background Interview	RDT-RDT-5

FORMER CYBERCRIMINALS (NA / EE / MENA / SEA / WE)

No.	Alias	Description	Year	Type	Code
1	Jeremy	Former Western European Hacker 1	NA	In Person / 38.56	WE-(F)H-1
2	Sean	Former Western European Cybercriminal 1	NA	In Person / 73.01 and Written Communication	WE-(F)CC-
3	Dave	Former Expatriate Cybercriminal Based in Southeast Asia 1	NA	In Person / 68.22	SEA(E)-(F) CC-1
4	Noah	Former North American Cybercriminal 1	NA	In Person / 37.25	NA-(F)CC-1
5	Ahmed	Former Southeast Asian Cybercriminal 1	NA	Phone / Unrecorded Interview	SEA-(F)CC-
6	Casper	Former Western European Cybercriminal 2	NA	In Person / 43.56	WE-(F)CC-
7	Scott	Former North American Cybercriminal 2	NA	Written Communication	NA-(F)CC-2
8	Claudiu	Former Eastern European Cybercriminal 1	NA	In Person / Informal Discussion	EE-(F)CC-1
9	Lance	Former North American Cybercriminal 3	NA	Phone / 50.47	NA-(F)CC-3
10	Don	Former North American Cybercriminal 4	NA	Written Communication	NA-(F)CC-4
11	Andrey	Former Eastern European Cybercriminal 2	NA	Written Communication	EE-(F)CC-2
12	Jim	Former North American Cybercriminal 5	NA	Written Communication	NA-(F)CC-5
13	Ivan	Former Eastern European Cybercriminal 3	NA	Written Communication	EE-(F)CC-3
14	Mohammed	Former Middle East and North African Cybercriminal 1	NA	Written Communication	MENA-(F) CC-1
15	Tan	Former Southeast Asian Cybercriminal 2	NA	Written Communication	SEA-(F)CC-
16	Thiago	Former South American Cybercriminal 1	NA	In Person / Unrecorded Interview	SA-(F)CC-1
17	Theodore	Former Cybercriminal (Undisclosed Location / Nationality) 1	NA	Written Communication / Informal Discussion	UDL-(F)CC
18	Jonas	Former Western European Cybercriminal 3	NA	Phone / 64.19	WE-(F)CC-3
19	Leonid	Former Eastern European Cybercriminal 4	NA	Written Communication	EE-(F)CC-4
20	Konstantin	Former Eastern European Cybercriminal 5	NA	Written Communication / Informal Discussion	EE-(F)CC-5

Appendix 2

Data and Methods

This appendix outlines the data and methods used in this study. The first section addresses the research style adopted for the project. The second section describes data sources and methods of data collection. The third section discusses the scope of the study, including aspects of sampling and limitations therein. The final section addresses important ethical considerations.

Research Style

This study makes use of qualitative methodologies, in part because the lack of credible cybercrime statistics limits conventional quantitative work on the subject.[1] Some scholars have found creative ways to carry out quantitative studies, which often require coding cybercriminal communications from law enforcement data or data scraped from forums. But for the present study, a qualitative approach is more appropriate. Cybercrime is still a poorly understood phenomenon, with many knowledge gaps. A qualitative study can provide a broad understanding of the industry of cybercrime and how cooperation functions within it. My focus here has been on mechanisms cybercriminals have developed to enhance cooperation and establish a functioning industry. The study of mechanisms is often well served by qualitative work, while quantitative approaches are often better suited to determining correlations.

As flagged in the Introduction, the core approach of this book is *exploratory*. It cannot be easily labeled using common academic distinctions such as empirical versus theoretical, deductive versus inductive, or explanatory versus interpretivist. From the beginning of the project, I have engaged in this work as an exploration, but along the way, input has come from various academic quarters encouraging me to fit my research into one of two boxes. Box one could be summarized as focused on hypothesis testing. It draws on existing theory, and is centrally interested in what the specific case of cybercrime might tell us about that theory. It starts with hypotheses and relies on deductive logic to test them. While this approach is most familiar to quantitative researchers, it can be applied successfully to qualitative work.[2] Box two is a more anthropological approach, ethnographic and strongly empirical. It begins with the fieldwork and data, and then uses inductive logic to develop theory. But often the intent is to focus tightly on a particular group or case, rather than to generalize much more broadly.[3]

While at different points, I did attempt to fit my research into one or the other of these boxes, it ultimately seemed to be a futile exercise. In terms of box one, the main challenge was developing testable hypotheses. The scope of this project is wide and, despite my years of fieldwork, the data remain largely suggestive. Although 238 interview participants constitute a substantial qualitative sample, they are but a tiny fraction of the cybercriminals, law enforcement agents, and technology sector employees engaged in this field. While I reached *saturation* and began, toward the end of the study, to hear subjects repeat similar points, further work may unearth new findings. Certainly there was wide variation in the sample, which is not a surprise given the levels of specialization and geographical dispersion evident in cybercrime. My attempts to craft specific hypotheses often ran up against data that did not speak with one voice. While hypothesis testing can be carried out with qualitative data, this is much more readily done with a narrower research agenda—as in focused examinations of case studies, in which variation can be limited, data contained, and hypotheses stated in a more specific way.[4] The scale of this project was simply too large.

Nonetheless, the fact that box one did not apply did not mean that box two was more appropriate. Ethnography conventionally employs inductive reasoning, assembling insights from a rich description of a culture to arrive at theoretical suppositions. This book employs a different approach, beginning with both key theory and research questions, to be investigated through the collected data. This study has its roots in existing theory on cooperation and governance, particularly as it relates to crime and extra-legal groups.[5] From the beginning, I focused on one question: how do cybercriminals successfully cooperate when dealing with anonymous criminal partners? One would expect trust to be difficult to attain in such circumstances, yet a large cybercriminal industry has evolved. While I don't employ hypothesis testing, I have had a clear theoretical focus from the outset and, throughout the project, I have undertaken fieldwork with this central question in mind.

Of secondary importance, the methods employed in this study also differ from conventional ethnography, especially in that I did not embed myself within a specific community to observe its behaviors and practices. With the development of online communities has come the advent of online ethnography, which allows researchers to engage virtually with these groups from the comfort of their own environs. I did not engage in this approach, partly because there are already publicly available data from archived forums and other meeting places to paint a picture of their workings. But there are also significant ethical issues raised by embedding oneself in these groups, tied to notifying one's role as a researcher, and whether and when informed consent needs to be attained. In addition, there are barriers to entry in joining such groups, which might require evidence of past criminality, and such tests become increasingly pronounced as one attempts to communicate with more elite and secretive actors. This represents a line academics cannot cross, unlike undercover agents from government and even the private sector who have their own methods of producing such evidence. Thus, ironically, one of the very topics of this study—mechanisms to weed out non-criminals—reduces opportunities to study these mechanisms. Finally, and most importantly, even if one can make contact with participants and interview them online, the interactions are effectively with their online personae rather than their offline selves. These can be very different people with very different perspectives. This is coupled with the dangers of interviewing active cybercriminals who may have an incentive to lie or hide aspects of the truth.

Instead of taking a virtual approach, this study is built around conventional offline fieldwork. But this still does not fit within the ethnographic model, which traditionally is focused on participant observation. For the present study, the fieldwork was largely composed of meetings where interviews took place. While some observation of interview subjects occurred during these encounters, and broader observations of the countries and cities that I visited were extremely beneficial for understanding context, the interviews themselves were the primary data source. The ethnographic approach is often focused on the depth of information that can be attained about a specific group. While this can be done comparatively, the time and resources required often limit the number of distinct groups that can be included.[6] The focus of this study is on breadth rather than depth. It is effectively a study of variation. A core part of this was the need to piece together and comprehend the complexity of the global cybercrime industry, which exists in many countries and therefore leads to inherent diversity.

The approach here takes some elements from the theoretical, deductive, explanatory camp and other elements from the empirical, inductive, interpretivist camp—but it subscribes to neither of them. It is led by theory and a specific research question, but does not engage in hypothesis testing. It features extensive data collection, but is not an ethnography of a group. It has a specific interest in the case of cybercrime, but also asks what this case can tell us about existing theory. It cannot be fitted neatly into either category because it is exploratory in nature. It is an early voyage into largely uncharted waters. Once more is known about cybercrime, studies that fit neatly into these categories could be more easily undertaken. But at this stage, the focus is on better understanding the topic and effectively drawing a map of this new world.

Data Sources

This book draws on four main forms of data. It makes use of legal documents, such as indictments. It draws on various communications among cybercriminals, such as forum screenshots and archives. It incorporates relevant open-source material, such as media articles on cybercrime and interviews with cybercriminals. Most importantly, the core data source of the study is 238 interviews carried out from 2011 to 2017 with law enforcement agents, members of the technology sector, former cybercriminals, and others with detailed knowledge of the subject.

The legal documents are largely from the public sphere and often publicly accessible. For instance, US indictments and other documents associated with cybercrime cases are often published online by the Department of Justice. Some of those which have not been published by the government have been made available by journalists and others. In the UK, similar documents are not as easily available. The closest equivalent is prosecutorial opening notes, which present similar information to indictments. These are often not published in the same way, but can be obtained by purchasing court transcripts or from prosecutors themselves. I also obtained some material from officials and agents that was not in the public domain or accessible to the general public, but which provided important detail on certain cases.

US and UK documents formed the bulk of records analyzed. Both countries are active in cyber law enforcement. In particular, the US engages with major international cases involving offenders from multiple jurisdictions. Unfortunately, it was not possible within the scope of this project to access such legal records across many jurisdictions included in this study. It would have involved an extensive investment of time and resources to overcome the numerous language barriers and bureaucratic hurdles.

Another valuable data source consisted of screenshots, logs, and archives of cybercriminal communications. These allowed analysis of cybercriminals speaking to each other in the wild. As mentioned above, access to active forums was not involved, as many screenshots and archives of cybercriminal forums are available online. Some such forums are now defunct, while others have suffered leaks but continue to exist. The web archive known as the Wayback Machine also offers snapshots of the historical Internet, giving some idea of forums that were not otherwise well archived. Screenshots can also be found in some of the legal documents mentioned above. Various participants also furnished me with forum archives from the past, or with chat logs.

There are also numerous open-source materials available that make for useful data. These include published interviews of active and former cybercriminals, and biographical and autobiographical accounts in books and articles. Media articles tracking cybercriminal cases, organizations, and endeavors continue to accumulate. Some of the best of this work comes from writers embedded in cybercriminal communities or who have strong relationships with active sources.

Finally, serving as the fundamental data source for this project are the semi-structured interviews I carried out, starting from 2011, with 238 participants. Interviews are better suited than more impersonal surveys to investigating sensitive topics.[7] Given the difficulties of accessing participants, it is also important to extract information that is as rich as possible from those who do participate. I interviewed a range of subjects with a strong knowledge of cybercrime, coming from a variety of backgrounds. But most participants were former cybercriminals, current and former law enforcement agents, or technology sector employees. Some people crossed these category boundaries, such as former cybercriminals or former law enforcement agents who went on to work in the private sector. The next section covers how participants were selected for interview, how they were approached, and sampling issues therein. A list of all participants is found in

Appendix 1. In all, 20 admitted or known former cybercriminals participated in this study.

All the field visits in this study followed the same model. They were short,
ranging from a few days to a few weeks, and scheduled well in advance to
include as many interviews as possible. Many interviews were arranged before my arrival, while a smaller number were arranged on the ground,
sometimes with the help of other interview subjects. The purpose of these
trips was to gather as much data as possible in the form of interviews in
each location, rather than to spend considerable time in a location and build
a thick ethnographic description of a specific community. Generally two interviews were scheduled each day. Surprisingly, it was only on a handful of
occasions that an interview subject failed to show for a planned meeting.

I met with most participants face-to-face. Some could not meet in person
due to scheduling or geography, or preferred not to due to privacy or other
concerns. In these cases, interviews were conducted by phone (or online
equivalent) or via electronic communication such as email or chat. Most
interviews were somewhat formal, following a protocol of core questions,
but often the conversation strayed into other areas according to the knowledge and interests of the participant. In many instances, these interviews
were recorded. When participants preferred not to be recorded, I took notes
and, after the meeting, spent time fleshing them out. I also recorded my general observations about the locations I was in, capturing contextual details,
such as economic or cultural factors, that might be relevant to the local
cybercrime situation.

Other researchers have noted that recording interviews can lead to eva-
sive answers.[8] Primarily for this reason, I offered a choice at the beginning
of interviews, which proved an effective strategy. Presumably those who
chose not to be recorded were more forthcoming than they would have
been if recording had taken place. At times participant choices appeared to
be influenced by culture or norms. For instance, in Hong Kong, no local
citizen wished to be recorded. By contrast, in many other jurisdictions,
I was somewhat surprised by the high proportion who were willing to be
recorded, given the sensitivity of issues involved. Some even preferred to be
recorded, whether to make matters easier for me as a researcher or to ensure that their comments were captured verbatim. Occasionally I was asked
to turn off the recorder so that something could be divulged that the participant did not want on tape. A high proportion of former cybercriminals
were happy to be recorded, despite providing perhaps the most sensitive
information. This might reflect the open nature of cyber actors, and uto-
pian online ideals of unbounded information sharing. Perhaps it was for

other reasons. Overall, interviews often proceeded more fluidly when they were recorded; as the conversation flowed, the recorder was scarcely noticed.[9] Note-taking was often an obstruction that slowed discussions down.

A smaller number of participants opted for informal discussions, often happy to assist yet preferring a further barrier between them and the official research output. Always focused on the comfort of subjects, I acquiesced to such requests. In fact, I usually offered the informal discussion option up front to those who had agreed to an interview, but where other complications were apparent. For instance, in some jurisdictions, legal professionals don't publicly state their views on particular matters. While I took notes in many of these conversations, I used the information only for background. Accordingly, I do not directly cite these informal subjects as sources of particular pieces of information. Appendix 1 clarifies who participated in this way.

Scope, Sampling, and Limitations

One of the main challenges in undertaking this study was defining its scope. Cybercrime is a vast subject area. The internal boundaries between the different groups and activities that fall under this banner have not been clearly demarcated. This made it difficult to choose a case-study-based approach, as there was not much evidence to identify and then justify the choice of specific examples. One could have chosen certain forums or countries as cases, but it was not clear how these fit into the broader economy of cybercrime. In fact, much of this project's fieldwork was devoted to gaining a more detailed and nuanced understanding of cybercrime than could be gleaned from existing literature. It was essential to have this context before addressing the research questions relating to cybercriminal cooperation and industrialization. The broader benefit may be that it contributes to identifying what groups, countries, or other entities may serve as suitable case studies in future projects.

My thinking on the subject of case studies evolved as my understanding of cybercrime increased. In the early days, I believed that case studies were not possible with regard to cybercrime, because it is such a transnational phenomenon with near-invisible actors meeting online. But I have come around to the view that fruitful case studies could be carried out on specific cybercriminal groupings, by drawing together data relating to the group in question and seeking to interview those with specific knowledge of it. While the transnational nature of these groups might make data collection more challenging, it remains possible. When more than one group is working together, one would also need to determine where one enterprise ends and the other begins. It might also be rewarding to engage in case studies of countries or other geographical units. There appears to be significant variation in styles of cybercrime by region, country, and perhaps even town. The research community could benefit from gaining a better understanding of the specific flavor of cybercrime found in such local contexts.

This case study approach is not adopted here. This is partly because I identified suitable cases only by having completed this project in the first place. But the approach in the book is also intentionally broad by design. It seeks to survey profit-driven cybercrime as a whole, and to answer the key research question of how cybercriminals have collectively established a functioning industry. As part of this, it brings in theoretical assumptions to be applied to the topic of cybercrime. This theory cuts across many aspects of cybercrime, and humanity as a whole. Thus, it is the variation (or lack thereof) among manifestations of cybercrime that is of central interest. And rather than being limited to one or two cases of cybercrime, a much broader approach allows significantly more variation. This offers a more nuanced investigation of how cooperation works and fits within the broader world of cybercrime.

GEOGRAPHICAL SAMPLING

Sampling for this study involved two sets of decisions. First, as I couldn't carry out fieldwork in every country in the world, choices about geographical focus had to be made. Second, there were sampling questions regarding how interview subjects were chosen. To begin with the question of geography first, this aspect of sampling evolved over the course of the study, largely due to knowledge developed along the way. The first phase of this project began in 2011 with a small study of cybercrime in the United Kingdom, which constituted my masters dissertation and effectively served as a pilot for this current work. One of those early participants offered a view that was not widely challenged by other subjects: that cybercrime was a universal phenomenon that didn't differ significantly between countries. In research following this pilot, this became an early supposition that I tested, as I continued to investigate the central research question and to gather background information.

Phase 2 effectively involved visits to countries that were chosen somewhat at random. This might be viewed as a form of accidental, opportunistic, or convenience sampling.[10] These were often places that I was passing through or visiting for other purposes, but where I also took some time to carry out fieldwork. Given the supposition that cybercrime was the same in each country, the specific choice should not matter. The first country visited following the UK was Singapore. Immediately, the idea that cybercrime was the same everywhere was challenged, because there appeared to be very little evidence that local cybercrime existed there beyond a small number of very minor cases. This is perhaps unsurprising. Singapore has low rates of crime in general likely owing partly to economics, but also to its strict laws and punishments, and a culture of obedience that emerged from this. Other countries where I conducted fieldwork during this phase included Australia, Hong Kong, Malaysia, Switzerland, Thailand, and some other parts of Europe that are redacted for the protection of certain participants. During this time, I also carried out work in the United States, but this relates more closely to Phase 3, which will be discussed below.

Visiting these countries was essential to understanding the variation involved in cybercrime. Because many of these countries were not cybercrime hotspots, strong positive findings relating to the research question were often limited. But this was not necessarily undesirable, as it contributed to the overall strength of the study in several ways. First, the data collected here served to improve my understanding of cybercrime. Even if local cybercrime situations were not severe, there were nonetheless global experts on cybercrime located in these countries. These countries also provided important variation in the sample, as those cases where cybercrime was not prevalent could be contrasted with those jurisdictions where cybercrime was a major challenge. Second, through expert opinion, research in these locations helped identify those cybercrime hotspots that were essential for me to visit as part of my study (to be discussed below). Third, the very lack of strong positive findings in these visits helped to confirm that expert opinion and the literature had not missed some key cybercrime hotspots. Finally, there were some surprises in these locations that made them worthwhile research ventures. In certain countries I found high-value interview subjects, such as former cybercriminals who happened to be residing in these jurisdictions but were not necessarily from there in the first place. In other instances I made unexpected discoveries, such as the physical presence of a significant number of Nigerian scammers in Malaysia. This was a phenomenon that I was then able to track throughout other countries.

The third and final phase of the project involved a concerted effort to visit cybercrime hotspots. Expert opinion from earlier phases had identified certain locations as having high concentrations of cybercriminals. These locations included Russia (two visits), Romania (two visits), China, Ukraine, Nigeria, and Brazil. While some other hotspots had also been mentioned in interviews, time and resources did not allow for visiting all of them. For instance, particular former Soviet Bloc countries were linked by some to large-scale cybercrime. Russia, Ukraine, and Romania were chosen because they came up most often as key hubs in Eastern Europe. Such views were also supported by known cases and public source material. In most of these locations, the expert opinion were borne out by data I obtained. The only exception was China, which many in the cybersecurity field focus on, given the large number of cyberattacks associated with it. But one of the key discoveries there was that the cybercriminal sphere is relatively immature. The main activities appeared to relate instead to cyber-espionage. Brazil justified its reputation as a hotspot by virtue of the large scale and intensity of the problem there, even if its impact is not of major local or international concern.

There were also countries I visited for other specific reasons, such as to meet certain people of interest. For instance, both the United States and the Netherlands have their share of cybercriminals, but they are also leading hubs for law enforcement agencies and security companies. Other countries I visited for specific thematic reasons based on tips and suggestions from earlier interviews and meetings. In Latvia, for example, I tried to examine connections between cybercrime and money laundering. In India, I looked into purported links between cybercrime and Indian call centers. In neither case did I find strong positive results (though they may appear with further research), but the trips turned out to be useful in other ways.

I also had to make strategic choices within countries I visited. I focused on cities and towns that were suspected hubs of cybercrime. Often this meant going to a capital or major city, such as Moscow, where law enforcement agents and technology companies were also located. I also targeted more regional cybercrime hubs based on past interviews and background research. In Romania, for example, I visited the infamous online fraud center of Râmnicu Vâlcea, as well as Bucharest (and Alexandria). In Ukraine, along with carrying out interviews in Kiev, I made sure to visit Odessa, which plays an important role in the history of cybercrime. But budget, time, and other practicalities also limited my going to further locations. In Nigeria, I based myself in Lagos but was not able to visit other hubs. In Ukraine, I could not visit Donetsk due to the ongoing conflict in the east, but felt that sufficient data were gained in Kiev and Odessa alone.

Though largely chronological, these phases should reflect shifts in research strategy, rather than strict delineations in time. For instance, I visited the United States while still undertaking Phase 2 research in places like Thailand. Being based in the United Kingdom, I also continued to carry out

UK-related research throughout all phases. Over the years, from the comfort of my office, I conducted interviews by phone and through correspondence with participants based in a range of locations.

PURPOSIVE SAMPLING

The other key aspect of sampling for this study relates to the participants themselves. This project made use of both purposive and snowball sampling. Having no prior contacts in the area at the beginning of the project, it began with purposive sampling.[11] In fact, this form of sampling remained the key approach even later in the study when some snowballing was possible (this was due to some key weaknesses in the latter style with regard to this study, which will be explained in the subsection below). From the outset, I reached out to people from a range of backgrounds with a strong knowledge of cybercrime. Among those I interviewed were former cybercriminals, hackers, law enforcement agents, lawyers, government officials, international civil servants, NGO employees, journalists, private sector cyber investigators and cyber intelligence practitioners, security company employees, malware experts, banking and financial institution employees, and engineers.

Early on, I identified three clear categories—former cybercriminals, law enforcement agents (current and former), and technology sector professionals with a focus on cybercriminals—as most relevant for my study because these groups have the strongest connections to cybercrime. Yet, having learned that some meetings can be unexpectedly useful, I also continued conducting some interviews outside these core groups with individuals I suspected might have a deep knowledge of the area. As a general rule, those with direct knowledge of cybercrime were most valuable in closely answering my research question. Former cybercriminals obviously have detailed understandings of how cybercriminals operate. I focused on former rather than active cybercriminals because they have less reason to lie about their criminal behavior, as it is in the past. Other arguments in their favor are the greater ease of locating them, the lesser risks of danger to the researcher, and the lower possibility of getting caught up in an ongoing law enforcement investigation.

Some clarification is important here. It is not the case that I chose not to engage with active offenders at all. In one case, such an opportunity presented itself by way of an introduction from an existing contact, and I took it (though I nonetheless label this person as a "former cybercriminal" in Appendix 1 to camouflage and therefore better protect him). I also have strong suspicions that in other instances I was actually interviewing active offenders, who simply did not admit this fact. Usually members of the technology sector, these individuals often spoke in generalities or described criminal activities of others they knew—of which they seemed to have very detailed knowledge. It would be accurate to say, however, that I pursued former cybercriminals more aggressively than I did active offenders, and the inquiries I made to the latter usually went unanswered. In a few cases, participants and others offered to make introductions to active offenders, but these interviews often did not materialize. In the one case where the introduction was successful, the individual was extremely cagey and did not engage in detailed discussions. These unsuccessful experiences pursuing active offenders helped shape my approach. Ultimately, I believed that strongly pursuing the "former" group offered the most value for the limited time I could invest. I also had fewer doubts concerning the authenticity of their claims, as they had less fear of arrest than active offenders and could speak more openly, providing more detailed and reliable data.

This last point is worthy of further discussion, given that there is a strong social science tradition of interviewing active offenders, some of them violent. Classics like William Foote Whyte's *Street Corner Society* pioneered the use of active offenders as study participants.[12] Other exponents of the approach followed.[13] Some of these studies illustrate certain challenges involved, but the practice has become generally accepted in researching criminal populations. Why might the case of cybercrime challenge this tradition? The key difference is that cybercriminals operate in much more secretive ways than conventional criminals, because shielding their true identities is often an essential part of doing business. Their crimes are also virtually invisible, making them more difficult to locate in the physical world and, when they are found, less likely to be fully forthcoming about their activities. The higher the level of business-minded offender, the more likely they will operate in a more guarded way, which includes not speaking openly (or at all) with researchers. Even if active cybercriminals were contacted in online spaces, as noted above, questions remain about both ethical access to certain elite groupings and verifying exactly who or what version (persona) of that person is being interviewed.

A separate distinction between traditional criminological research and cybercrime studies is that the risks to the researcher are not the same. Violence might be a heightened concern with some conventional subjects, but with cybercriminals the real difference is that, once you are in their world, you cannot leave. Urban ethnographers can depart dangerous neighborhoods confident that physical threats will not follow them. But cybercrime researchers could stir up virtual threats capable of following them wherever they go in the world. In light of this, extra caution might be taken when considering engaging widely with active cybercriminals. This lack of conventional territoriality also makes it harder to know if certain individuals are under police investigation. Interviewing a criminal under investigation can have adverse effects for both the researcher and the participant, such as a demand for the release of confidential data that has been collected.

As for the latter two participant categories, I chose to speak to law enforcement agents because they also have strong knowledge of cybercrime, having spent much time investigating it. The question of why the technology sector provides a good source of participants requires further explanation. Given the challenges of cyber law enforcement, hampered by both technical requirements for investigation and a transnational threat that can make arrests more difficult, a number of private sector companies and other organizations have evolved in part to fill the void. Some are entities created for the sole purpose of gathering intelligence on cybercriminals or carrying out forensic investigations, while others are units that large companies have developed or acquired to carry out these functions. Some organizations protect themselves with large in-house teams. Other companies are serviced by external security teams. A number of these security companies also partner with law enforcement agencies and assist them in their investigations. In some instances and contexts, they can take on major responsibilities. As a result, those with law-enforcement-like experience in the private sector also became a valuable group within the project's sample.

Most participants were located through online searches. In the early days of the project, I often identified law enforcement agencies and companies that I believed would be relevant and then made contact through their publicly listed channels. In some cases this was successful, with very helpful public-relations staff connecting me with appropriate participants. But in many cases, my inquiry either failed to elicit a response or the organization declined to participate. In some cases where an interview was arranged, the PR representative appeared to expect the organization to benefit in some specific way. Such quid pro quos might be acceptable in some journalistic quarters, but cannot sit comfortably with academic research.

As a result, I shifted to attempting to contact individuals directly. Extensive personal information is now available online which can be used to find and profile potential interview subjects. For instance, many people provide a wealth of information on LinkedIn (perhaps too much in personal security terms), even down to the specific responsibilities they carried out within a specific period and within a specific unit in their organization. This site also makes suggestions of other people who have similar profiles or are connected to a profile one is viewing. Over time, I developed a checklist of features that often suggested whether a subject might be suitable. For law enforcement this meant having experience investigating cybercrime. For the technology sector, it usually meant having experience in cyber intelligence or forensic investigation.

For former cybercriminals, one can use public case records and media reports to identify potential participants outside prison. Beyond this, some former offenders openly include their criminal backgrounds on their social media profiles or elsewhere. For those who are not publicly known, other signals can suggest possible connections to cybercrime. For instance, if someone came to cybercrime from a hacking background, he might list an involvement in "security" or the "security industry" at a very young age. Others might note past hacking exploits. Anyone listing a title of *penetration tester* or *ethical hacker* is signaling membership in the legitimate profession perhaps most associated with hacking. Some of these people, hired by organizations to test their security, gained their skills through formal training and certifications. Others taught themselves to hack. Over the course of the project I found that some in this latter category had prior experience in cybercrime. This often made them useful participants. Of course, there were also very many who had not been involved in cybercrime at all. But even some of these pentesters were familiar with that world and knew others who had been involved in it.

Contact with all three central groups was made primarily through email. An introductory email described the background to the project and requested an interview. Some of those contacted did not respond, but many did. Sometimes they responded immediately, but in many cases I followed up at least once. Persistence appeared to pay, as in many instances people agreed to an interview on second contact. Perhaps they were busy or forgot, or perhaps the second contact signaled a more genuine and specific interest in meeting them. I sometimes made contact a third time, if a subject I considered very important had not replied, and this led to occasional success. Whenever people declined, I would, of course, bother them no further.

In the simplest cases, contact details were publicly available. In the more difficult cases, other email addresses for the organization were available online or otherwise in my possession, and this template could be used to determine the target's specific email address. In the most difficult cases, no such format was known and I had to guess the template through trial and error, often leading to multiple bounces. In cases where I couldn't determine someone's contact details at all, I sometimes tried contacting them directly through social media such as LinkedIn. Finding contact details was sometimes as, if not more, time-consuming as identifying a potential participant in the first instance.

Cybercriminals can be difficult to locate and it is important to avoid studying only the low-hanging fruit that can be more easily accessed. Approaching those in the manner discussed above often led to a slightly skewed sample. I did manage to speak with cybercriminals of all levels, from those who flirted with it to well-known veterans of the industry. I also managed to cover a range from the very technical to those more oriented to the money side. But the sample tended to skew more toward the technical, and often, though not always, participants had subsequently found gainful employment in the technology sector. With some very notable exceptions, the sample also skewed toward medium- and lower-level offenders.

As a result, I undertook one further activity to improve the sample's quality: interviewing prison inmates. Elite cybercriminals are held in prisons around the world, and potentially provide a very useful resource.[14] Including them also helps to overcome the problem of dealing only with self-identified cybercriminals whose veracity might be questioned. While I did not have doubts about the bona fides of those I spoke to (and a number did have criminal records but had been released), this potential bias remains a concern for some.[15] Doing a small amount of prison research was very valuable in increasing the number of high-level cybercriminals in the sample. It also allowed for some more interviews with those primarily on the money side, rather than the technical side, who tend to be more difficult to access in the outside world.

My initial intention was to conduct in-person interviews with inmates. But it soon became clear that this would not be practical. Accessing prisons for research has become an increasingly difficult and time-consuming process. Furthermore, cybercriminals are incarcerated in a range of prisons, sometimes in locations far from major cities, increasing the time and financial resources required. Prisoners are also occasionally moved, creating the risk that one might travel to a remote location only to find the prisoner no longer on site.

Instead, I conducted prisoner interviews by mail and electronic communications. I drew inspiration from prior prison researchers who engaged in research by letter.[16] In this case, the approach differed in that I wasn't attempting to study prisoners per se, but cybercriminals who happened to be in prison. Rather than advertising my project in different institutions and hoping for responses, I drew up a list of desired participants and then contacted them directly. The lists were largely drawn from known cases and media reports. Those in the US prison system proved far simpler to access than those in the UK system, as there is a public website that provides information on incarcerated people and where they are held. In the UK, privacy restrictions prevent such a system and make locating inmates far more time-consuming. I did not attempt to access prisoners in other jurisdictions. This was largely due to practical considerations in terms of limited time and resources, and difficulties in accessing inmates in some countries. But, as will be discussed below, there were also ethical considerations in terms of engaging inmates in some locations where their mistreatment might be more likely.

Once the location of a prisoner was determined, I would send a letter outlining the study. Those who were interested could communicate with me by phone, letter, or the closed communication system available to some prisoners that approximates email but does not allow general access to the Internet. This electronic system proved the most popular and effective form of communication. Prisoners have considerable time on their hands and several participants engaged in extensive communications with me, going into detail beyond what would have been possible in face-to-face interviews. While this form of communication did not allow me to read body language or assess other cues, I believed the richness of the data more than made up for this. Any misunderstandings due to lack of tone or otherwise could be clarified in follow-up messages. This method presents various advantages, reducing time, cost, and access issues, while increasing standardization across interviews and requiring no subsequent transcription.

Those who wrote to me through letters usually did so because they did not have, or were not allowed, access to the electronic communications system. This approach provided some useful information but messages were generally shorter, due to the need for handwriting or using a typewriter, and there were much longer delays in our exchanges. (Meanwhile, detailed electronic messages sometimes came more regularly than I could easily respond to them). The delays made it more difficult to build up rapport and trusting relationships. They also made it more difficult to go as deeply into details. Nonetheless, such letters from cybercriminals can still provide gems that cannot be accessed elsewhere. Communicating by phone did not raise specific issues beyond some scheduling complications, as inmates have to call out rather than the researcher calling in. For ethical reasons, I do not signify the inmates to whom I spoke as part of this study. As will be discussed further below, I also provide what I consider to be the minimum necessary contextual information on inmates, to prevent particular individuals from being identified.

SNOWBALL SAMPLING

While purposive sampling was the primary approach used in this project, snowball sampling supplemented this where possible.[17] Snowballing was more difficult than has been the case with some other qualitative studies, where it is commonly used. Because the study engaged three core participant samples across different jurisdictions, snowballing was bound to face challenges. Rather than one large snowball, the use of smaller snowballs by country or by category was more reasonable. In some sense, the process is begun anew each time a new location is visited. But even this type of focused snowballing proved somewhat difficult. This may be because the world of cybersecurity happens to have more than its share of paranoid people, on both the criminal and the enforcement sides. On various occasions, interview subjects offered to connect me with other possible participants, but the interviews failed to happen. When such meetings could be arranged, they did not necessarily snowball any further. Outside a small number of cases, these failures of snowballing were particularly apparent among former offenders.

Nonetheless, snowball sampling was still achieved in some instances. Referrals from existing participants connected me to subjects I might not have located on my own. Such referrals broadened the sample, and generally led to a higher level of participation than direct, cold contacts did. In fact, occasionally, referrals led to interviews with participants who had previously failed to respond to my cold contact messages. Obviously, issues of trust applied to myself as well.[18] Referrals are very effective in conducting this type of research, especially when the referee is well respected. Snowball sampling corrected some of the possible deficiencies of purposive sampling and added many valuable interview subjects to the sample who could not be accessed through other means.

As would be expected, snowballing was most difficult in the early days of the project but improved over time. By the end of the project, I had built an extensive list of contacts across many countries and professions. Among these were certain individuals who acted as what might be called *global gatekeepers*. Given the transnational nature of cybercrime and its enforcement, certain international networks have formed often among leading players. Each time I visited a new location, I would contact one or more of the gatekeepers that I suspected had the deepest contacts in that region. This usually led to suggestions of interview subjects. Sometimes, these suggested contacts became local gatekeepers and in turn introduced me to further participants. Other particularly helpful participants performed this role after we met. There were even some who didn't meet with me who kindly served this role, offering contacts they believed were more appropriate, or similar to them in cases when they were unavailable.

ACCURACY AND LIMITATIONS

Over the course of the study, many hundreds of individuals (and organizations) were contacted. While there was some variation among countries, generally 25–30 percent of those contacted agreed to be interviewed. Another 25–30 percent responded to my inquiry but did not meet for the interview, either because they declined or it did not take place for some other reason. The remainder did not respond at all. As with most qualitative studies, there may be some non-response bias in the sample, but the nature of this bias is challenging to determine. Factors in non-response might include: apprehension of communicating with a stranger, a lack of confidence in their knowledge, a lack of confidence in their language ability, being overly busy, forgetting to respond, or traveling during the interview period. In contrast, factors in successful response might include: a strong interest in academic research or the world of cybercrime, an altruistic personality, cultural norms that encourage hosting visitors, an international outlook or desire to meet a (foreign) visitor, boredom, or free time during the workday.

The preceding sections have included some reference to possible flaws and limitations in the data. This is always the case with qualitative studies, which often make use of non-random samples. But in many instances, measures were taken to counteract the impact of these challenges. These measures fall under the key concept of triangulation.[19] The central idea is that multiple data sources and perspectives can be brought together to limit the weaknesses within any specific source. This was achieved through many means in the study. First, the project draws on data from three groupings of participants. Each group has its own perspectives and its own possible weaknesses as informants. For instance, some might worry about those in the technology sector overemphasizing the threat of cybercrime as a business strategy. Others might be concerned that law enforcement would emphasize their own success in counteracting cybercrime. Still others might be concerned about former cybercriminals hiding certain sensitive pieces of information about their past actions. All these and more are genuine concerns, but are lessened by having all the participant categories combined, which provides internal cross-checks and increases accuracy.

Second, the study also draws on other forms of data that can be compared to the interview results, including legal records and cybercriminal communications. Unless there is an elaborate feedback mechanism occurring, multiple independent forms of data pointing to the same conclusion suggest higher levels of accuracy.

Additionally, one need not wait until all data are collected to triangulate. It is also important to ensure that each interview is as accurate as possible while carrying it out. The skill of the interviewer plays a significant role in qualitative research.[20] Through good interview technique, information can be tested against other already collected data or information already provided within that same interview. It is important to begin interviews with broad, open questions, which allow participants to answer without the interviewer prompting them and avoid pushing them toward specific responses they might otherwise not provide. But once these responses have been given and the interviewer can ascertain the participant's unvarnished views, more direct follow-up questions can be asked if necessary.

These questions can be either closed or simply more specific. Their purpose is to verify or expand aspects of the account that has been given. If something that has been said conflicts with what is known from existing data, the relevant topic can be raised more directly. If the subject continues to display good confidence in the account, it is at least clear they believe it with certainty. This means that the area might require further investigation to harmonize or otherwise resolve the conflicting data points. If the participant quickly backtracks from a point when questioned directly on it, then one knows to view it with caution, and might privilege other more credible data over these claims.[21]

Such checks on accuracy need not only occur externally, but can also be done internally. For instance, the background of the participant in question and the certainty with which they speak can influence how responses should be interpreted. If a law enforcement agent from country x makes a confident statement about cybercrime in that country, it is likely of higher value than a statement made by someone with no connection to x whatsoever, or who seems uncertain but willing to offer an opinion nonetheless. One can also flag seemingly contradictory statements that are made within the same interview. If the subject can effectively resolve the apparent contradiction, then the data are more likely to be sound. If not, then the data, again, should be used with caution. In some instances, a participant's general account may appear credible, but may not connect closely with the central interests of the study and a more direct prompt may be required to gain their insights on these topics.

In terms of carrying out interviews, providing anonymity to participants was vital to the overall accuracy of this study. Anonymous reporting will be discussed below in relation to ethics, but it had practical advantages, as well. First, it improved access to interview subjects and expanded the sample. A number of participants directly and indirectly indicated that they would not have participated without this assurance. These were often, though not always, those with strong knowledge of the subject and included law enforcement agents and former cybercriminals. Yet, there were others in these categories who indicated that anonymity was not a major concern for them. Second, providing anonymity also likely improved the openness with which people participated and the amount of information they offered. Some participants said they could provide information that they would not be able to talk about if it would be tied back to either themselves or their organization. For instance, in one case I became aware that one of my subjects was a former cybercriminal only during the course of the interview and solely because anonymity was provided. Partway through answering my questions, he double-checked: "This is all anonymous, right?" Then he proceeded to outline his past criminal endeavors in some detail, providing some of the most useful data I collected over the course of the project.

Third, by offering anonymity, I believe I also improved the quality of the information I received. Evidence for this came from the proportion of the sample who had previously given media interviews (sometimes the interviews that made me aware of them in the first place). The ways in which the information I collected from participants differed from their on-the-record statements was somewhat counterintuitive. Despite having their name against the quote, interviewees appeared to allow less accurate information to go into the public record. Although it was not always clear what role the journalists might have played in this, sometimes this would be due to hyperbole such as overstating the threat of cybercrime or the involvement of organized crime groups. In other instances, these exaggerations were intended to demonstrate the effectiveness of their organization or company in fighting cybercrime. In terms of former cybercriminals who went on the record, some played up their past criminality and others played it down. Those who highlighted their past deeds often did so as a form of promotion perhaps to secure or improve their place in the security industry. But for others, there were clear attempts to sanitize their past deeds and downplay particularly destructive acts, their motivations at the time, or aspects of their personal lives that might not encourage people to work with them as they sought to build new lives.

When participants came to speak to me under the protection of ano-nymity, a number pulled back from their on-the-record statements, and often offered far more measured accounts. Part of this might be thanks to the academic nature of this project, if participants felt some greater obliga-tion to speak accurately than they would in a journalistic interview. Ulti-mately, I believe that providing anonymity to all participants improved overall accuracy by reducing any tendency they had to promote other agendas.

Also helping the accuracy of findings is the extent of data collection for this study. While a case study may provide rich data, what is learned may not be very generalizable. The broad approach taken in this project draws on many cases from many jurisdictions, greatly increasing its external validity.[22] The substantial variation within the sample is also helpful in avoiding se-lection on the dependent variable.[23] To properly comprehend the presence of a phenomenon (the dependent variable)—cybercriminal cooperation, in this instance—one should also study cases where that phenomenon is not present. These would be failures of cooperation. Otherwise, one might fail to determine which independent variables are necessary for the pres-ence of the phenomenon under study, and which are present regardless of whether that phenomenon occurs or not. In this study, this variation was provided in three ways. First, cases were examined over time, through pe-riods where cybercriminal cooperation was successful and others where it was less so. Second, geographical variation also meant that some countries saw high levels of cooperation among their local cybercriminals, while in others cooperation was hindered. Third, the accounts of the cybercriminals themselves also provided micro-level instances of where they succeeded at cooperating and where they failed.

Ultimately, despite these measures, there will always remain some biases and limitations. This is the case with all research, but there are particular challenges that relate specifically to qualitative research. While little can be done to address such questions, it is important to acknowledge these biases and limitations and factor this into the overall analysis. First, all interview data face similar questions over credibility. It is possible that interview sub-jects may provide misinformation intentionally or accidentally, may hide aspects of their account, or may forget certain details over time. As noted, companies might play up the threat of cybercrime, while law enforcement from a specific country might downplay it to present a rosy picture to out-siders. The measures described above, such as triangulation, reduce such risks but some will always remain. Second, the samples of participants along with the other data used are not random, so it is difficult to generalize the findings in a concrete way. Instead, the results of studies like this one offer more suggestive findings and outcomes. Jane Ritchie and colleagues explain such sampling in this way: "The sample is not intended to be statistically representative: the chances of selection for each element are unknown but, instead, the characteristics of the population are used as the basis of selection. It is this feature that makes them well suited to small-scale, in-depth studies."[24]

There are also points peculiar to this study that should be acknowledged. It is possible that the sample does not include certain key participants who might alter the results. The nature of law enforcement and private sector involvement in the cybercrime sphere is possible to delineate and I made significant efforts to include a reflective cross section of these groups and the range of participants in them. For cybercriminals this is more difficult, largely due to issues of access. While I also believe I have a good cross section of cybercriminals across countries, areas of specialization, and ranging from low-level to high-level offenders, there remains at least some possibility that certain key participants might be missing from the sample. First, for the reasons described above, mostly former cybercriminals are included in the sample. There may be something qualitatively different between former cybercriminals and those who remain in the business. Active cybercriminals have not been arrested yet, and nor have they chosen to retire. Some information is provided on this group by the former cybercriminals who dealt with them, but largely they are not heard from directly in this study. This is a possible bias that must be acknowledged but cannot be directly counteracted.

It is not entirely clear what the impact of this data hole is on the accuracy of the study. There might be little difference between the two cybercriminal categories, if it is simply a matter of time before various active cybercriminals become former ones. It is possible, however, that the two samples are quite different. For instance, those that voluntarily retire from cybercrime might be less committed to the business and have other opportunities they can turn to than those who remain involved. A different concern in traditional criminological studies is that convicted offender populations might overrepresent low-level street offenders, as these people make easy targets for arrest. This skew might mean that higher-level actors are not well-represented in a sample of convicted participants. But in cybercrime, the situation appears to be different. There are simply too many cases for law enforcement agencies to investigate. While some small fish are arrested, in many cases the policing strategy appears to be taking out high-value and high-profile targets, maximizing the impact of minimal resources, perhaps as part of a strategy of deterrence. If anything, this means those that are arrested could skew to the higher echelons of cybercrime—those worth arresting—rather than the small-timers (see also note 14).

If there is a segment of cybercriminals missing from the sample, it is most likely those who are extremely cautious. It is those actors who raise their heads too high that appear to get caught. The "smart ones" avoid high-profile targets that are likely to attract the full force of a law enforcement agency, even if that means a lower payoff. They might also be more careful in their personal lives, not going on holidays to locations where they are more likely to be arrested and extradited, as is somewhat common among international cybercriminals. They probably also do not participate in academic research projects and give out information on their criminal dealings. They may not make the most money in the industry, but if these ghosts exist, they are likely missing from this sample (other than in the accounts others give of them).

Ethics

This project made use of standard ethical protocols for carrying out qualitative research and interviews in particular. Gaining informed consent is the foundation of such studies.[25] To obtain participants' consent, I carefully explained the nature of the study. According to my university ethics clearance, it was standard procedure to present each interview participant in this project with a form that also outlined the key aspects of the study. Many participants consented in writing. A substantial number consented orally instead. In countries where signed documents are viewed with suspicion, oral consent was common. But it was also a personal decision regardless of context, with some preferring not to have an official paper trail linked to them.

Given there are sensitivities around both the topics and the participants involved in this research, anonymity and confidentiality were also essential. Codes and randomly assigned pseudonyms have been substituted for all participant names. In addition, Appendix 1 only lists the most critical information about interviewees. For instance, I do not identify specific law enforcement agencies in each country. The world of cybercrime remains a fairly small one, for offenders and enforcers alike, and some ostensibly innocuous details could help uncover identities. Some participants reside in countries that differ from their nationalities. In certain cases, revealing this might disclose the identity of someone who is one of just a few people of that nationality working in the security sector of a particular country. In such cases, I have typically included them in their nationality category, particularly if the information they provided relates largely to that context. If the information they provided does not primarily relate to their national context, I list them more broadly as an expatriate of no stated nationality residing in the relevant country. For similar reasons, I provide only the year of each meeting to avoid clear references to specific conferences where someone might have been interviewed and attendee lists might be accessed. In rare cases, I have also subsumed certain nationalities together. For instance, while I didn't visit numerous former Soviet countries, I did encounter some of these nationalities in locations such as Russia. Rather than isolate these nationalities, where there is sometimes only a small community of known security experts, I list them in the country where I interviewed them.

With regard to former cybercriminal participants, I took the further step of identifying them only by region rather than by nationality. This is due to the extra sensitivity involved with these participants and the small pool of known offenders, of whom some are included in this study. For similar reasons, I also do not differentiate between those who are, or were, in prison and those who have not been incarcerated. Nor do I specify the year(s) in which the interviewing took place. In rare cases, I may make mention of arrest in the text if it is essential to the point being made, but I try to avoid too much detail that might be used to narrow down cases. In certain instances, I interviewed members of the IT sector in various countries that I suspected might have had past or ongoing involvement in cybercriminal activities. Unless these participants actively acknowledged their involvement, I do not report these suspicions. Without providing such sensitive information, I therefore include them in the general lists of interview subjects, rather than the list of former cybercriminals. Mark Israel and Iain Hay provide a useful overview of similar precautions that have been employed by scholars in other studies.[26] Nonetheless, all direct quotes from these participants are verbatim, or as close as transcription allowed. In the case of written interviews, the words are left as they are, but for basic readability, there has been some very minor editing for spelling, punctuation, and formatting.

For the most part, this study did not engage with subjects from particularly vulnerable populations. No subject was under the age of 18 or suffering from known mental disabilities. Former cybercriminals are likely most at risk, but the risk is still somewhat low, given that any criminal behavior was in the past and often known by others or with some degree of public record. It would also be wrong to assume that police are strongly interested in research on this subject as a possible source of evidence. Currently, there is no shortage of cybercrime cases for law enforcement to pursue, leaving

little interest for them to compel a researcher such as myself to divulge information on past offenders (which I would in any case refuse to do). In
fact, I interviewed a large number of law enforcement agents who were
aware that I was also interviewing former cybercriminals. No such requests
were made or even suggested, with most participants across all groups being
aware of the importance of independent academic research. This appears
to differ from some other researcher experiences, where scholars have faced
unwanted interest from law enforcement agents and others.[27]

Nonetheless, there was one class of former cybercriminals in a more vulnerable position: prison inmates. I address the ethical means with which
I approached this group below.

INMATES AND ETHICS

Doing research with prisoners presents ethical considerations. Nonetheless,
if a researcher applies the correct measures, these issues can be overcome.
At present, the British Society of Criminology Statement of Ethics (BSCSE),
the most relevant protocol of its kind for this project, provides only limited
guidance for conducting research with prisoners.[28] While making use of the
elements of the BSCSE that do apply, along with an application of its general principles, I also examined the relevant literature in this area, which
provides the more direct guidance on ethical issues regarding inmates.[29]

Below I outline the key concerns that I needed to be aware of in conducting this research and the appropriate measures that I undertook. In
most cases, these issues related to gaining informed consent in these special circumstances. As I did not physically visit the prisons, consent was attained through writing. Given the vulnerable nature of prisoners, it did not
seem appropriate to require signed consent forms from them, especially
when such forms could not be presented in person. Many outside prison
are already intimidated by signing what looks to them to be a formal binding
document (even though such a form largely spells out the protections
participants will receive). Prisoners would also have to mail forms back to
me, thereby accruing (unnecessary and sometimes international) postage
costs. As a result, the standard approach I adopted was to present the information contained on the consent form as key points the prisoner participants
needed to understand. For those communicating by letter, this information
was in a document without a space for a signature. For those communicating
electronically, I cut and pasted the same information into a message that I
sent them. Rather than require them to sign anything, I specified that they
should read the material and let me know if they had any questions. We
would only proceed with the interview once they were satisfied and felt

comfortable. Some seemed to have few concerns with the nature of the study; others engaged in a long back and forth with me about different aspects of how the information would be used. After this discussion had addressed their concerns, or various limitations on their participation had been stated, they then indicated whether they were happy to proceed. Overall, the consent process in writing was perhaps even clearer than it would be in person.

INCRIMINATING ADMISSIONS

During interviews, inmates may provide information on crimes that have not been the subject of legal proceedings. This could put both the researcher and the participant in a difficult situation. The BSCSE explains this issue by way of a "frequently asked question":

> Q1: "One of my interviewees in prison has told me about getting away with various offences. He told me he is in prison for three burglaries, but there are several other offences that the police don't know about. What should I do?"
> A1: It should have been made clear to participants in the research at the outset the limits of confidentiality for those involved in the study. Research in sensitive settings such as prisons is particularly likely to raise issues of this kind.

Bearing this in mind, I adopted the approach of offering inmates complete confidentiality and a promise to report data anonymously, changing participants' names and key details that could be used to identify them.[30] But I was aware of the issues raised above, the potential complications involved, and the risks I was taking on. As a result, I specified to inmates that they should answer questions only with regard to crimes for which they had been tried and convicted. I indicated the importance of steering away from sensitive topics to avoid potential legal issues for both the inmate and myself. While it is beyond the focus of the project, I also specified that the interview should not cover behavior inside the relevant prison, to avoid knowledge of potentially sensitive information in this regard, which a researcher might feel some compulsion to disclose. The tension between maintaining confidentiality and, for example, knowledge of a purported prison break or internal assaults is a difficult one. This is generally regarded as a complex grey area, and it is ultimately up to the researcher to best decide what action to take in the specific circumstances.[31] Fortunately, this issue did not arise in the course of my fieldwork.

INFORMED CONSENT AND POTENTIAL COERCION

In terms of the BSCSE and the discussion above, informed consent is a vital requirement of participant-based research. In the case of prisoners, issues of potential coercion can complicate this process. Carol Matfin outlines the problem:

> Despite public perception to the contrary, prisoners are an extremely vulnerable group of people, without the freedom to walk away from a situation or the normal recourse to legal help and advice. They cannot pick up the telephone at will or pop into a friend's house to discuss what they should do. They may feel that to co-operate might be detrimental to their position but that not to co-operate could have even worse consequences for them. They are a powerless group of people about whose lives others take all the decisions, whether they like those decisions or not.[32]

The most important measure to take in this regard is to be aware of the vulnerability of prisoners and to be extremely careful in gaining informed consent. With all participants, I took care to explain the research fully—both what they were participating in and its potential implications. But in the case of prisoners, the voluntary nature of participation was also stressed. As I dealt directly with prisoners and did not require a prison officer as an intermediary, this reduced the potential for accidental coercion. Consent was gained directly from each inmate and, as previously noted, we often engaged in several back-and-forth communications before beginning, to make sure that the project information I provided was understood and the inmate was satisfied with how matters would proceed.

With all this said, I believe that inmates generally viewed their participation in this study as a positive experience. The rapid-fire and detailed responses I received from some indicated that this activity was something they were happy to spend considerable time on. Carrying out research by mail, Mary Bosworth and her coauthors find something similar: the prisoners enjoyed participating in projects because it gave them something to do, engaged their minds, was an opportunity to express themselves and potentially make a difference, or allowed broader social contact.[33] As Matfin puts it:

> One distinct advantage of carrying out research among such a literally captive audience is that the refusal rate is usually low. Prison

is an excruciatingly boring place and the boredom often makes prisoners willing to participate. Once the research has been explained to the inmates and staff, and if the prisoner understands that s / he *need* not comply with the request for an interview, then consent to participate is very much dependent on the individual skills that the researcher needs to employ. Can the researcher offer *anything* the prisoner wants? It is very unlikely that the inmate will agree to an interview if the answer is no. Prisoners agree to be interviewed because they will get something out of it for themselves. This is known as the *research bargain*. Whilst no inducements may be offered, that does not mean the prisoner does not weigh up whether there is likely to be any other advantage attached to the interview. For the researcher, working out exactly what that advantage might be can be complex, but it is the key to why inmates agree to be interviewed and then often reveal deeply private information. In some circumstances, the bargain may be as straightforward as the prisoner simply wanting to talk to someone different about almost anything other than their immediate surroundings.[34]

Regarding the inmates included in this book, I believe the subject matter was particularly important to them. Across this study I interviewed former cybercriminals whose passion for technology and cybersecurity went beyond their criminal endeavors. Sometimes they indicated that they enjoyed speaking with me about the issues I was studying and even asked me questions on the topic following the conclusion of the interview. For inmates, the pool of people they can speak to about these issues can be limited. One prisoner indicated that he appreciated our communications because he had no one else at his facility who understood anything about the subject. Another possible motivation was that some enjoyed sharing their expertise and being acknowledged for their abilities, while also seeing their input making research more accurate on the subject of cybercrime. While inmates may have felt they benefitted by participating in the research, I did also make clear to inmates that participation carried no specific rewards or, for that matter, disadvantages.

WEAKENED ANONYMITY AND CONFIDENTIALITY

Finally, while confidentiality and anonymity were offered to every subject in this study, it is important to note that communications with those in prison may be monitored by prison officials. Despite offering this full confidentiality and anonymity, I also had to make this possible surveillance clear to each inmate at the outset. At various points, when I felt subjects were sharing information too liberally, I reminded them to take care already. Certain inmates appeared to be very aware that their communications were being monitored and would self-censor. For instance, they would not use the names of former collaborators who had not been arrested or would indicate to me that they had removed certain details from an account that might be sensitive.

Notes

1. INTRODUCTION

1. Del Quentin Wilber and Chris Strohm, "Accused Russian Hacker on Tropical Holiday Nabbed by U.S. Agents," Bloomberg, March 11, 2015, https://www.bloomberg.com/news/articles/2015-03-11/accused-russian-hacker-on-tropical-holiday-nabbed-by-u-s-agents.

2. For published photos see "Russian MP's Son to Remain in Custody in Seattle until Hacking Trial," RT [Russia Today] (website), August 16, 2014, https://www.rt.com/news/180752-seleznyov-seattle-custody-trial/; Mike Carter, "Accused Hacker Should Pay Defense Cost, Prosecutors Say," *Seattle Times,* March 20, 2015, http://www.seattletimes.com/seattle-news/crime/accused-hacker-should-pay-defense-cost-prosecutors-say/; Levi Pulkkinen, "Piles of Cash, Bunches of Bling and a Public Defender?" *Seattle Post-Intelligencer,* January 16, 2015, http://www.seattlepi.com/local/article/Piles-of-cash-bunches-of-bling-and-a-public-6021422.php.

3. USA v. Roman Seleznev, 2:11-cr-00070-RAJ, Document 5 (Western District of Washington) [2011 Indictment].

4. Carter, "Accused Hacker Should Pay Defense Cost, Prosecutors Say."

5. USA v. Roman Zolotarev and others, 2:12-cr-00004-APG-GWF, Document 1 (District of Nevada) [2012 Indictment].

6. Wilber and Strohm, "Accused Russian Hacker on Tropical Holiday Nabbed by U.S. Agents."

7. Nicole Perlroth, "Russian Hacker Sentenced to 27 Years in Credit Card Case," *New York Times,* April 21, 2017, https://www.nytimes.com/2017/04/21/technology/russian-hacker-sentenced.html.

8. For a survey of different estimates see Steve Morgan, "Cyber Crime Costs Projected to Reach $2 Trillion by 2019," *Forbes,* January 17, 2016, http://www.forbes.com/sites/stevemorgan/2016/01/17/cyber-crime-costs-projected-to-reach-2-trillion-by-2019. But these figures should be viewed with caution. This is a controversial area known for loose claims, limited data, and certain agendas that may benefit from hyping the threat. While the problem is undoubtedly large, some scholars have pushed back and advocated for a more careful approach in estimating the costs of cybercrime: Ross Anderson, Chris Barton, Rainer Böhme,

et al., "Measuring the Cost of Cybercrime," in *The Economics of Information Security and Privacy*, ed. Rainer Böhme (Berlin: Springer, 2013), 265–300.

9. UNODC, *Comprehensive Study on Cybercrime*, United Nations Office on Drugs and Crime, Vienna, draft February 2013, 28, https://www.unodc.org/documents/organized -crime/UNODC_CCPCJ_EG.4_2013/CYBERCRIME_STUDY_210213.pdf.

10. On broader definitional issues see John Nightingale, "On the Definition of 'Industry' and 'Market,'" *Journal of Industrial Economics* 27, no. 1 (1978): 31–40.

11. See Jeffrey R. Church and Roger Ware, *Industrial Organization: A Strategic Approach* (Boston: Irwin, McGraw-Hill, 2000); Donald A. Hay and Derek J. Morris, *Industrial Economics: Theory and Evidence* (Oxford: Oxford University Press, 1991).

12. Paolo Campana and Federico Varese, "Cooperation in Criminal Organizations: Kinship and Violence as Credible Commitments," *Rationality and Society* 25, no. 3 (2013): 263–289, 265.

13. Diego Gambetta, *The Sicilian Mafia: The Business of Private Protection* (Cambridge, MA: Harvard University Press, 1993); Diego Gambetta, *Codes of the Underworld: How Criminals Communicate* (Princeton, NJ: Princeton University Press, 2009); Federico Varese, *The Russian Mafia: Private Protection in a New Market Economy* (Oxford: Oxford University Press, 2001); Campana and Varese, "Cooperation in Criminal Organizations"; David Skarbek, "Governance and Prison Gangs," *American Political Science Review* 105, no. 4 (2011): 702–716; Michael Levi, *The Phantom Capitalists: The Organization and Control of Long-Firm Fraud* (Aldershot, UK: Ashgate, 2008); Peter Reuter, *Disorganized Crime: The Economics of the Visible Hand* (Cambridge, MA: MIT Press, 1983).

14. Jonathan Lusthaus, "Trust in the World of Cybercrime," *Global Crime* 13, no. 2 (2012): 71–94; Jonathan Lusthaus, "How Organised Is Organised Cybercrime?" *Global Crime* 14, no. 1 (2013): 52–60; Thomas J. Holt and Eric Lampke, "Exploring Stolen Data Markets Online: Products and Market Forces," *Criminal Justice Studies* 23, no. 1 (2010): 33–50; Nir Kshetri, *The Global Cybercrime Industry: Economic, Institutional and Strategic Perspectives* (Berlin: Springer, 2010).

15. Peter N. Grabosky, "Virtual Criminality: Old Wine in New Bottles?" *Social & Legal Studies* 10, no. 2 (2001): 243–249; Susan W. Brenner, "Organized Cybercrime? How Cyberspace May Affect the Structure of Criminal Relationships," *North Carolina Journal of Law & Technology* 4, no. 1 (2002): 1–50; Majid Yar, *Cybercrime and Society* (Thousand Oaks, CA: Sage, 2006); David S. Wall, *Cybercrime: The Transformation of Crime in the Information Age* (Cambridge: Polity, 2007); David S. Wall, *Crime and the Internet* (London: Routledge, 2001).

16. David S. Wall, "What Are Cybercrimes?" *Criminal Justice Matters* 58, no. 1 (2004): 20–21, 20.

17. David S. Wall, "Catching Cybercriminals: Policing the Internet," *International Review of Law, Computers & Technology* 12, no. 2 (1998): 201–218, 201–202.

18. Grabosky, "Virtual Criminality: Old Wine in New Bottles?" 243.

19. Thomas J. Holt and Adam M. Bossler, "An Assessment of the Current State of Cybercrime Scholarship," *Deviant Behavior* 35, no. 1 (2014): 20–40, 21.

20. See, for example, Steven Furnell, *Cybercrime: Vandalizing the Information Society* (Boston: Addison-Wesley, 2002), 22.

21. Samuel C. McQuade, *Understanding and Managing Cybercrime* (Boston: Allyn and Bacon, 2006), 16.

22. One former law enforcement agent took the debate to the extreme, even arguing that cybercrime is so pervasive and intertwined with conventional crime that it is "time to drop the concept of this cyber thing. This is life" (US-(F)LE-5).

23. David S. Wall, "Cybercrime and the Internet," in *Crime and the Internet,* ed. David S. Wall (London: Routledge, 2001), 3–7.

24. With thanks to Benoît Dupont on this point.

25. Jonathan Lusthaus, "Electronic Ghosts," *Democracy* 31 (Winter 2014), https://democracyjournal.org/magazine/31/electronic-ghosts/.

26. In reality, some blurring of these categories is inevitable. For example, a cyber-criminal might carry out an action for multiple reasons, such as hacking something because it is both enjoyable and brings financial reward, or might engage in multiple, distinct activities each of which has a different motivation behind it. He might carry out hacks for fun or political activism, but also engage in credit card fraud to make some money on the side, or be coopted by a national intelligence agency to carry out certain tasks in a freelance (but perhaps mandatory) capacity. No typology can accurately place every case in one, and only one, category, but a functional typology capable of demarcating basic boundaries, is a useful tool in understanding cybercrime.

27. Among the rare studies that have addressed such issues, see Alice Hutchings, "Cyber-crime Trajectories: An Integrated Theory of Initiation, Maintenance and Desistance," in *Crime Online: Correlates, Causes, and Context,* ed. Thomas J. Holt, 3rd ed. (Durham, NC: Carolina Academic Press, 2016); and National Cyber Crime Unit, Prevent Team, "Pathways into Cyber Crime," Intelligence Assessment, National Crime Agency, London, January 13, 2017, http://www.nationalcrimeagency.gov.uk/publications/791-pathways-into-cyber-crime/file.

28. See "Frequently Asked Questions" at http://hacks.mit.edu/Hacks/misc/faq.html.

29. See, for instance, Paul Babiak and Robert D. Hare, *Snakes in Suits: When Psychopaths Go to Work* (New York: Reagan Books, 2006).

30. "Gary McKinnon Profile: Autistic 'Hacker' Who Started Writing Computer Programs at 14," *Telegraph,* January 23, 2009, http://www.telegraph.co.uk/news/worldnews/northamerica/usa/4320901/Gary-McKinnon-profile-Autistic-hacker-who-started-writing-computer-programs-at-14.html.

31. Nicola Harley, "Teenage Boy Brought Down Websites of Cambridge University, Microsoft and Sony Then Made £386k Selling the Software to Criminals," *Telegraph,* April 21, 2017, http://www.telegraph.co.uk/news/2017/04/21/teenage-boy-brought-websites-cambridge-university-microsoft/.

32. Rebecca Ledingham and Richard Mills, "A Preliminary Study of Autism and Cyber-crime in the Context of International Law Enforcement," *Advances in Autism* 1, no. 1 (2015): 2–11.

33. At the time of writing, the author was aware of some ongoing efforts in this area, but the results had yet to be published and so could not be addressed herein.

34. Kevin Poulsen, *Kingpin: How One Hacker Took Over the Billion-Dollar Cybercrime Underground* (New York: Crown, 2011).

35. The database can be viewed at http://www.cl.cam.ac.uk/~ah793/cccd.html. While the dataset is regularly updated, Alice Hutchings kindly provided me with a copy for statistical analysis in July 2017, which is the data presented in this book. The database has missing fields for certain cases. This analysis of gender incorporates only those cases where gender is known and listed.

36. For a more detailed study on gender and cybercrime see Alice Hutchings and Yi Ting Chua, "Gendering Cybercrime," in *Cybercrime through an Interdisciplinary Lens,* ed. Thomas J. Holt (Abingdon: Routledge, 2017).

37. United States Department of Justice, "Former U.S. Nuclear Regulatory Commission Employee Pleads Guilty to Attempted Spear-Phishing Cyber-Attack on Department of Energy Computers," Office of Public Affairs, press release, February 2, 2016, https://www.justice.gov/opa/pr/former-us-nuclear-regulatory-commission-employee-pleads-guilty-attempted-spear-phishing-cyber.

38. Kim Zetter, "DarkMarket Ringleader Pleads Guilty in London," Wired, January 21, 2010, https://www.wired.com/2010/01/jilsi-pleads-guilty/.

39. On this subject see Travis Hirschi and Michael Gottfredson, "Age and the Explanation of Crime," *American Journal of Sociology* 89, no. 3 (1983): 552–584; Lawrence E. Cohen and Kenneth C. Land, "Age Structure and Crime: Symmetry versus Asymmetry and the Projection of Crime Rates through the 1990s," *American Sociological Review* 52, no. 2 (1987): 170–183.

40. For a small database, with a mean of 25, see Mira Carignan, *L'origine Géographique en tant que facteur explicatif de la cyberdélinquance* (Master's Thesis, Université de Montréal, 2015), https://papyrus.bib.umontreal.ca/xmlui/handle/1866/12549. The Cambridge Computer Crime Database has incomplete data on age of offense: the exact age is known for 134 individuals, with an age range provided for 99 further individuals. The mean for exact age is 29.69. Taking the median of the age range for the remaining individuals, the mean of that group is quite similar at 29.44. Of course, age is not static and offending can take place over a period of time.

41. Shiv Malik, "Teenagers Jailed for Running £16m Internet Crime Forum," *The Guardian,* March 2, 2011, https://www.theguardian.com/uk/2011/mar/02/ghostmarket-web-scam-teenagers.

42. Lawrence E. Cohen and Marcus Felson, "Social Change and Crime Rates: A Routine Activity Approach," *American Sociological Review* 44, no. 4 (1979): 588–608, 589.

43. Jack Katz, *Seductions of Crime: Moral and Sensual Attractions in Doing Evil* (New York: Basic Books, 1988).

44. There is a small but growing computer science literature investigating more human aspects. See, for example, Jason Franklin, Vern Paxson, Adrian Perrig, and Stefan Savage, "An Inquiry into the Nature and Causes of the Wealth of Internet Miscreants," in *Proceedings of the 14th ACM Conference on Computer and Communications Security,* Alexandria VA, October 2007, 375–388; Furnell, *Cybercrime: Vandalizing the Information Society;* Marti Motoyama, Damon McCoy, Kirill Levchenko, Stefan Savage, and Geoffrey M. Voelker, "An Analysis of Underground Forums," in *Proceedings of the 2011 ACM SIGCOMM Conference on Internet Measurement (IMC'11),* Berlin, November 2011, 71–80; Sadia Afroz, Vaibhav Garg, Damon McCoy, and Rachel Greenstadt, "Honor among Thieves: A Common's Analysis of Cybercrime Economies," Presentation, 2013 APWG eCrime Researchers Summit, San Francisco, CA, September 2013; Andreas Haslebacher, Jeremiah Onaolapo,

and Gianluca Stringhini, "All Your Cards Are Belong to Us: Understanding Online Carding Forums," Presentation, 2017 APWG Symposium on eCrime, Scottsdale, AZ, April 2017; Damon McCoy, Andreas Pitsillidis, Grant Jordan, et al., "Pharmaleaks: Understanding the Business of Online Pharmaceutical Affiliate Programs," Presentation, 21st USENIX Security Symposium, Bellevue, WA, August 2012; Shuang Hao, Kevin Borgolte, Nick Nikiforakis, et al., "Drops for Stuff: An Analysis of Reshipping Mule Scams," Presentation, ACM Conference on Computer and Communications Security, Denver, October 2015.

45. See, for instance, Tim Jordan and Paul Taylor, "A Sociology of Hackers," *Sociological Review* 46, no. 4 (1998): 757–780; Wall, *Crime and the Internet*.

46. A selection of examples include: Lusthaus, "Trust in the World of Cybercrime"; Alice Hutchings, "Hacking and Fraud: Qualitative Analysis of Online Offending and Victimization," in *Global Criminology: Crime and Victimization in a Globalized Era*, ed. K. Jaishankar and Natti Ronel (Boca Raton, FL: CRC Press, 2013); David Décary-Hétu and Benoît Dupont, "The Social Network of Hackers," *Global Crime* 13, no. 3 (2012): 160–175; Holt and Lampke, "Exploring Stolen Data Markets Online"; Marleen Weulen Kranenbarg, *Cyber-offenders versus Traditional Offenders: An Empirical Comparison* (PhD Thesis, Vrije Universiteit Amsterdam, 2018); Lisa Sugiura, *Respectable Deviance and Purchasing Medicine Online: Opportunities and Risks for Consumers* (Cham: Palgrave Macmillan, 2018); Andrew Mell, "Reputation in the Market for Stolen Data," Discussion Paper No. 611, Department of Economics, University of Oxford, June 2012, https://www.economics.ox .ac.uk/materials/papers/12045/paper611.pdf; E. Rutger Leukfeldt, Edward R. Kleemans, and Wouter P. Stol, "Cybercriminal Networks, Social Ties and Online Forums: Social Ties versus Digital Ties within Phishing and Malware Networks," *British Journal of Criminology* 57, no. 3 (2017): 704–722; E. Rutger Leukfeldt, Anita Lavorgna, and Edward R. Kleemans, "Organised Cybercrime or Cybercrime That Is Organised? An Assessment of the Conceptualisation of Financial Cybercrime as Organised Crime," *European Journal on Criminal Policy and Research* 23, no. 3 (2017): 287–300.

47. For instance, Wall, *Cybercrime: The Transformation of Crime in the Information Age*; Susan W. Brenner, *Cybercrime: Criminal Threats from Cyberspace* (Westport, CT: Praeger, 2010); Yar, *Cybercrime and Society*.

48. Kshetri, *The Global Cybercrime Industry*.

49. Poulsen, *Kingpin*; Joseph Menn, *Fatal System Error: The Hunt for the New Crime Lords Who Are Bringing Down the Internet* (New York: PublicAffairs, 2010); Misha Glenny, *DarkMarket: Cyberthieves, Cybercops and You* (London: Bodley Head, 2011); Brian Krebs, *Spam Nation: The Inside Story of Organized Cybercrime—From Global Epidemic to Your Front Door* (Naperville, IL: Sourcebooks, 2014).

50. Holt and Lampke, "Exploring Stolen Data Markets Online"; Thomas J. Holt, "Exploring the Social Organisation and Structure of Stolen Data Markets," *Global Crime* 14, no. 2/3 (2013): 155–174; Roderic Broadhurst, Peter N. Grabosky, Manoun Alazab, and Steve Chon, "Organizations and Cyber Crime: An Analysis of the Nature of Groups Engaged in Cyber Crime," *International Journal of Cyber Criminology* 8, no. 1 (2014): 1–20; David Décary-Hétu and Benoît Dupont, "Reputation in a Dark Network of Online Criminals," *Global Crime* 14, no. 2/3 (2013): 175–196; Benoît Dupont, Anne-Marie Côté, Claire Savine, and David Décary-Hétu, "The Ecology of Trust among Hackers," *Global Crime* 17, no. 2 (2016): 129–151. A rare exception, which examined complete databases of forums that had been "leaked," is

Motoyama et al., "An Analysis of Underground Forums." In a similar vein, see Benoît Dupont, Anne-Marie Côté, Jean-Ian Boutin, and José Fernandez, "Darkode: Recruitment Patterns and Transactional Features of 'the Most Dangerous Cybercrime Forum in the World,'" *American Behavioral Scientist* 61, no. 11 (2017): 1219–1243.

51. Holt and Lampke, "Exploring Stolen Data Markets Online."

52. Décary-Hétu and Dupont, "Reputation in a Dark Network of Online Criminals."

53. Benoît Dupont, "Skills and Trust: A Tour Inside the Hard Drives of Computer Hackers," in *Crime and Networks,* ed. Carlo Morselli (New York: Routledge, 2014), 195–216.

54. Benoît Dupont, "Skills and Trust," 211.

55. Thomas J. Holt, "Examining the Forces Shaping Cybercrime Markets Online," *Social Science Computer Review* 31, no. 2 (2013): 165–177; Motoyama et al., "An Analysis of Underground Forums"; Michael Yip, Craig Webber, and Nigel Shadbolt, "Trust among Cybercriminals? Carding Forums, Uncertainty and Implications for Policing," *Policing and Society* 23, no. 4 (2013): 516–539; Thomas J. Holt, Olga Smirnova, Yi Ting Chua, and Heith Copes, "Examining the Risk Reduction Strategies of Actors in Online Criminal Markets," *Global Crime* 16, no. 2 (2015): 81–103; Dupont et al., "The Ecology of Trust among Hackers."

56. Bill McCarthy, John Hagan, and Lawrence E. Cohen, "Uncertainty, Cooperation, and Crime: Understanding the Decision to Co-Offend," *Social Forces* 77, no. 1 (1998): 155–184.

57. Partha Dasgupta, "Trust as a Commodity," in *Trust: Making and Breaking Cooperative Relations,* ed. Diego Gambetta (Oxford: Basil Blackwell, 1988), 51.

58. James S. Coleman, *Foundations of Social Theory* (Cambridge, MA: Belknap Press of Harvard University Press, 1990), 91.

59. Russell Hardin, "Conceptions and Explanations of Trust," in *Trust in Society,* ed. Karen S. Cook (New York: Russell Sage Foundation, 2001).

60. Piotr Sztompka, *Trust: A Sociological Theory* (Cambridge: Cambridge University Press, 1999), ch. 4.

61. See, among others, Robert Axelrod, *The Evolution of Cooperation,* rev. ed. (New York: Basic Books, 2006); Benjamin Klein and Keith B. Leffler, "The Role of Market Forces in Assuring Contractual Performance," *Journal of Political Economy* 89, no. 4 (1981): 615–641; Dilip Abreu, "On the Theory of Infinitely Repeated Games with Discounting," *Econometrica* 56, no. 2 (1988): 383–396.

62. Thomas C. Schelling, *The Strategy of Conflict* (Cambridge, MA: Harvard University Press, 1963), 134–135.

63. Avinash K. Dixit, *Lawlessness and Economics: Alternative Modes of Governance* (Princeton, NJ: Princeton University Press, 2004); Elinor Ostrom, *Governing the Commons: The Evolution of Institutions for Collective Action* (Cambridge: Cambridge University Press, 1990).

64. Ernst Fehr and Simon Gächter, "Cooperation and Punishment in Public Goods Experiments," *American Economic Review* 90, no. 4 (2000): 980–994; Ernst Fehr and Herbert Gintis, "Human Motivation and Social Cooperation: Experimental and Analytical Foundations," *Annual Review of Sociology* 33 (2007): 43–64.

65. Gambetta, *The Sicilian Mafia*; Varese, *The Russian Mafia*; Dixit, *Lawlessness and Economics.*

66. Karen S. Cook, Russell Hardin, and Margaret Levi, *Cooperation without Trust?* (New York: Russell Sage Foundation, 2005), 37.

67. Schelling, *The Strategy of Conflict,* 22.

68. Thomas C. Schelling, *Strategies of Commitment and Other Essays* (Cambridge, MA: Harvard University Press, 2006), 1.

69. Schelling, *The Strategy of Conflict,* 43–44.

70. Gambetta, *Codes of the Underworld,* 66.

71. Campana and Varese, "Cooperation in Criminal Organizations."

72. Gambetta, *Codes of the Underworld,* 62–64.

73. Gambetta, *Codes of the Underworld,* 63.

74. The difficulties of scaling cooperation from small groups to larger ones are well known see, for instance, Mancur Olson, *The Logic of Collective Action: Public Goods and the Theory of Groups* (Cambridge, MA: Harvard University Press, 1971).

75. Douglass C. North, "Institutions," *Journal of Economic Perspectives* 5, no. 1 (1991): 97–112, 97.

76. North, "Institutions," 97.

77. Thomas Hobbes, *Leviathan* (Oxford: Oxford University Press, 2012).

78. See, for instance, Friedrich A. von Hayek, *The Constitution of Liberty* (London: Routledge, 2006); Friedrich A. von Hayek, *The Fatal Conceit* (London: Routledge, 1988).

79. Dixit, *Lawlessness and Economics.*

80. Thomas C. Schelling, "What Is the Business of Organized Crime?" *Journal of Public Law* 20, no. 1 (1971): 71–84, 72.

81. Schelling, "What Is the Business of Organized Crime?" 74.

82. Federico Varese, "What Is Organized Crime?" in *Organized Crime: Critical Concepts in Criminology,* ed. Federico Varese (New York: Routledge, 2010).

83. Gambetta, *The Sicilian Mafia.*

84. Varese, "What Is Organized Crime?" 14, 17.

85. Nicholas Pileggi, *Wiseguy: Life in a Mafia Family* (New York: Pocket Books, Simon & Schuster, 1985), 56–57.

86. Axelrod, *The Evolution of Cooperation;* Robert Gibbons, "Trust in Social Structures: Hobbes and Coase Meet Repeated Games," in *Trust in Society,* ed. Karen S. Cook (New York: Russell Sage Foundation, 2001); Karen S. Cook, Chris Snijders, Vincent Buskens, and Coye Cheshire, eds., *eTrust: Forming Relationships in the Online World* (New York: Russell Sage Foundation, 2009).

2. FROM LONE WOLVES TO INDUSTRIALIZATION

1. David S. Wall, *Cybercrime: The Transformation of Crime in the Information Age* (Cambridge: Polity, 2007); Majid Yar, *Cybercrime and Society* (Thousand Oaks, CA: Sage, 2006).

2. See, for example, Steven Levy, *Hackers: Heroes of the Computer Revolution,* 25th anniv. ed. (Sebastopol, CA: O'Reilly Media, 2010); Suelette Dreyfus and Julian Assange, *Underground: Tales of Hacking, Madness and Obsession on the Electronic Frontier* (Edinburgh, UK: Canongate, 2012).

3. Susan W. Brenner, *Cybercrime: Criminal Threats from Cyberspace* (Westport, CT: Praeger, 2010), ch. 2.

4. Misha Glenny, *DarkMarket: Cyberthieves, Cybercops and You* (London: Bodley Head, 2011); Kevin Poulsen, *Kingpin: How One Hacker Took Over the Billion-Dollar Cybercrime*

Underground (New York: Crown, 2011); Joseph Menn, *Fatal System Error: The Hunt for the New Crime Lords Who Are Bringing Down the Internet* (New York: Public Affairs, 2010); Brian Krebs, *Spam Nation: The Inside Story of Organized Cybercrime—From Global Epidemic to Your Front Door* (Naperville, IL: Sourcebooks, 2014).

5. Levy, *Hackers: Heroes of the Computer Revolution*, ch. 1.

6. Levy, *Hackers: Heroes of the Computer Revolution*, ch. 2.

7. Yar, *Cybercrime and Society*, 6–7; Brenner, *Cybercrime: Criminal Threats from Cyberspace*, 15; Katie Hafner and Matthew Lyon, *Where Wizards Stay Up Late: The Origins of the Internet* (New York: Simon & Schuster, 1998).

8. Brenner, *Cybercrime: Criminal Threats from Cyberspace*, 13–14. See also Philip Lapsley, *Exploding the Phone: The Untold Story of the Teenagers Who Hacked Ma Bell* (New York: Grove Press, 2013).

9. Jonathan Littman, "The Last Hacker: He Called Himself Dark Dante. His Compulsion Led Him to Secret Files and, Eventually, the Bar of Justice," *Los Angeles Times*, September 12, 1993, http://articles.latimes.com/1993-09-12/magazine/tm-34163_1_kevin-poulsen; Jonathan Littman, *The Watchman: The Twisted Life and Crimes of Serial Hacker Kevin Poulsen* (New York: Little, Brown, 1997).

10. Kevin D. Mitnick and William L. Simon, *Ghost in the Wires: My Adventures as the World's Most Wanted Hacker* (New York: Little, Brown, 2011); Brenner, *Cybercrime: Criminal Threats from Cyberspace*, 23–26.

11. Michelle Slatalla and Joshua Quittner, *Masters of Deception: The Gang That Ruled Cyberspace* (London: Vintage, 1995). See also http://cultdeadcow.com and http://www.ccc.de/en/.

12. Clifford Stoll, *The Cuckoo's Egg: Tracking a Spy through the Maze of Computer Espionage* (New York: Pocket Books, Simon & Schuster, 2000).

13. USA v. Robert Tappan Morris, 928 F. 2d 504 (2nd Circuit, 1991); Timothy B. Lee, "How a Grad Student Trying to Build the First Botnet Brought the Internet to Its Knees," *Washington Post*, November 1, 2013, https://www.washingtonpost.com/news/the-switch/wp/2013/11/01/how-a-grad-student-trying-to-build-the-first-botnet-brought-the-internet-to-its-knees/?noredirect= on&utm_term=.4b422cdec5e9.

14. Brenner, *Cybercrime: Criminal Threats from Cyberspace*, 30–36.

15. Donn B. Parker, *Fighting Computer Crime* (New York: Scribner, 1983), 110.

16. Federal Bureau of Investigation, "A Byte Out of History: $10 Million Hack, 1994-Style," FBI News, January 31, 2014, https://www.fbi.gov/news/stories/a-byte-out-of-history-10-million-hack.

17. Associated Press, "Theft of Credit Card Numbers from Internet Leads to Arrest," *New York Times*, May 23, 1997, https://www.nytimes.com/1997/05/23/us/theft-of-credit-card-numbers-from-internet-leads-to-arrest.html.

18. Poulsen, *Kingpin*, 38.

19. Cormac Herley and Dinei Florêncio, "Nobody Sells Gold for the Price of Silver: Dishonesty, Uncertainty and the Underground Economy," in *Economics of Information Security and Privacy*, ed. Tyler Moore, David Pym, and Christos Ioannidis (Boston: Springer, 2010), 33–53.

20. George A. Akerlof, "The Market for 'Lemons': Quality Uncertainty and the Market Mechanism," *Quarterly Journal of Economics* 84, no. 3 (1970): 488–500.

21. See Poulsen, *Kingpin*, 73–75; Glenny, *DarkMarket*, part II; Menn, *Fatal System Error*, ch. 9.

22. Poulsen, *Kingpin*, 73–74.

23. "Carding. Interview with Script'om," Xakep.ru [*Hacker* magazine] 39 (2002), 48–50.

24. In the course of this project, it became apparent that cybercriminals read widely and have often encountered mainstream articles and books written on the subject. While interview subjects remained firm in their convictions, it is possible that the strong CarderPlanet narrative found, for instance, in the books referenced above might have influenced some of their thoughts on the matter.

25. Poulsen, *Kingpin*, 73–74.

26. Glenny, *DarkMarket*, 66–67.

27. For numerous examples of meetings and socializing, see also Sergey Pavlovich, *How to Steal a Million: The Memoirs of a Russian Hacker* (self-pub., 2018).

28. Poulsen, *Kingpin*, 73–74.

29. US law enforcement document and offline archived elements of CarderPlanet.

30. Jonathan Lusthaus, "Trust in the World of Cybercrime," *Global Crime* 13, no. 2 (2012): 71–94, 80.

31. Poulsen, *Kingpin*, 75.

32. Glenny, *DarkMarket*, 76.

33. "Carding. Interview with Script'om."

34. US law enforcement document.

35. United States Department of Justice, "Ukrainian National Who Co-Founded Cyber-crime Marketplace Sentenced to 18 Years in Prison," Office of Public Affairs press release, December 12, 2013, http://www.justice.gov/opa/pr/ukrainian-national-who-co-founded -cybercrime-marketplace-sentenced-18-years-prison.

36. "Tracking the Russian Scammers," Wired, January 31, 2007, http://archive.wired.com /politics/onlinerights/news/2007/01/72605.

37. Brian Krebs, "Ukrainian Cybercrime Boss Leads Political Party," *Washington Post*, March 13, 2008, http://voices.washingtonpost.com/securityfix/2008/03/ukranian_cybercrime _boss_leads.html.

38. Golubov's profile page on the Verkhovna Rada of Ukraine official web portal can be accessed at http://itd.rada.gov.ua/mps/info/page/18074.

39. US law enforcement document.

40. Brian Grow and Jason Bush, "Hacker Hunters," Bloomberg Businessweek, May 30, 2005, https://www.bloomberg.com/news/articles/2005-05-29/hacker-hunters.

41. USA v. Andrew Montovani and others, SSC/2003R01260 (District of New Jersey) [Indictment].

42. Poulsen, *Kingpin*, 76.

43. United States Department of Justice, "Six Defendants Plead Guilty in Internet Identity Theft and Credit Card Fraud Conspiracy," Cybercrime press release, November 17, 2005, https://www.justice.gov/archive/criminal/cybercrime/press-releases/2005/mantovaniPlea .htm.

44. USA v. Montovani and others.

45. Poulsen, *Kingpin*.

46. R v. Renu Subramaniam and John McHugh, Blackfriars Crown Court, 2010 [Opening Note].

47. "Organiser of Darkmarket Fraud Website Jailed," BBC News, February 26, 2010, http://news.bbc.co.uk/1/hi/uk/8539680.stm.

48. Poulsen, *Kingpin;* Glenny, *DarkMarket.*

49. Joseph D. Pistone and Richard Woodley, *Donnie Brasco: My Undercover Life in the Mafia* (London: Coronet, 1997).

50. Botnet is short for robot network, meaning a network of computers that have been infected by malware and are now controlled by a "bot herder" or "bot master." Botnets can be used to carry out DDoS attacks, send spam, or harvest data from victim computers.

51. Vulnerabilities are essentially weak spots in computer software that can be exploited by attackers. A zero-day vulnerability is one that has not yet been publicly disclosed and therefore remains unpatched.

52. Past and present examples of more specialized forums include, for instance, Hack-Forums.net, TheRealDeal, BlackHatWorld.com, and Spamdot.biz.

53. There appears to be some uncertainty around when anti-chat.ru came into existence. Participant estimations ranged from the late 1990s to the early to mid-2000s.

54. An exploit kit automates the exploitation of vulnerabilities to deliver malicious code.

55. Brian Krebs, "The Darkode Cybercrime Forum, Up Close," KrebsonSecurity, July 15, 2015, http://krebsonsecurity.com/2015/07/the-darkode-cybercrime-forum-up-close/.

56. A Trojan horse is a malicious piece of software that masquerades as a safe one.

57. Leo Kelion, "Cryptolocker Ransomware Has 'Infected About 250,000 PCs,'" BBC News, December 24, 2013, http://www.bbc.co.uk/news/technology-25506020; Brian Krebs, "'Operation Tovar' Targets 'Gameover' ZeuS Botnet, CryptoLocker Scourge," KrebsonSecurity, June 14, 2014, http://krebsonsecurity.com/2014/06/operation-tovar-targets-gameover-zeus-botnet-cryptolocker-scourge/. On the group connected to earlier Zeus activity, see USA v. Evgeniy Mikhaylovich Bogachev, 4:14-mj-03034-CRZ, Document 1 (District of Nebraska) [2014 Criminal Complaint].

58. "Cyber-Attack: Europol Says It Was Unprecedented in Scale," BBC News, May 13, 2017, http://www.bbc.co.uk/news/world-europe-39907965.

59. James Verini, "The Great Cyberheist," *New York Times Magazine,* November 10, 2014, https://www.nytimes.com/2010/11/14/magazine/14Hacker-t.html.

60. Steve Ragan, "Eight Arrested in Moscow after Allegedly Stealing Millions Using Carberp Trojan," Security Week (website), March 21, 2012, http://www.securityweek.com/eight-arrested-moscow-after-allegedly-stealing-millions-using-carberp-trojan. On the other hand, the progammers who created the malware itself appeared to operate more remotely from different locations around Ukraine: Julia Ryabchun, "System Error: A Group of Hackers Was Neutralized," *Kommersant,* February 4, 2013, http://www.kommersant.ua/doc/2160535.

61. Krebs, *Spam Nation.*

62. United States Department of Justice, "Ukrainian National."

63. USA v. Liberty Reserve S. A. and others, 13 CRIM368 (Southern District of New York) [2013 Indictment].

64. Olga Kharif, "The Criminal Underworld Is Dropping Bitcoin for Another Currency," Bloomberg, January 2, 2018, https://www.bloomberg.com/news/articles/2018-01-02/criminal

-underworld-is-dropping-bitcoin-for-another-currency; Jeff John Roberts, "Criminals Drop Bitcoin for Other Cryptocurrencies," *Fortune,* January 22, 2018, http://fortune.com/2018/01/22/bitcoin-monero-cryptocurrency-crime/.

65. Some hosting providers favored by criminals may not be intentionally bulletproof, but rather simply unable to deal with takedown requests because they are small operations with limited capacity. With thanks to Alice Hutchings on this point.

66. James Graham, Rick Howard, Ralph Thomas, and Steven Winterfeld, eds., *Cyber Fraud: Tactics, Techniques, and Procedures* (Boca Raton, FL: CRC Press, 2009), 171–172.

67. Brian Krebs, "Shadowy Russian Firm Seen as Conduit for Cybercrime," *Washington Post,* October 13, 2007, http://www.washingtonpost.com/wp-dyn/content/article/2007/10/12/AR2007101202461.html.

68. Krebs, *Spam Nation,* 17–24.

69. Graham et al., eds., *Cyber Fraud,* 173.

70. Graham et al., eds., *Cyber Fraud,* 202–207.

71. On such topics see, for example, Tim Maurer, *Cyber Mercenaries: The State, Hackers and Power* (Cambridge: Cambridge University Press, 2018); Lucas Kello, *The Virtual Weapon and International Order* (New Haven: Yale University Press, 2017); Florian Egloff, "Cybersecurity and the Age of Privateering," in George Perkovich and Ariel E. Levite, eds., *Understanding Cyber Conflict* (Washington, DC: Georgetown University Press, 2017), 231–247; Jamie Collier, "Proxy Actors in the Cyber Domain: Implications for State Strategy," *St Antony's International Review* 13, no. 1 (2017): 25–47.

72. David E. Sanger, David Barboza, and Nicole Perlroth, "Chinese Army Unit Is Seen as Tied to Hacking Against U.S.," *New York Times,* February 19, 2013, http://www.nytimes.com/2013/02/19/technology/chinas-army-is-seen-as-tied-to-hacking-against-us.html.

73. Josh Rogin, "NSA Chief: Cybercrime Constitutes the 'Greatest Transfer of Wealth in History,'" *Foreign Policy,* July 9, 2012, http://foreignpolicy.com/2012/07/09/nsa-chief-cybercrime-constitutes-the-greatest-transfer-of-wealth-in-history/.

74. "Cyber-attack: US and UK Blame North Korea for WannaCry," BBC News, December 19, 2017, http://www.bbc.com/news/world-us-canada-42407488.

75. On North Korean hackers seeking profit, see Sam Kim, "Inside North Korea's Hacker Army," Bloomberg Businessweek, February 7, 2018, https://www.bloomberg.com/news/features/2018-02-07/inside-kim-jong-un-s-hacker-army.

76. For an overview, see Alan Dupont, *East Asia Imperilled: Transnational Challenges to Security* (Cambridge: Cambridge University Press, 2001), 23–31, 173–193.

77. Thomas C. Schelling, "What Is the Business of Organized Crime?" *Journal of Public Law* 20, no. 1 (1971): 71–84; Diego Gambetta, *The Sicilian Mafia: The Business of Private Protection* (Cambridge, MA: Harvard University Press, 1993); Yiu Kong Chu, *The Triads as Business* (London: Routledge, 2000); Annelise Graebner Anderson, *The Business of Organized Crime: A Cosa Nostra Family* (Stanford, CA: Hoover Institution Press, 1979); Peter Reuter, "The Organization of Illegal Markets: An Economic Analysis," National Institute of Justice, U.S. Department of Justice, Washington, DC, February 1985.

78. Chu, *The Triads as Business;* Gambetta, *The Sicilian Mafia;* Federico Varese, *The Russian Mafia: Private Protection in a New Market Economy* (Oxford: Oxford University Press, 2001).

79. Letizia Paoli, Victoria A. Greenfield, and Peter Reuter, *The World Heroin Market: Can Supply Be Cut?* (Oxford: Oxford University Press, 2009); Ko-lin Chin and Sheldon X. Zhang,

The Chinese Heroin Trade: Cross-Border Drug Trafficking in Southeast Asia and Beyond (New York: New York University Press, 2015); Damián Zaitch, *Trafficking Cocaine: Colombian Drug Entrepreneurs in the Netherlands* (The Hague: Kluwer Law International, 2002); Steven Levitt and Sudhir Venkatesh, "An Economic Analysis of a Drug-Selling Gang's Finances," *Quarterly Journal of Economics* 115, no. 3 (2000): 755–789.

80. Michael Levi, *The Phantom Capitalists: The Organization and Control of Long-Firm Fraud,* rev. ed. (Aldershot, UK: Ashgate, 2008); Tomson H. Nguyen, "The Business of Illegal Gambling: An Examination of the Gambling Business of Vietnamese Cafés," *Deviant Behavior* 25, no. 5 (2004): 451–464.

3. MAKING SENSE OF THE CYBERCRIME INDUSTRY

1. See, for example, Jeffrey R. Church and Roger Ware, *Industrial Organization: A Strategic Approach* (Boston: Irwin McGraw-Hill, 2000); Donald A. Hay and Derek J. Morris, *Industrial Economics: Theory and Evidence* (Oxford: Oxford University Press, 1991).

2. See, for instance, David Décary-Hétu and Benoît Dupont, "The Social Network of Hackers," *Global Crime* 13, no. 3 (2012): 160–175.

3. See David G. Rand, Samuel Arbesman, and Nicholas A. Christakis, "Dynamic Social Networks Promote Cooperation in Experiments with Humans," *Proceedings of the National Academy of Sciences* 108, no. 48 (2011): 19193–19198; Edoardo Gallo and Chang Yan, "The Effects of Reputational and Social Knowledge on Cooperation," *Proceedings of the National Academy of Sciences* 112, no. 12 (2015): 3647–3652.

4. Mark Granovetter, "Economic Action and Social Structure: The Problem of Embeddedness," *American Journal of Sociology* 91, no. 3 (1985): 481–510, 504. Around the topic of networks as an encompassing versus a distinct concept, see Grahame Thompson, Jennifer Frances, Rosalind Levačić and Jeremy Mitchell, eds., *Markets, Hierarchies and Networks: The Coordination of Social Life* (London: Sage Publications, 1991).

5. Adam Smith, *The Wealth of Nations* (London: Penguin, 1999), 109–110.

6. Dune Lawrence, "An Identity Thief Explains the Art of Emptying Your Bank Account," *Bloomberg Businessweek,* July 15, 2015, https://www.bloomberg.com/news/articles/2015-07-15/an-identity-thief-explains-the-art-of-emptying-your-bank-account.

7. It is likely also the case that automation can supersede certain specialties and lead to greater efficiency and productivity (IRE-CSP-2).

8. Douglass C. North, "Institutions," *Journal of Economic Perspectives* 5, no. 1 (1991): 97–112, 99.

9. On the Soviets and science, see Kendall E. Bailes, *Technology and Society under Lenin and Stalin: Origins of the Soviet Technical Intelligentsia, 1917–1941* (Princeton, NJ: Princeton University Press, 1978); Loren R. Graham, *Science in Russia and the Soviet Union: A Short History* (Cambridge: Cambridge University Press, 1993); Loren R. Graham, *What Have We Learned about Science and Technology from the Russian Experience?* (Stanford, CA: Stanford University Press, 1998).

10. Sergey Pavlovich, *How to Steal a Million: The Memoirs of a Russian Hacker* (self-pub., 2018), ch. 33.

11. David Belson, ed., "Akamai's [State of the Internet] Q3 2015 Report," *Akamai Technologies* 8, no. 3 (2015), https://www.akamai.com/us/en/multimedia/documents/report/q3-2015-soti-connectivity-final.pdf.

12. Jonathan Lusthaus and Federico Varese, "Offline and Local: The Hidden Face of Cybercrime," *Policing*, July 28, 2017.

13. For a rare study, see Michael Yip, "An Investigation into Chinese Cybercrime and the Applicability of Social Network Analysis," Poster Presentation, 3rd Annual Conference on Web Science, Koblenz, Germany, June 2011.

14. On Chinese hackers, see Scott J. Henderson, *The Dark Visitor: Inside the World of Chinese Hackers* (self-pub., 2007). Available at http://www.lulu.com/items/volume_62/2048000 /2048958/4/print/2048958.pdf; Doug Mackey, *The Diffusion of Network Penetration Skills in the People's Republic of China* (Master's Thesis, Georgia Institute of Technology, 2014).

15. Ransomware was another form of cybercrime that was regularly noted as a critical threat in a great number of jurisdictions I visited. But case by case, it was often unclear if the attackers were local, from abroad, or a combination of the two.

16. On professionalization, see Stanley Parker, *The Sociology of Industry* (Boston: Allen and Unwin, 1981), ch. 12; Stuart R. Timperley and Michael D. Osbaldeston, "The Professionalization Process: A Study of an Aspiring Occupational Organization," *Sociological Review* 23, no. 3 (1975): 607–627; Terence J. Johnson, *Professions and Power* (London: Routledge, 2016), ch. 2.

17. See, for instance, Brian Krebs, "Feds Charge Carding Kingpin in Retail Hacks," KrebsonSecurity, July 8, 2014, https://krebsonsecurity.com/2014/07/feds-charge-carding -kingpin-in-retail-hacks/#more-26782.

18. Brian Krebs, *Spam Nation: The Inside Story of Organized Cybercrime—From Global Epidemic to Your Front Door* (Naperville, IL: Sourcebooks, 2014), ch. 4.

19. Hugh Gravelle and Ray Rees, *Microeconomics* (Harlow: Prentice Hall, 2004), 3.

20. Ronald H. Coase, *The Firm, the Market and the Law* (Chicago: University of Chicago Press, 1988), 7.

21. Thomas J. Holt, "Exploring the Social Organisation and Structure of Stolen Data Markets," *Global Crime* 14, no. 2/3 (2013): 155–174; Thomas J. Holt, "Examining the Forces Shaping Cybercrime Markets Online," *Social Science Computer Review* 31, no. 2 (2013): 165–177; Thomas J. Holt and Eric Lampke, "Exploring Stolen Data Markets Online: Products and Market Forces," *Criminal Justice Studies* 23, no. 1 (2010): 33–50; David Décary-Hétu and Benoît Dupont, "Reputation in a Dark Network of Online Criminals," *Global Crime* 14, no. 2/3 (2013): 175–196; Alice Hutchings and Thomas J. Holt, "A Crime Script Analysis of the Online Stolen Data Market," *British Journal of Criminology* 55, no. 3 (2015): 596–614.

22. Kevin Poulsen, *Kingpin: How One Hacker Took Over the Billion-Dollar Cybercrime Underground* (New York: Crown, 2011); Misha Glenny, *DarkMarket: Cyberthieves, Cybercops and You* (London: Bodley Head, 2011).

23. USA v. Roman Zolotarev and others, 2:12-cr-APG-GWF, Document 1 (District of Nevada) [2012 Indictment].

24. Arthur Sullivan and Steven M. Sheffrin, *Economics: Principles in Action* (Upper Saddle River, NJ: Pearson Prentice Hall, 2003), 29.

25. Ronald H. Coase, "The Nature of the Firm," *Economica* 4, no. 16 (1937): 386–405. For a relevant review of the literature on firms see Robert Gibbons, "Four Formal(izable) Theories of the Firm?" *Journal of Economic Behavior & Organization* 58, no. 2 (2005): 200–245.

26. On firms and traditional organized crime, see Peter Reuter, *Disorganized Crime: The Economics of the Visible Hand* (Cambridge, MA: MIT Press, 1983); Diego Gambetta, *The Sicilian Mafia: The Business of Private Protection* (Cambridge, MA: Harvard University Press, 1993).

27. Steve Ragan, "Eight Arrested in Moscow after Allegedly Stealing Millions Using Carberp Trojan," SecurityWeek (website), March 21, 2012, https://www.securityweek.com/eight-arrested-moscow-after-allegedly-stealing-millions-using-carberp-trojan.

28. Krebs, *Spam Nation*, ch. 2; James Graham, Rick Howard, Ralph Thomas, and Steven Winterfeld, eds., *Cyber Fraud: Tactics, Techniques, and Procedures* (Boca Raton, FL: CRC Press, 2009).

29. USA v. Liberty Reserve S. A. and others, 13 CRIM368 (Southern District of New York) [2013 Indictment].

30. Krebs, *Spam Nation*.

4. NICKNAMES AND IDENTITY

1. David W. Maurer and Allan W. Futrell, "Criminal Monickers," *American Speech* 57, no. 4 (1982): 243–255, 248.

2. Diego Gambetta, *Codes of the Underworld: How Criminals Communicate* (Princeton, NJ: Princeton University Press, 2009), ch. 9.

3. Federico Varese, *The Russian Mafia: Private Protection in a New Market Economy* (Oxford: Oxford University Press, 2001), Appendix A.

4. For other approaches, see Barbara H. Zaitzow, "Nickname Usage by Gang Members," *Journal of Gang Research* 5, no. 3 (1998): 29–40; Sharon Black, Brad Wilcox, and Brad Platt, "Nicknames in Prison: Meaning and Manipulation in Inmate Monikers," *Names* 62, no. 3 (2014): 127–136; Craig Wilson, "What's in a Name? Gang Monikers," *FBI Law Enforcement Bulletin* 65, no. 5 (1997): 14–17.

5. For more detail on these points, see Varese, *The Russian Mafia*, 193–194.

6. Gambetta, *Codes of the Underworld*, 239–246.

7. Varese, *The Russian Mafia*, 195–197.

8. USA v. Roman Zolotarev and others, 2:12-cr-APG-GWF, Document 1 (District of Nevada) [2012 Indictment].

9. Dumps are card details stolen from hacked point-of-sale systems.

10. Kevin Poulsen, *Kingpin: How One Hacker Took Over the Billion-Dollar Cybercrime Underground* (New York: Crown, 2011), 127.

11. United States Department of Justice, "Retail Hacking Ring Charged for Stealing and Distributing Credit and Debit Card Numbers from Major U.S. Retailers," Cybercrime press release, August 5, 2008, https://www.justice.gov/archive/opa/pr/2008/August/08-ag-689.html; Kim Zetter, "Ukrainian Carding King 'Maksik' Was Lured to Arrest," Wired, July 28, 2010, https://www.wired.com/2010/07/maksik-lured-to-arrest/.

12. In all contexts, even without direct nickname connections, thorough investigations can sometimes trace back links among nicknames, logins, email addresses, and other digital footprints that might begin with a younger, more naive user who originally did not take operational security into mind.

13. "I Was a Cybercrook for the FBI," Wired, January 30, 2007, http://archive.wired.com/politics/onlinerights/news/2007/01/.

14. Jonathan Lusthaus, "Call Me I$Hm@El," *Pacific Standard*, November 6, 2013, https://psmag.com/social-justice/call-ihmel-crybercrime-nickname-internet-67238.

15. Kevin Poulsen, "One Hacker's Audacious Plan to Rule the Black Market in Stolen Credit Cards," Wired, December 22, 2008, https://www.wired.com/2008/12/ff-max-butler/.

16. USA v. Zolotarev and others.

17. Poulsen, *Kingpin*.

18. See Diego Gambetta, "Signaling," in *The Oxford Handbook of Analytical Sociology*, ed. Peter Hedström and Peter Bearman (Oxford: Oxford University Press, 2009); Michael Spence, "Job Market Signaling," *Quarterly Journal of Economics* 87, no. 3 (1973): 355–374; Amotz Zahavi, "Mate Selection: A Selection for a Handicap," *Journal of Theoretical Biology* 53, no. 1 (1975): 205–214.

19. Poulsen, *Kingpin*.

5. HOW CYBERCRIMINALS COOPERATE ONLINE

1. Piotr Sztompka, *Trust: A Sociological Theory* (Cambridge: Cambridge University Press, 1999), ch. 4.

2. While beyond the scope of this chapter, it is possible to view issues of cybercriminal appearance through a signaling theory framework. For attempts at applying signaling theory to cybercrime, see Jonathan Lusthaus, "Trust in the World of Cybercrime," *Global Crime* 13, no. 2 (2012): 71–94; David Décary-Hétu and Anna Leppänen, "Criminals and Signals: An Assessment of Criminal Performance in the Carding Underworld," *Security Journal* 29, no. 3 (2016): 442–460; Thomas J. Holt, Olga Smirnova, and Alice Hutchings, "Examining Signals of Trust in Criminal Markets Online," *Journal of Cybersecurity* 2, no. 2 (2016): 137–145. On signaling theory more generally see Michael Spence, "Job Market Signaling," *Quarterly Journal of Economics* 87, no. 3 (1973): 355–374; Diego Gambetta, "Signaling," in *The Oxford Handbook of Analytical Sociology*, ed. Peter Hedström and Peter Bearman (Oxford: Oxford University Press, 2009).

3. Kevin Poulsen, *Kingpin: How One Hacker Took Over the Billion-Dollar Cybercrime Underground* (New York: Crown, 2011), 119.

4. Joseph D. Pistone, *Donnie Brasco: My Undercover Life in the Mafia* (New York: New American Library, 1987), 46.

5. Money mules are those tasked with moving illicit funds rather than drugs, often through nonphysical methods like online bank transfers or international money transfers.

6. On topics relating to reviewed vendors see Thomas J. Holt, "Examining the Forces Shaping Cybercrime Markets Online," *Social Science Computer Review* 31, no. 2 (2013): 165–177, 173; Thomas J. Holt and Eric Lampke, "Exploring Stolen Data Markets Online: Products and Market Forces," *Criminal Justice Studies* 23, no. 1 (2010): 33–50, 43–44; Michael Yip, Craig Webber, and Nigel Shadbolt, "Trust among Cybercriminals? Carding Forums, Uncertainty and Implications for Policing," *Policing & Society* 23, no. 4 (2013): 516–539, 528.

7. Diego Gambetta, *Codes of the Underworld: How Criminals Communicate* (Princeton, NJ: Princeton University Press, 2009), 16–18.

8. See Robert Axelrod, *The Evolution of Cooperation*, rev. ed. (New York: Basic Books, 2006); Benjamin Klein and Keith B. Leffler, "The Role of Market Forces in Assuring Contractual Performance," *Journal of Political Economy* 89, no. 4 (1981): 615–641; Dilip Abreu, "On the Theory of Infinitely Repeated Games with Discounting," *Econometrica* 56, no. 2 (1988): 383–396.

9. Thomas C. Schelling, *The Strategy of Conflict* (Cambridge, MA: Harvard University Press, 1963), 134–135.

10. Marti Motoyama, Damon McCoy, Kirill Levchenko, Stefan Savage, and Geoffrey M. Voelker, "An Analysis of Underground Forums," in *Proceedings of the 2011 ACM SIGCOMM Conference on Internet Measurement,* Berlin, November 2011, 71–80, 75.

11. There is a growing literature examining the importance of reputation within the cryptomarket drug trade. See, for example, Wojtek Przepiorka, Lukas Norbutas, and Rense Corten, "Order without Law: Reputation Promotes Cooperation in a Cryptomarket for Illegal Drugs," *European Sociological Review* 33, no. 6 (2017): 752–764; David Décary-Hétu and Olivier Quessy-Doré, "Are Repeat Buyers in Cryptomarkets Loyal Customers? Repeat Business between Dyads of Cryptomarket Vendors and Users," *American Behavioral Scientist* 61, no. 11 (2017): 1341–1357; Robert Augustus Hardy and Julia R. Norgaard, "Reputation in the Internet Black Market: An Empirical and Theoretical Analysis of the Deep Web," *Journal of Institutional Economics* 12, no. 3 (2016): 515–539.

12. Mark Granovetter, "Economic Action and Social Structure: The Problem of Embeddedness," *American Journal of Sociology* 91, no. 3 (1985): 481–510, 490.

13. Elinor Mills, "Q&A: FBI Agent Looks Back on Time Posing as a Cybercriminal," CNET News, June 29, 2009, https://www.cnet.com/news/q-a-fbi-agent-looks-back-on -time-posing-as-a-cybercriminal/.

14. David Décary-Hétu and Benoît Dupont, "Reputation in a Dark Network of Online Criminals," *Global Crime* 14, no. 2 / 3 (2013): 175–196.

15. Motoyama et al., "An Analysis of Underground Forums," 75.

16. R v Gary Paul Kelly and others, Southwark Crown Court, 2011, 35 [Case Summary].

17. Holt, "Examining the Forces Shaping Cybercrime Markets Online," 173; Holt, "Exploring the Social Organization and Structure of Stolen Data Markets," 165.

18. See, for instance, R v Kelly and others.

19. See Chrysanthos Dellarocas, "The Digitization of Word of Mouth: Promise and Challenges of Online Feedback Mechanisms," *Management Science* 49, no. 10 (2003): 1407–1324; Paul Resnick and Richard Zeckhauser, "Trust among Strangers in Internet Transactions: Empirical Analysis of eBay's Reputation System," in *The Economics of the Internet and E-Commerce,* ed. Michael R. Baye (Amsterdam: Elsevier Science, 2002); Andreas Diekmann, Ben Jann, and David Wyder, "Trust and Reputation in Internet Auctions," in *eTrust: Forming Relationships in the Online World,* ed. Karen S. Cook, Chris Snijders, Vincent Buskens, and Coye Chester (New York: Russell Sage Foundation, 2009).

20. Paul R. Milgrom, Douglass C. North, and Barry R. Weingast, "The Role of Institutions in the Revival of Trade: The Law Merchant, Private Judges, and the Champagne Fairs," *Economics & Politics* 2, no. 1 (1990): 1–23; Avner Greif, "Reputation and Coalitions in Medieval Trade: Evidence on the Maghribi Traders," *Journal of Economic History* 49, no. 4 (1989): 857–882.

21. Milgrom, North, and Weingast, "The Role of Institutions in the Revival of Trade."

22. Benoît Dupont, "Skills and Trust: A Tour Inside the Hard Drives of Computer Hackers," in *Crime and Networks,* ed. Carlo Morselli (New York: Routledge, 2014).

23. Poulsen, *Kingpin,* 168.

24. Names of associates are also removed to maintain anonymity.

25. Brian Krebs, "The World Has No Room for Cowards," KrebsonSecurity, March 15, 2013, http://krebsonsecurity.com/2013/03/the-world-has-no-room-for-cowards/.

26. Caroline Davies, "Welcome to DarkMarket—Global One-Stop Shop for Cybercrime and Banking Fraud," *The Guardian*, January 14, 2010, http://www.guardian.co.uk /technology/2010/jan/14/darkmarket-online-fraud-trial-wembley.

27. Sean O'Neill, "Girl, 8, Raped to Order on the Internet," *The Telegraph*, February 14, 2001, http://www.telegraph.co.uk/news/uknews/1322551/Girl-8-raped-to-order-on-the -Internet.html.

28. Holt, "Exploring the Social Organization and Structure of Stolen Data Markets"; Holt and Lampke, "Exploring Stolen Data Markets Online"; Yip et al., "Trust among Cyber-criminals?"

29. Davies, "Welcome to DarkMarket."

30. It is interesting to note that escrow appears far less reliable within the online drug trade. There have been a number of "exit scams," where administrators have disappeared with large sums that the site had held in escrow. One of the largest and most notable cases involved $12 million being stolen: Nicky Wolf, "Bitcoin 'Exit Scam': Deep-Web Market Operators Disappear with $12m," *The Guardian*, March 18, 2015, https://www.theguardian.com /technology/2015/mar/18/bitcoin-deep-web-evolution-exit-scam-12-million-dollars.

31. Douglass C. North, "Institutions," *Journal of Economic Perspectives* 5, no. 1 (1991): 97–122.

32. Federico Varese, *Mafias on the Move* (Princeton, NJ: Princeton University Press, 2011), 114–120.

33. Federico Varese, *The Russian Mafia: Private Protection in a New Market Economy* (Oxford: Oxford University Press, 2001); Robert Nozick, *Anarchy, State and Utopia* (Oxford: Blackwell, 1974), 3–25; Diego Gambetta, *The Sicilian Mafia: The Business of Private Protection* (Cambridge, MA: Harvard University Press, 1993).

34. Federico Varese, "What Is Organized Crime?" in *Organized Crime: Critical Concepts in Criminology*, ed. Federico Varese (New York: Routledge, 2010).

35. See Jonathan Lusthaus, "How Organised Is Organised Cybercrime?" *Global Crime* 14, no. 1 (2013): 52–60, 56.

36. Lusthaus, "How Organised Is Organised Cybercrime?" 56.

37. Milgrom, North, and Weingast, "The Role of Institutions in the Revival of Trade."

38. See, for example, Center for Strategic and International Studies, "Net Losses: Estimating the Global Cost of Cybercrime," McAfee-CSIS joint report, June 2014, https://csis -prod.s3.amazonaws.com/s3fs-public/legacy_files/files/attachments/140609_rp_economic _impact_cybercrime_report.pdf.

39. Gary King, Robert O. Keohane, and Sidney Verba, *Designing Social Inquiry: Scientific Inference in Qualitative Research* (Princeton, NJ: Princeton University Press, 1994), 129–137.

40. Avinash K. Dixit, *Lawlessness and Economics: Alternative Modes of Governance* (Princeton, NJ: Princeton University Press, 2004), 12.

6. THE OFFLINE DIMENSION

1. For rare examples see Jonathan Lusthaus, "Honour among (Cyber)Thieves?" Working Paper No. 2016-1, Extra-Legal Governance Institute, University of Oxford, 2016, http://www

.exlegi.ox.ac.uk/images/Papers/HonourAmongCyberThieves.pdf; Jonathan Lusthaus and Federico Varese, "Offline and Local: The Hidden Face of Cybercrime," *Policing*, July 28, 2017; E. Rutger Leukfeldt, Edward R. Kleemans, and Wouter P. Stol, "Cybercriminal Networks, Social Ties and Online Forums: Social Ties versus Digital Ties within Phishing and Malware Networks," *British Journal of Criminology* 57, no. 3 (2017): 704–722; E. Rutger Leukfeldt, "Cybercrime and Social Ties," *Trends in Organized Crime* 17, no. 4 (2014): 231–249.

2. Peter Reuter, *Disorganized Crime: The Economics of the Visible Hand* (Cambridge, MA: MIT Press, 1983).

3. Kevin Poulsen, *Kingpin: How One Hacker Took Over the Billion-Dollar Cybercrime Underground* (New York: Crown, 2011).

4. Steve Ragan, "Eight Arrested in Moscow after Allegedly Stealing Millions Using Carberp Trojan," Security Week (website), March 21, 2012, http://www.securityweek.com/eight-arrested-moscow-after-allegedly-stealing-millions-using-carberp-trojan.

5. James Graham, Rick Howard, Ralph Thomas, and Steven Winterfeld, eds., *Cyber Fraud: Tactics, Techniques, and Procedures* (Boca Raton, FL: CRC Press, 2009), 171–172; Brian Krebs, *Spam Nation: The Inside Story of Organized Cybercrime—From Global Epidemic to Your Front Door* (Naperville, IL: Sourcebooks, 2014), 17–24.

6. For further detail, see Forward-Looking Threat Research Team, "The Rove Digital Takedown," Research Paper, Trend Micro Inc., Cupertino, CA, 2012, http://www.trendmicro.co.uk/media/misc/rove-digital-takedown-research-paper-en.pdf.

7. Jake Halpern, "Bank of the Underworld," *The Atlantic*, May 2015, http://www.theatlantic.com/magazine/archive/2015/05/bank-of-the-underworld/389555/.

8. Arrows are based overseas because victims might be wary of sending money directly to Romania. There are also cases of cybercriminals from elsewhere in the world operating from different jurisdictions than their own. Sometimes this is to assist scams carried out locally or cash out operations in those jurisdictions. It is also relatively common for cybercriminals to move jurisdictions if they appear to be attracting too much attention from local law enforcement, or simply because they wish to enjoy their money (and the high life) in another location (RUS-(F)LE-1, EE-(F)CC-2).

9. The type of scam itself can be traced further back in history and does not appear to be a Nigerian invention in the first instance. See, for example, "An Old Swindle Revived," *New York Times*, March 20, 1898, https://timesmachine.nytimes.com/timesmachine/1898/03/20/102108294.pdf.

10. On Nigerian cybercrime, see Joshua Oyeniyi Aransiola and Suraj Olalekan Asindemade, "Understanding Cybercrime Perpetrators and the Strategies They Employ in Nigeria," *Cyberpsychology, Behavior, and Social Networking* 14, no. 12 (2011): 759–763.

11. Yudhijit Bhattacharjee, "Welcome to Hackerville: The Romanian Cybercriminal Hotspot," Wired, February 7, 2011, http://www.wired.co.uk/magazine/archive/2011/03/features/welcome-to-hackerville.

12. On the nature of Silicon Valley see Martin Kenney, ed., *Understanding Silicon Valley: The Anatomy of an Entrepreneurial Region* (Stanford, CA: Stanford University Press, 2000); Christophe Lécuyer, *Making Silicon Valley: Innovation and the Growth of High Tech, 1930–1970* (Cambridge, MA: MIT Press, 2006). On the network effects of knowledge transfer and

innovation see, for instance, Ray Reagans and Bill McEvily, "Network Structure and Knowledge Transfer: The Effects of Cohesion and Range," *Administrative Science Quarterly* 48, no. 2 (2003): 240–267.

13. James S. Coleman, "Social Capital in the Creation of Human Capital," *American Journal of Sociology* 94, Supplement: Organizations and Institutions (1988): S95–S120, S98–S99.

14. Coleman, "Social Capital in the Creation of Human Capital," S99.

15. Paolo Campana and Federico Varese, "Cooperation in Criminal Organizations: Kinship and Violence as Credible Commitments," *Rationality and Society* 25, no. 3 (2013): 263–289, 281.

16. Diego Gambetta, *Codes of the Underworld: How Criminals Communicate* (Princeton, NJ: Princeton University Press, 2009), 63.

17. Ryan Singel, "Turkish Police Arrest Alleged ATM Hacker-Kidnapper," Wired, September 12, 2008, https://www.wired.com/2008/09/turkish-police/.

18. A version of the photo can be viewed at Kevin Poulsen, "Hacker Reportedly Kidnaps and Tortures Informant, Posts Picture as a Warning to Others," Wired, August 15, 2008, https://www.wired.com/2008/08/hacker-reported.

19. Chima Aguazue, *The Role of a Culture of Superstition in the Proliferation of Religio-Commercial Pastors in Nigeria* (Bloomington, IN: Author House, 2013).

20. See Charlotte Baarda, "Human Trafficking for Sexual Exploitation from Nigeria into Western Europe: The Role of Voodoo Rituals in the Functioning of a Criminal Network," *European Journal of Criminology* 13, no. 2 (2015): 257–273; Paolo Campana, "The Structure of Human Trafficking: Lifting the Bonnet on a Nigerian Transnational Network," *British Journal of Criminology* 56, no. 1 (2016): 68–86, 81.

21. See Aransiola and Asindemade, "Understanding Cybercrime Perpetrators"; Oludayo Tade, "A Spiritual Dimension to Cybercrime in Nigeria: The 'Yahoo Plus' Phenomenon," *Human Affairs* 23, no. 4 (2013): 689–705.

22. Michael Levi, *The Phantom Capitalists: The Organization and Control of Long-Firm Fraud*, rev. ed. (Aldershot, UK: Ashgate, 2008); Reuter, *Disorganized Crime*; Letizia Paoli, Victoria A. Greenfield, and Peter Reuter, *The World Heroin Market: Can Supply Be Cut?* (Oxford: Oxford University Press, 2009).

7. CYBERCRIME, ORGANIZED CRIME, AND GOVERNANCE

1. Avinash K. Dixit, *Lawlessness and Economics: Alternative Modes of Governance* (Princeton, NJ: Princeton University Press, 2004).

2. James Densley, *How Gangs Work: An Ethnography of Youth Violence* (New York: Palgrave Macmillan, 2013); Heather Hamill, *The Hoods: Crime and Punishment in Belfast* (Princeton, NJ: Princeton University Press, 2011); David Skarbek, "Governance and Prison Gangs," *American Political Science Review* 105, no. 4 (2011): 702–716; Diego Gambetta, *The Sicilian Mafia: The Business of Private Protection* (Cambridge, MA: Harvard University Press, 1993); Anja Shortland and Federico Varese, "The Protector's Choice: An Application of Protection Theory to Somali Piracy," *British Journal of Criminology* 54, no. 5 (2014): 741–764.

3. Thomas C. Schelling, "What Is the Business of Organized Crime?" *Journal of Public Law* 20, no. 1 (1971): 71–84.

4. Federico Varese, *Mafias on the Move: How Organized Crime Conquers New Territories* (Princeton, NJ: Princeton University Press, 2011), ch. 5.

5. Brian Krebs, *Spam Nation: The Inside Story of Organized Cybercrime—From Global Epidemic to Your Front Door* (Naperville, IL: Sourcebooks, 2014), 17–24.

6. Krebs, *Spam Nation*, 20.

7. Krebs, *Spam Nation*, 18.

8. John Blau, "Russia—a Happy Haven for Hackers," ComputerWeekly.com, May 2004, http://www.computerweekly.com/feature/Russia-a-happy-haven-for-hackers.

9. David Goldman, "The Cyber Mafia Has Already Hacked You," CNN Money, July 27, 2011, http://money.cnn.com/2011/07/27/technology/organized_cybercrime/.

10. For similar arguments see David S. Wall, "Internet Mafias? The Dis-Organization of Crime on the Internet," in *Organized Crime, Corruption and Crime Prevention*, ed. Stefano Caneppele and Francesco Calderoni (Cham, Switzerland: Springer, 2014); Rob McCusker, "Transnational Organised Cyber Crime: Distinguishing Threat from Reality," *Crime, Law and Social Change* 46, no. 4–5 (2006): 257–273; Anita Lavorgna, "Exploring the Cyber-Organised Crime Narrative: The Hunt for a New Bogeyman?" in *Narrative on Organised Crime in Europe: Criminals, Corrupters & Policy*, ed. Petrus C. Van Duyne, Miroslav Scheinost, Georgios A. Antonopoulos, Jackie Harvey, and Klaus Von Lampe (Oisterwijk, NL: Wolf Legal Publishers, 2016), 193–220; E. Rutger Leukfeldt, Anita Lavorgna, and Edward R. Kleemans, "Organised Cybercrime or Cybercrime That Is Organised? An Assessment of the Conceptualisation of Financial Cybercrime as Organised Crime," *European Journal on Criminal Policy and Research* 23, no. 3 (2017): 287–300.

11. McCusker, "Transnational Organised Cyber Crime," 257.

12. Joseph D. Pistone, *Donnie Brasco: My Undercover Life in the Mafia* (New York: New American Library, 1987).

13. Peter Reuter, *Disorganized Crime: The Economics of the Visible Hand* (Cambridge, MA: MIT Press, 1983).

14. James Graham, Rick Howard, Ralph Thomas, and Steven Winterfeld, eds., *Cyber Fraud: Tactics, Techniques, and Procedures* (Boca Raton, FL: CRC Press, 2009), 173; Krebs, *Spam Nation*, 22–23.

15. Nicole Hong, "More Street Gangs Turn to Financial Crimes," *Wall Street Journal*, March 7, 2016, http://www.wsj.com/articles/more-street-gangs-turn-to-financial-crimes-1457379074.

16. Richard Edwards, "'Lord' Masterminded Plot to Steal £229 million by Hacking into City Bank Computers," *Telegraph*, January 22, 2009, https://www.telegraph.co.uk/news/uknews/4307731/Lord-masterminded-plot-to-steal-229-million-by-hacking-into-City-bank-computers.html.

17. Federico Varese, *Mafia Life: Love, Death and Money at the Heart of Organised Crime* (London: Profile Books, 2017), 156–157.

18. See Joseph Menn, *Fatal System Error: The Hunt for the New Crime Lords Who Are Bringing Down the Internet* (New York: Public Affairs, 2010).

19. Jordan Robertson and Michael Riley, "The Mob's IT Department: How Two Technology Consultants Helped Drug Traffickers Hack the Port of Antwerp," Bloomberg Businessweek, July 7, 2015, http://www.bloomberg.com/graphics/2015-mob-technology-consultants-help-drug-traffickers/.

20. For a broader analysis of how strong trust networks interact with and survive political rule across a range of historical settings, see Charles Tilly, *Trust and Rule* (Cambridge: Cambridge University Press, 2005).

21. "Tracking the Russian Scammers," Wired, January 31, 2007, http://archive.wired.com /politics/onlinerights/news/2007/01/72605.

22. Krebs, *Spam Nation*, 150–153.

23. Associated Press in Seattle, "Russian MP Allegedly Plotted with Imprisoned Son to Escape US Custody," *The Guardian,* October 8, 2015, https://www.theguardian.com/world /2015/oct/08/russia-mp-valery-seleznev-plotted-son-escape-us-custody.

24. Graham et al., eds., *Cyber Fraud,* 173.

25. Krebs, *Spam Nation,* 17–18.

26. Menn, *Fatal System Error,* 150–152.

27. See Jonathan Lusthaus and Federico Varese, "Offline and Local: The Hidden Face of Cybercrime," *Policing,* July 28, 2017, 6.

28. See, for instance, Transparency International's "Corruption Perceptions Index, 2017," https://www.transparency.org/news/feature/corruption_perceptions_index_2017.

29. Regarding drug investigations on Silk Road, US law enforcement agents Carl Force and Shaun Bridges were arrested for misappropriating bitcoins: Nate Raymond, "Ex-Agent in Silk Road Probe Gets More Prison Time for Bitcoin Theft," Reuters, November 8, 2017, https://www.reuters.com/article/us-usa-cyber-silkroad/ex-agent-in-silk-road-probe-gets -more-prison-time-for-bitcoin-theft-idUSKBN1D804H.

30. Shawn Hogan, "What Does Carmen Electra, Cyber-Terrorism And Meg Whitman Have In Common? EBay!" Shawn Hogan Fan Club (website), August 2, 2010, https:// shawnhogan.com/2010/08/what-does-carmen-electra-cyber-terrorism-and-meg-whitman -have-in-common-ebay.html.

31. See Federico Varese, "Pervasive Corruption," in *Economic Crime in Russia,* ed. Alena V. Ledeneva and Marina Kurkchiyan (The Hague: Kluwer Law International, 2000).

32. Dixit, *Lawlessness and Economics.*

33. Varese, "Pervasive Corruption"; Alena V. Ledeneva, *Russia's Economy of Favours: Blat, Networking and Informal Exchange* (Cambridge: Cambridge University Press, 1998); Alena V. Ledeneva, *How Russia Really Works: The Informal Practices that Shaped Post-Soviet Politics and Business* (Ithaca, NY: Cornell University Press, 2006).

34. Gilles Favarel-Garrigues, *Policing Economic Crime in Russia: From Soviet Planned Economy to Privatisation* (London: C Hurst, 2011).

35. Favarel-Garrigues, *Policing Economic Crime in Russia,* 3.

36. Federico Varese, *The Russian Mafia: Private Protection in a New Market Economy* (Oxford: Oxford University Press, 2001), 59.

37. Varese, *The Russian Mafia,* 59–61.

38. Varese, *The Russian Mafia,* 61–68. On the Russian context see also Mark Galeotti, *The Age of Anxiety: Security and Politics in Soviet and Post-Soviet Russia* (London: Routledge, 2014); Vadim Volkov, *Violent Entrepreneurs: The Use of Force in the Making of Russian Capitalism* (Ithaca, NY: Cornell University Press, 2002).

39. Sergey Pavlovich, *How to Steal a Million: The Memoirs of a Russian Hacker* (self-pub., 2018), Foreword.

8. CONCLUSION

1. Isak Ladegaard, "We Know Where You Are, What You Are Doing and We Will Catch You: Testing Deterrence Theory in Digital Drug Markets," *British Journal of Criminology* 58, no. 2 (2018): 414–433; David Décary-Hétu and Luca Giommon, "Do Police Crackdowns Disrupt Drug Cryptomarkets? A Longitudinal Analysis of the Effects of Operation Onymous," *Crime, Law and Social Change* 67, no. 1 (2017): 55–75. Time will tell whether the latest law enforcement operation against AlphaBay and Hansa produces different results: Brian Krebs, "After AlphaBay's Demise, Customers Flocked to Dark Market Run by Dutch Police," KrebsonSecurity, July 20, 2017, https://krebsonsecurity.com/2017/07/after-alphabays-demise-customers-flocked-to-dark-market-run-by-dutch-police/.

2. Michael Levi, Alan Doig, Rajeev Gundar, David S. Wall, and Matthew Williams, "Cyberfraud and the Implications for Effective Risk-Based Responses: Themes from UK Research," *Crime, Law and Social Change* 67, no. 1 (2017): 77–96; Benoît Dupont, "Bots, Cops, and Corporations: On the Limits of Enforcement and the Promise of Polycentric Regulation as a Way to Control Large-Scale Cybercrime," *Crime, Law and Social Change* 67, no. 1 (2017): 97–116.

3. Alice Hutchings and Thomas J. Holt, "The Online Stolen Data Market: Disruption and Intervention Approaches," *Global Crime* 18, no. 1 (2017): 11–30, 23.

4. See, in relation to traditional forms of crime, David Weisburd, Laura A. Wyckoff, Justin Ready, John E. Eck, Joshua C. Hinkle, and Frank Gajewski, "Does Crime Just Move around the Corner? A Controlled Study of Spatial Displacement and Diffusion of Crime Control Benefits," *Criminology* 44, no. 3 (2006): 549–591; Rob T. Guerette and Kate J. Bowers, "Assessing the Extent of Crime Displacement and Diffusion of Benefits: A Review of Situational Crime Prevention Evaluations," *Criminology* 47, no. 4 (2009): 1331–1368.

5. Zachary K. Goldman and Damon McCoy, "Deterring Financially Motivated Cybercrime," *Journal of National Security Law & Policy* 8, no. 3 (2016): 595–619.

6. Jonathan Lusthaus and Federico Varese, "Offline and Local: The Hidden Face of Cybercrime," *Policing*, July 28 (2017).

7. For varying accounts that are drawn on see Kevin Poulsen, *Kingpin: How One Hacker Took Over the Billion-Dollar Cybercrime Underground* (New York: Crown, 2011), 49–53; Ariana Cha, "A Tempting Offer for Russian Pair," *Washington Post*, May 19, 2003.

APPENDIX 2

1. On qualitative approaches to studying fraud and organized crime more broadly see Michael Levi, "Qualitative Research on Elite Frauds, Ordinary Frauds, and "organized crime," in *The Routledge Handbook of Qualitative Criminology*, ed. Heith Copes and J. Mitchell Miller (Abingdon: Routledge, 2015).

2. Gary King, Robert O. Keohane, and Sidney Verba, *Designing Social Inquiry: Scientific Inference in Qualitative Research* (Princeton, NJ: Princeton University Press, 1994).

3. On anthropological and ethnographic approaches, see H. Russell Bernard, *Research Methods in Anthropology*, 5th ed. (Lanham, MD: AltaMira, 2011); Lisa Maher, *Sexed Work: Gender, Race and Resistance in a Brooklyn Drug Market* (Oxford: Clarendon Press, 1997).

4. See, as an example, Federico Varese, *Mafias on the Move: How Organized Crime Conquers New Territories* (Princeton, NJ: Princeton University Press, 2011)

5. Avinash K. Dixit, *Lawlessness and Economics: Alternative Modes of Governance* (Princeton, NJ: Princeton University Press, 2004); Diego Gambetta, *The Sicilian Mafia: The Business of Private Protection* (Cambridge, MA: Harvard University Press, 1993); Diego Gambetta, *Codes of the Underworld: How Criminals Communicate* (Princeton, NJ: Princeton University Press, 2009); Federico Varese, *The Russian Mafia: Private Protection in a New Market Economy* (Oxford: Oxford University Press, 2001); Thomas C. Schelling, *The Strategy of Conflict* (Cambridge, MA: Harvard University Press, 1963).

6. For a rare exception see Martín Sánchez Jankowski, *Islands in the Street: Gangs and American Urban Society* (Berkley: University of California Press, 1991).

7. Julia Brannen, "The Study of Sensitive Subjects," *Sociological Review* 36, no. 3 (1988): 552–563, 553; Grant McCracken, *The Long Interview* (Newbury Park, CA: Sage, 1988), 9–11.

8. Varese, *The Russian Mafia*, 12.

9. For similar arguments see Robin Legard, Jill Keegan, and Kit Ward, "In-Depth Interviews," in *Qualitative Research Practice*, ed. Jane Ritchie and Jane Lewis (Thousand Oaks, CA: Sage, 2003), 166–167.

10. See Joseph A. Maxwell, *Qualitative Research Design: An Interactive Approach* (Thousand Oaks, CA: Sage, 1996), 70–71; Robert G. Burgess, *In the Field: An Introduction to Field Research*, rev. ed. (London: Routledge, 1990), 44; J. J. Honigmann, "Sampling in Ethnographic Fieldwork," in *Field Research: A Sourcebook and Field Manual*, ed. Robert G. Burgess (London: Allen & Unwin, 1982), 80–82; Rick H. Hoyle, Monica J. Harris, and Charles M. Judd, *Research Methods in Social Relations*, 7th ed. (Fort Worth, TX: Wadsworth, 2002), 186.

11. Jane Ritchie, Jane Lewis, and Gillian Elam, "Designing and Selecting Samples," in *Qualitative Research Practice*, ed. Jane Ritchie and Jane Lewis (Thousand Oaks: Sage, 2003), 78–80, 96–104; Hoyle, Harris, and Judd, *Research Methods in Social Relations*, 187–188.

12. William Foote Whyte, *Street Corner Society: The Social Structure of an Italian Slum* (Chicago: University of Chicago Press, 1943).

13. See, for instance, Sheldon X. Zhang, *Chinese Human Smuggling Organizations: Families, Social Networks, and Cultural Imperatives* (Stanford, CA: Stanford University Press, 2008); Alexandra K. Murphy and Sudhir Alladi Venkatesh, "Vice Careers: The Changing Contours of Sex Work in New York City," *Qualitative Sociology* 29, no. 2 (2006): 129–154; Alice Goffman, *On the Run: Fugitive Life in an American City* (Chicago: University of Chicago Press, 2014); Sánchez-Jankowski, *Islands in the Street.*

14. Some might view inmates as a different form of low-hanging fruit, with suggestions that those criminals in prison skew toward the incompetent. This was an expectation of Michael Levi, *The Phantom Capitalists: The Organization and Control of Long-Firm Fraud*, rev. ed. (Aldershot, UK: Ashgate, 2008). In this study of conventional fraudsters in the UK, Levi notes that major arrests just prior to his research led to a "better class" of fraudster being available to him (327). Within the world of cybercrime, I believe that there are structural factors that mean such a class of offenders can somewhat regularly be found in prison. The number of cybercrimes around the world is vast, so law enforcement agencies cannot possibly investigate every case. Credible cybercrime statistics are also sparse. This means police are less likely to get sucked into a political game of improving their arrest statistics by

sweeping for low-level offenders, as might be the case with drug offenders at street level. Given they currently cannot demonstrate their worth through statistics, major arrests of "big fish" present cybercrime units with a better alternative. Agents appear to focus their limited investigative resources on those cases which can lead to a high-profile arrest, perhaps thereby disrupting the underground or deterring other cybercriminals. This is what leads to a "better class" of cybercrime inmate than might be expected in other forms of crime. For further methodological detail on carrying out interviews with convicted fraudsters see Michael Levi, *The Organisation and Control of Long-Firm Fraud* (PhD Thesis: University of Southampton), ch. 3.

15. See Benoît Dupont, "Skills and Trust: A Tour Inside the Hard Drives of Computer Hackers," in *Crime and Networks*, ed. Carlo Morselli (New York: Routledge, 2014), 195–196.

16. See, for instance, Mary Bosworth, Debi Campbell, Bonita Demby, Seth M. Ferranti, and Michael Santos, "Doing Prison Research: Views from Inside," *Qualitative Inquiry* 11, no. 2 (2005): 249–264.

17. On snowball sampling see Ritchie, Lewis, and Elam, "Designing and Selecting Samples," 94–95; Hoyle, Harris, and Judd, *Research Methods in Social Relations*, 188–189.

18. Some (criminal) subjects may suspect a researcher to be an undercover agent: Bruce A. Jacobs, "The Case for Dangerous Fieldwork," in *The Sage Handbook of Fieldwork*, ed. Dick Hobbs and Richard Wright (Thousand Oaks, CA: Sage, 2006), 158–159. In my case, some participants in certain jurisdictions brought up this question, often in the form of a joke. I could only assure these participants that I was not an agent, and explain that no agent would go to the lengths that I have for my research to maintain a cover. Ultimately my research output, such as this book, would vindicate my true status.

19. Michael Quinn Patton, *Qualitative Research and Evaluation Methods*, 3rd ed. (Thousand Oaks, CA: Sage, 2002), 555–563; Norman K. Denzin, *The Research Act: A Theoretical Introduction to Sociological Methods* (London: Routledge, 2017), ch. 12.

20. Steinar Kvale, *Interviews: An Introduction to Qualitative Research Interviewing* (Thousand Oaks, CA: Sage, 1996); Herbert J. Rubin and Irene S. Rubin, *Qualitative Interviewing: The Art of Hearing Data*, 2nd ed. (Thousand Oaks, CA: Sage, 2005), 12.

21. Existing literature delves into these challenges and provides further detail on carrying out effective interviews. See, for instance, Legard, Keegan, and Ward, "In-Depth Interviews," 148–165.

22. Hoyle, Harris, and Judd, *Research Methods in Social Relations*, 32–33, 41–42.

23. See King, Keohane, and Verba, *Designing Social Inquiry*, 129–137.

24. Ritchie, Lewis, and Elam, "Designing and Selecting Samples," 78.

25. See Mark Israel and Iain Hay, *Research Ethics for Social Scientists* (Thousand Oaks, CA: Sage, 2006), ch. 5.

26. Israel and Hay, *Research Ethics for Social Scientists*, ch. 6.

27. Israel and Hay, *Research Ethics for Social Scientists*, 85–90; Jacobs, "The Case for Dangerous Fieldwork," 158.

28. The latest version of the British Society of Criminology's Statement of Ethics can be found at: http://www.britsoccrim.org/documents/BSCEthics2015.pdf. Before this iteration of the statement was released, I relied on a previous version, which was very similar in content with regard to this issue. There are also other codes with a more medical focus that I

have consulted, but that are not directly relevant to social science research. See, for instance: http://www.hhs.gov/ohrp/policy/prisoner.html.

29. Carol Matfin, "Doing Research in a Prison Setting," in *Doing Criminological Research*, ed. Victor Jupp, Pamela Davies, and Peter Francis (London: Sage, 2000); Roy D. King, "Doing Research in Prisons," in *Doing Research on Crime and Justice,* ed. Roy D. King and Emma Wincup (Oxford: Oxford University Press, 2000); Alison Liebling, "Doing Prison Research: Breaking the Silence?" *Theoretical Criminology* 3, no. 2 (1999): 147–173; Robert C. Sorensen, "Interviewing Prison Inmates," *Journal of Criminal Law and Criminology* 41, no. 2 (1950): 180–182; Rose Giallombardo, "Interviewing in the Prison Community," *Journal of Criminal Law, Criminology* 57, no. 3 (1967): 318–324.

30. In general, there is no UK legal obligation for researchers to reveal undisclosed criminal actions to law enforcement unless compelled by them to do so. The statute covering this is the Criminal Law Act 1967 s.4 and s.5.

31. Matfin, "Doing Research in a Prison Setting," 229; Donald J. Newman, "Research Interviewing in Prison," *Journal of Criminal Law, Criminology* 49, no. 2 (1958): 127–132, 131–132.

32. Matfin, "Doing Research in a Prison Setting," 222.

33. Bosworth et al., "Doing Prison Research," 254–256.

34. Matfin, "Doing Research in a Prison Setting," 228.

Acknowledgments

This book would not have been possible without the participation of my interview subjects, who number close to 250. I began working on cyber-crime in 2011 with no knowledge at all of the topic. From the beginning, participants generously shared their time and wisdom with me. They educated me. Some went further and took it upon themselves to champion this study, opening their networks and recommending other potential interview subjects, sending me relevant sources to read, and taking me under their protection so that I felt welcome (and safe) in foreign countries. As much as I have woven this study together from a range of different sources, at a foundational level it encapsulates the experiences, knowledge, and insights of these subjects. This book is as much theirs as it is mine. Due to the restrictions of maintaining their anonymity, I cannot acknowledge them by name. But I owe them the greatest thanks.

I also benefited greatly from the help of many others who were not formal participants in the study. Many were friends or colleagues already, while others were people I encountered along the journey who wished to help. All showed me great kindness. Some made introductions to potential subjects; others offered travel and safety tips. Some met me for meals or let me sleep on their couches! I won't name everyone who helped me along the way for fear that I would almost certainly forget someone (and also extend these acknowledgments by many pages). Moreover, it would not seem appropriate to thank individuals in this category by name, while those above remain anonymous. But, again, my gratitude to all those who helped me is deep.

This was a costly study to undertake, because it involved so much travel. I was forced to carry out many of the trips in a miserly fashion, often undertaking research when I had other reasons for passing through a country. There were certain field visits that would not have been possible without the generous support of others. Nuffield College provided a substantial research allowance each year, which contributed to a number of trips. The college also provided two travel fund grants that specifically allowed me to visit China and Nigeria. I was also the beneficiary of a John Fell Fund grant, alongside Professor Federico Varese, which allowed a second visit to Romania. Finally, I thank the Commonwealth Bank of Australia for generously providing a no-strings-attached donation to cover research costs toward the end of the project. This made it possible to visit some essential locations that remained on my list of hotspots, most notably Ukraine. Following this, the bank's generous sponsorship of the Human Cybercriminal Project at Oxford allowed me the time to finish writing this book, as the Commonwealth Bank Fellow. I particularly thank the bank for understanding the value of independent academic research. Ian Narev provided great support from the top. I am also incredibly grateful to Brett Winterford and Ben King for becoming true partners in this research and driving it forward. And a special acknowledgment must be paid to Ben Heyes, who championed this research. In many ways, he ensured this book could come to fruition. I owe him a debt.

In academic terms, I wish to thank those who read parts or all of this book—or related components—at various points, and provided a range of helpful comments. A number of study participants and family members fall into this category, along with David Dixon, Laurin Weissinger, Paolo Campana, Jamie Collier, Michael Hart, Andrew Conway, Gianluca Miscione, Edoardo Gallo, Ask Neve, Alan Dupont, Rebecca Ledingham, Alice Hutchings, Benoît Dupont, David Skarbek, Ross Anderson, Robert McArdle, Bas von Schaik, and Jaap van Oss.

I also thank all those involved in my doctoral project at the University of Oxford. Heather Hamill and Paolo Campana acted as examiners for my Transfer of Status. David Kirk and Lucas Kello played the same role in my Confirmation of Status. David Kirk and Mike Levi served as my final examiners for the viva, and have both generously continued to advise me on my research since. The points of support and challenge in these meetings were equally valuable in clarifying my thinking and enhancing this project. My doctorate was undertaken as a Clarendon Scholar. My studies would not have been possible without the joint support of the Clarendon Fund and Nuffield College. I am also extremely grateful to the Department of Sociology—under the past and present heads of department, Melinda Mills and Christiaan Monden—for agreeing to house my research program and supporting my efforts, and to Nuffield College for providing me with such a positive environment and community.

In terms of the preparation of the manuscript, I thank everyone involved in the Harvard University Press process, from the office of the director to the Board of Syndics to the reviewers who all saw something in this book and supported its publication. I also thank all those involved in the production process, especially Julia Kirby for her efforts in "punching up" the text and smoothing out the reading experience, and Anne McGuire for her rigorous checking of the notes. Outside of HUP, Ben Taaffe provided speedy and thorough copy editing on an earlier draft, while Ellada Larionidou assisted me with translation from Russian. Special thanks must go to my editor at HUP, Ian Malcolm, who has believed in this book from when we first met and has fought for it at every step in the process. While this is my first experience with an editor, I suspect there are few more supportive or effective editors out there.

I express enormous gratitude to my former supervisor (and now colleague), Federico Varese. I could not have hoped for a better one. Before, during, and after my time as his student, he has been a constant source of encouragement and support. From the beginning, he has helped in framing the project. I benefited greatly from his incisive mind, and particularly his ability to see each project on its own terms, rather than offering a cookie-cutter view of how good research must be done. While the writing and ideas contained herein are all my own, the intellectual parentage is clear. I also wish to thank Valeria Pizzini-Gambetta, who supervised my Masters thesis, which was the origin of this project and remains strongly connected to this final product. I also thank Diego Gambetta in more indirect terms, for establishing a style of research on organized crime at Oxford that continues to be very influential to my way of thinking. Equally, Misha Glenny may be unaware that a seminar he gave in Oxford opened my eyes to the cybercriminal underground and set me on a path to research it.

I pay tribute to my wife. She has been my companion throughout the journey, both metaphorically and literally. Her patient agreement to spend our holidays largely in cybercrime hotspots has played a huge role in allowing this study to be completed. Through this process, she has become somewhat of an expert on cybercrime herself! She has been a constant source of support and someone to bounce ideas off. She assisted me greatly in the final stages of finishing this project, ensuring that everything came together in time. I quite simply couldn't have done it without her.

I would also like to thank my whole family, whose love and support travels with me wherever I go. In particular, I honor the unbreakable bond with my siblings, and also my grandparents. I dedicate this book to my parents. My father had dreams of being a political economist, but life went another way. He had a fascination with China and Russia and it is perhaps fitting that my research on cybercrime led me both to economic sociology and an opportunity to study such countries. I hope very much that he would have enjoyed reading this book. My mother has fought for me my entire life and constantly challenged me to pursue big ideas. This book is a testament to how she has raised me, and I hope lives up to the model that she set for me.

Index